The Quest
for the Shaman

The Quest
for the Shaman

SHAPE-SHIFTERS, SORCERERS AND
SPIRIT-HEALERS OF ANCIENT EUROPE

Miranda & Stephen Aldhouse-Green

with 134 illustrations, 24 in color

Thames & Hudson

To Juliet and John

FRONTISPIECE *This figure is depicted on a gilded silver cauldron probably made in the 2nd–1st century* BC, *and found in a peat-bog at Gundestrup in Jutland. The cauldron, dismantled before burial, was a votive offering. The antlered image may represent a shaman during trance, with his animal helper beside him.*

First published in 2005 in hardcover in the United States of America by Thames & Hudson Inc., 500 Fifth Avenue, New York, New York 10110

thamesandhudsonusa.com

Library of Congress Catalog Card Number 2004112869

ISBN-13: 978-0-500-05134-4
ISBN-10: 0-500-05134-8

Designed by Liz Rudderham

Printed and bound in Singapore by Star Standard Industries Pte Ltd

CONTENTS

1 *Reconstruction drawing of a man wearing an antler headdress from Star Carr, Yorkshire.*

PREFACE

It was entirely fortuitous, but highly auspicious that, as we finished the Epilogue to *The Quest for the Shaman*, we embarked on a holiday to Chilean Patagonia for – unwittingly – we were to experience a living shamanistic landscape. Much of southern Chile's indigenous population is known as the Mapuche ('People of the Earth'), a term embracing a range of Amerindian peoples and, throughout our journey, from Santiago to San Rafael, we were to encounter 'shamanic' mythologies and material culture, particularly in the Chilote Archipelago, a wilderness of waterways and small islands formed from a drowned glaciated landscape. Chiloé, we were told, is a *locus sanctus*, a focus for ceremony and ritual involving close encounters with the spirit-world. It is easy to see why, for the intimate interaction between land and water, the myriad tiny islands, waterfalls, rapids, fjords and mountains that form the topography here and elsewhere in southern Chile, present an intensely liminal visual world, perceived as infested with spirits and supernatural forces.

Here, we met the *Machi*, Mapuche shamans who travel in a multi-layered cosmos and who use drums, marked with these layers, to call up the spirits. Most *Machi* are female, and those that are male cross-dress to become 'female'. And we met the curious life-size male and female wooden images, called *che-mamull*, used in funerary rituals and placed by newly made graves in order to enable the transformation of the dead to the world of the ancestors. We saw some of the musical instruments played in sacred ceremonies, the diving-rods and the paraphernalia used in the preparation and ingestion of trance-inducing hallucinogens that form the shaman's toolkit, and we found old sepia photographs of early twentieth-century Chilean Indian shamans, painting themselves as animals in preparation for their supervision of adolescents' *rites de passage*.

The glimpse we have had of the Mapuche sacred cosmos and its shamans contains strong resonances with the world of the ancient ritualists with whom this book is concerned. It has been a rare privilege for us to have encountered living shamanism in a wild, remote, beautiful and enchanted landscape which, although far removed in space and time from our chosen arena, nonetheless seves to convince us that 'shamanism', in its broadest sense, is and has been endemic to rural communities in much of the ancient and modern world. Our quest in the pages that follow is to identify the 'shaman's footprint'.

Chiloé
Southern Patagonia
Chile

1 SHAMANISM
An Introduction

Being a shaman is probably, in fact, the oldest profession, covering the roles which in industrial societies, are played separately by the doctor, psychotherapist, soldier, fortune-teller, priest and politician.
Piers Vitebsky, *The Shaman*[1]

This book was viewed from the outset as a journey through prehistory and into the early historic period, as far as the seventh century AD. The journey had a purpose: it was a quest for evidence of shamanism. We did not know at the outset what our conclusion would be. Nonetheless, it would be only honest to share with the reader the fact that we were both favourably disposed to the concept of the recognition of ancient shamanism. Think of this book, if you like, as a kind of 'road movie' (we have the films *Badlands* and *Bonnie and Clyde* particularly in mind): certain things will happen on our way, as we make our journey through time. We will enter caves and view monsters, part human and part animal, painted on the walls. By the flickering light of our wooden torches and oil lamps, these monsters and whole prides of lions and herds of rhinoceros will seem to move and come alive in the Stone Age darkness. We will see, in Chauvet Cave in the Ardèche, that bears – using the cave for hibernation – have done violence to the paintings created only last year by making deep scratches through them with their claws. We hear, or think we hear, strange sounds in the dark. Could it be that the bears are returning? In a different cave, 5,000 years later at 27,000 years ago, we will see stencils of apparently mutilated hands on the wall of Gargas Cave in the Pyrenees. We cannot say – because we were not present when the art was actually carried out – whether the hands recorded here were mutilated or not.

It may be that what we see is a shadow language, of a kind used by some Australian Aborigines during hunting and during periods of sacred silence,[2] 'fixed' onto the cave walls. So many questions and so few answers. Some of our ports of call were fun, like the exploding figurines of Dolní Věstonice, but many are scenes of untimely death, ritual murder or execution, such as the hanging of Tollund Man, and the drowning of the Windeby Girl. Occasionally, our breath is taken away by the sheer spectacle of some of the evidence, like the 'map of the cosmos' from Bronze Age Nebra in Germany, and our own minds are blown by discoveries of mind-altering narcotics in use: if the 'doctor' buried at Stanway in Essex, just on the cusp of the Roman conquest, used in life the objects interred with him, he must have enjoyed an interesting career as healer, diviner and drug-user!

Iron Age and Roman-period imagery shows us a world of two-spirit people, who exhibited their ability to cross boundaries between human and sacred worlds by changing gender or species. As our journey progresses, literature enables us to encounter real, named individuals who may well have been shamans: the Druid Diviciacus, the prophetess Veleda and, later still, the weird characters of Cú Chulainn, the skin-turner and the terrifying Irish goddess-phantoms who could change at will between young women, hags and ravens. All this we will meet in due course, but first we have some basic questions to consider: namely, what is shamanism and how can we recognize it archaeologically?

THE SHAMAN'S FOOTPRINTS

The quest

It is important at the beginning of our shamanic quest, to set out our position to explain what we are seeking to achieve. The present volume is not intended as an anthropological study, nor does it aim to explore the neuropsychology of trance states. It also does not seek to revisit in detail the evidence of cave art recently covered by David Lewis-Williams[3] in his book *The Mind in the Cave*. Rather, we approach the issue of shamans and shamanism as archaeologists, and what interests us is an examination of shamanism as a form of past ritual activity that leaves behind it residues of that behaviour.

Towards a definition

First, what do we mean by shamanism? What is a shaman? The word 'šaman' is a Siberian Tungus word and simply means 'the ecstatic one'. Shamanism is not even a 'religion' as such but rather a world-view system or a 'grammar' of the mind.[4] One scholar has gone so far as to suggest that 'as both a term and a notion, shamanism is entirely an academic creation'.[5] He adds, however, that 'as such it is certainly a useful tool serving to describe a pattern of ritual behaviour and belief found in strikingly similar form across much of the arctic and sub-arctic regions of the world'. But this similarity may be no more than skin deep, as Ronald Hutton's account of ritual and belief in Siberia shows:

> The ethnic and linguistic diversity of Siberian tribes was matched by an almost bewildering variety of religious beliefs and customs. All accepted the principle of animal sacrifice and regarded certain trees, stones or waters as particularly holy. Most had a notion of the world as divided into three levels, but not all did and those who shared the notion could differ over the level which they regarded as human. Many had a concept of a tree, column or post which unites the different levels of existence, but, again, not all. Some focused upon a single main deity, or two complementary deities, or two opposed deities, one good and one evil. Some had many divine beings and some just venerated spirits of nature and of ancestors. To some the sun was female and the moon male, to others the reverse was true. The same variety of attitudes applies to the genders of earth and sky. Many tribes feared the dead, yet some did not. Funeral customs were proportionately heterogeneous, rituals focusing on the three major modes of cremation, placement (exposed or covered) on platforms, and burial. The first two were most common, simply because of the practical difficulty of digging graves in permafrost. Some of the tribes built temples, others did not, and the same is true of the carving of images of deities or of spirits. There was never any such entity as 'Siberian religion' or 'Siberian mythology'; there were many.[6]

Shamanism is often a quite loosely defined term embracing the concepts of 'sorcerer', 'ritualist', or 'medicine man'. For Piers Vitebsky,[7] an anthropologist based at the Scott Polar Research Institute in the University of Cambridge, shamanism must involve soul journeys of persons chosen by the spirits: the shaman's soul must be able to use trance to leave the body, visit the spirit-world and negotiate there for the purposes of healing, hunting or some other communication with supernatural forces. The multifarious characteristics of a shaman may include perception of a three-tiered cosmos: the underworld where the ancestors and some maleficent spirits live; 'middle-earth', the abode of humans and animals; and the upper world, wherein abide the main assemblage of spirits. Shamanistic societies perceive that they inhabit an ensouled, numinous world, where everything around them possessed (or was possessed by) a spirit force, whether sky, sun, river, mountain, rock outcrop, cave, house or hunted creature.

Shamans must be able to transgress the boundaries between human and spirit worlds and, to do this, they invoke trance as the pathway through the 'tween-space'. In a trance state, an altered state of awareness, shamans may visit other worlds to negotiate with the spirits on behalf of their communities in order to avert or cure disease; they may intervene to prevent or stop famine, failure of the herds or pestilence; and intercede with the supernatural world to promote their people's prosperity and success. Liaising with the spirits is not without danger, for transference between worlds is itself full of risk and there is always a chance that the shaman may not be able to re-enter his or her own cosmic space. The danger is present, too, in the malevolence of certain spirits, and the shaman may have to do battle with inimical forces which have stolen the souls of the sick.

Shamanic trance

The shaman may travel to the spirit world in a number of ways, within the dream/trance state. Most common are sensations of flying or swimming. These may manifest themselves in shamanic art. In so far as an altered state of consciousness is important, shamanism may be described as an 'ecstatic' religion.[8] In visiting the spirit-world, the shaman must be able to control his/her trance and possess a mental map or chart of the cosmos. The attainment of shamanic trance – a feature that to some scholars[9] is essential to the actions of a shaman – may involve agencies that work on the shaman's mind, to alter it and render it receptive to its soul-journey. These *may* but do not necessarily mean the ingestion of narcotic substances, psychotropes that change the brain's chemistry. Other, equally effective, ways of achieving trance states might be quite natural: lack of sleep or sensory deprivation; repeated sounds including chanting, drumming, rattling or music; activity such as dancing or jumping; and breathing control or isolation. The drum is an important symbol and a significant 'indicator of transition'. It resonates physically but also resonates with meaning.[10] Hallucination involves all the senses, including sound.[11] Saami shamans interpret drum-beats in order to gain ingress to the past and the future.[12] Such drum-beats, chanting, clashing of metal ornaments, or the wearing of animal costume, all contribute to the drama of the shamanic experience. Words and music have power. 'Words make things happen.'[13] While in a trance state the shaman may utter weird sounds and may look strange as well, with grimaces or protruding eyes which signify the pain of transition.

Trance plays an important role not just in the shaman's soul-journey to the spirits but in the shaman's actions as a performer. The theatre of shamanic ritual is crucial, for the shaman has to be a public figure in order for the community to believe in the efficacy of the spirit-contact and share in the shamanic experience and have trust and confidence in the power of their spiritual leader. Thus, divinatory or healing rituals must be carried out in the presence of the people for whom the shaman is negotiating with the other world. Trance is central, for it enables transformation, and the shaman has to be transformed in order to enter the spirit-dimension.

Shamans as 'two-spirit' people

Shamans are transgressive: they move constantly between worlds and have multiple natures. They may therefore possess a dual persona, sometimes with opposed identities which may display ambiguities either in gender or in species, where there may be oscillation between human and animal. Cross-dressing may be an important part of the shaman's identity (Navajo and Chukchi are examples of peoples with transvestite shamans). Among the Chukchi, whose eastern Siberian territory extends from the Bering Strait to the Kolyma River valley, a woman may only become a shaman at or after the menopause, because reproductive capacity is seen to inhibit shamanistic power.[14] People described as 'two-spirits' may cross the gender-divide, perhaps in both dress and behaviour: they may actually live out a life in the opposite gender.[15] The notion of the shaman as a transformative 'two-spirit' is underpinned by the idea of his or her liminal, boundary state, constantly moving between worlds. In order both to enable and to express this double persona, the shaman may live a transposed life that sometimes involves a gender-shift, either during ritual or even in daily life, so that a male shaman may live, dress and work as a woman and *vice versa*.

Shape-shifting

The other way in which the shaman's transferent position may be expressed is in trans-species identity: thus, when in a trance state, shamans in many traditional communities experience transmogrification from human to animal form. Shamans may dress up in animal pelts, feathers or antler headdresses when about to contact the spirits. Indeed animals are usually crucial to shamanistic systems: thus, in hunter-gatherer and hunter-herder communities, a particular beast, often the one on which the group's survival most depends, may be perceived as an animal-helper, a creature that aids the shaman in transgressing between worlds and paving the way for negotiation with the spirits. Thus, for the San of southern Africa, the eland is the main spirit animal, just as it is the reindeer for the Saami of northern Scandinavia and the polar bear for some Siberian communities. The shaman may adopt an animal's persona partly to demonstrate his instability, partly in respect of 'performance', but also partly because humans define themselves in relation to differences and similarities between people and beasts. 'Becoming' an animal while in a trance state may be an important part of the shaman's experience.[16] The shaman's guardian spirits may be in animal form; they advise the shaman how to deal with hostile spirits.

The use of structures and equipment by the shaman

In their attainment of a transformative state, shamans may make use of symbols and equipment. The transformation itself may be symbolized by the use of fire, water and metals, all of which are associated with change. The shaman may have a special place in which to enact rituals: a tent, a cave, a sacred pool, river, mountain or other 'edgy' place. Shamans may use drums, not only as percussive instruments but as divining tools; they may use rods or other lot-casting devices; rattles, gongs or bells might be shaken or struck to call up the spirits; wands or staffs as badges of authority or as implements with which to strike, point or gesture. Special costumes may be worn; bodies are sometimes painted, perhaps to replicate the animal-helper or spirit-beast that acts as go-between. They may make use of images: figurines might be temporarily ensouled during ceremonies, and then ritually broken to release the supernatural energy accumulated within them. Trance/dream images may be painted on cave walls, or carved into rocks, to engage the community with the shaman's experience and act as an *aide mémoire* for the future.

The tiered cosmos

The notion of a three-tiered or layered cosmos or universe is common in shamanic societies. The cosmos may be divided vertically or horizontally but, as we have seen, generally consists of an upper world, inhabited by the spirits, a middle world for living people and animals, and an underworld inhabited by the dead, from which evil and disease may seep upwards and infect 'middle earth'.[17] Sometimes a physical structure or natural feature will symbolize the cosmos and access points between its layers. Thus, the Saami tent, with its threefold division, is the centre of its occupant's ritual cosmos. Again, the Saami underworld is an inversion of earth-world and the dead walk upside down in the footsteps of the living. For the Sora of Orissa in eastern India, the seasons in the underworld are inverted and the dead speak backwards.[18]

Access to the otherworld

Access points to the otherworld include such liminal places as estuaries, rapids, caves, islands and seasonal transition points. Sacrificial sites will often be in these edgy places. We will see, too, that the Breton passage graves are closely linked with the sea. Rock-art sites like Mont Bégo in southern France and Camonica Valley in northern Italy are in liminal situations, at the edge of the settled landscape, in a cleft within the mountains. It is useful to turn to modern or recent sacred landscapes whose meaning is informed by indigenous knowledge. Here, a study of the Algonkian peoples of Quebec provides considerable insight.[19]

According to traditions, shamans acted as a link between humans and supra-sensible powers. Such contact was effected in special places, including structures like the sweat-lodge or the shaking tent, or natural places in the landscape. These last particularly included rock formations, steep rocks, gushing springs, the base of cliffs, caves and fissures within caves. These were places of intersection of the tiers of the Algonkian cosmos. In line with practice in northern America, people who were about to become shamans went on vision quests where, through isolation and fasting, the proto-shaman experienced a trance in which he or she met a guardian spirit. Moreover, shamans sought out such lonely sites where they might gain sacred knowledge, sometimes via rocks known as 'teaching rocks', where the shaman gained contact with the spirit world through the use of songs and offerings. At such a time the shaman might use red ochre to create rock art in order to illustrate the vision received. Thus, a natural place became one of transcendental significance.

Caves, fissures and cracks in rock were deemed to be especially important because they served as access routes for spirits and the shaman could communicate with these spirits through sending his own guardian spirit or helper into these openings. Offerings were often placed in these situations. It is clear from field study of these sites that their natural acoustic properties, including associated sounds – such as the sighing of the wind or the lapping of waves – were of great importance and added to the characteristic drums, rattles, singing and chanting noises of shamanic ritual.

Symbolic dismemberment

Being a shaman might involve psychic and physical risk because of the link with spirits, travelling between worlds, and mind-bending (perhaps, in the last case, using dangerous hallucinogens and because he/she might meet inimical spirits). In order to become a shaman, a person might have to undergo a symbolic dissolution, dismemberment and reconstitution by the spirits.[20] The shamanic rite of passage might involve separation, marginalization and reincorporation.[21] Fire and water are important transformative agents. Thus, the cauldron could play a significant role in the ritual death, dismemberment and reconstitution of the shaman by cooking. The blacksmith, as a transformative being, might be involved with this process. The 'shamanic death' and reintegration are necessary, for they lead to a stronger mental state, enabling the shaman to negotiate more effectively with powerful spirits.

Divination

Divination is not always part of the shamanic 'grammar', but often may be. It may mean foretelling the future, perhaps predicting movements of game for hunting communities, but it may also mean telling what is happening at a distance, at different places as well as at different times. The shaman may communicate with spirits, including dead ancestors, who may be immensely powerful, by means of the divinatory rite. These otherworld beings hold the key to time: past, present and future, and the relationship between them is pivoted on the being of the shaman.

SHAMANISM AND ITS ARCHAEOLOGICAL RECOGNITION

We will range widely over space, time and evidence. Our focus is 'Europe', but we will draw analogies from as far afield as the Americas, Australasia and Africa, and we will travel across Asia to northern Siberia. We begin with the later Palaeolithic and end with medieval mythic literature on the western edge of our study area. We look at caves, chamber tombs, and other boundary places that might have been perceived as entrances to other worlds; we examine costumes and regalia; figurines and toolkits; divination and sacrifice; transformational imagery, indicative of shape-shifting and 'two-spirit' beings; and we try to identify shamanic burials and images of those who may have been ancient shamans.

The reader will, by now, have gained a few clues as to the kind of evidence which we will seek. There is a range of potential indicators although, clearly, these will become more convincing if a number are present at the same site. As we have seen, shamanic sites may very often be such natural places as caves or fissures, rock out-crops, lakes, pools, rivers, estuaries and coasts. They may also be structures set up in such places. The occurrence of potential sites in settings that possess this association with natural features is no more than indicative. The interpretation becomes more plausible, however, where it can be demonstrated that the locales are remote from contemporary settlements or are not themselves living sites, as for example with the Neolithic tombs of the Breton coast.

The concept and practice of trance is central to the recognition of shamanism. The clues here include the use of 'music' to induce trance through audio-driving. The instruments which are normally seen as key to this process, apart from the human voice, include drums and rattles. Archaeologically we see also the use of flutes and, in caves, the practice of striking resonant calcite draperies. In the latter case, it is possible to detect damage which seems to be limited to the area of panels of art or important natural cave features. Finally, there are so-called osteophones, large animal bones (often of mammoth) which seem to have been struck to create a tune.

It has been argued that trance is attested in other ways. The point has been strongly made by David Lewis-Williams and colleagues that all humankind pos-sesses the same neuropsychology and so all peoples have the same capacity to enter trance. According to Lewis-Williams, such trance states fall into a common pattern with three identifiable stages, each characterized by different suites of images seen in the 'mind's eye' of the subject. These images are called entoptics or phosphenes. Stage one images typically take the form of geometric shapes, whereas stage three images are more characteristically those of monsters, creatures that are often part human and part animal. Such depictions can be identified in the cave art of both the Ice Age and postglacial periods. It is fair to say, however, that there is an ongoing active debate about what has come to be called 'neurological determinism', a debate in which views have become extremely polarized. We will return to this.

Animals are usually crucial to shamanistic systems. We have already discussed the genesis and role of animal helpers. It may be that what we see in some of the depictions of stage three monsters (normally called 'therianthropes') are either shamans 'kitted out' to represent an animal or shamans shown as being in transition to animal form. The kind of evidence which survives includes actual headdresses, for example from the Mesolithic site of Star Carr in Yorkshire (Fig. 1), or the 25,000-year-old figurines showing shape-shifting in action from the Balzi Rossi caves of the Ligurian coast. These animal transformations represent an aspect of the trance journeys undertaken by shamans, which may involve, as the shaman understands it, flying through the air or diving down below the sea. Thus the symbols of birds may be suggestive of shamanic flight or those of fish may speak of quite a different sort of aqua-adventure.

Where burials are concerned, particular questions can be asked. Is the grave remote from settlement? Is the body that of a disabled person who might perhaps have been seen as 'other' and so touched by the divine? Are there unusual items interred with the corpse which might be suggestive of the accoutrements of a shaman? One thinks here of the ivory marionette found in what has been inter-preted as the grave of a shaman at Brno in the Czech Republic.

Shamanism is generally regarded as having been endemic to hunter-gatherer societies, because of the importance of its role in hunting. Hunter-gatherer soci-eties enjoy a close relationship with game animals, as exemplified by the beliefs and practices of the caribou-hunting Labrador Eskimo and Innu. Shamanism is above all a hunter's cosmology. Life is taken, in the context of appropriate sanctions and rituals, in order to provide nourishment. The shaman must negotiate with the spirits to neutralize the harmful effects of the theft from the natural world and to predict movements of game. These groups believed in a King of the Caribou who gave the caribou (reindeer) to the hunters. But they believed also that they would not appear unless the hunters showed them proper respect. Thus, the Innu believed that keeping the antlers together would ensure the continuity of the herds. The traveller William Brooks Cabot witnessed a heap of smashed caribou bones 3–4 m (10–13 ft) in diameter and several piles of caribou antlers, known as windrows. Sometimes such accumulations were placed in lakes to appease the spirits of the caribou.[22] Religion and hunting were thus closely linked.

Turning to later prehistory, the evidence takes on a different quality. Sites may produce evidence of the use of narcotics to facilitate entry into trance states. With bog bodies, we may even know the precise contents of their stomachs that, in the case of the men ritually killed at Tollund and Grauballe in Denmark, included the violent mind- and body-altering substance ergot, a parasite growing on rotten barley. Some of these victims of sacred murder were disabled, deformed or even deliberately mutilated, like some of our earlier candidates for shamans. We also have special burials, at late Iron Age sites like Stanway in southern England and La Chaussée in France, of individuals who may have been sacred healers or diviners. Most interesting of all is the evidence that manifests itself in ways that resonate with earlier prehistory: the shape-changers and gender-crossers and, as in these earlier symbolic systems, animals play a crucial role, even though the societies involved were by no means traditional hunter-gatherers but were organized into chiefdoms and states. The Bronze Age and Iron Age rock art of Alpine and northern Europe shows depictions that, like some of the earlier cave art, suggests the shared experience of the visionary. Once our journey reaches the literate past, we come face to face with people, like the Druids, who – so the Classical writers tell us – share so much with 'traditional' shamans that it is hard not to regard them as other than shamans in all but name.

2 BEYOND THE STONE GATES
Later Palaeolithic Ritual Practice

Forget the onslaught of a bull that is a man ... He does not exist. Hope for nothing: not even the wild beast in the darkness.

No aguardes la embestida del toro que es un hombre ... No existe. Nada esperes. Ni siquiera en el negro crepusculo la fiera.

J. L. Borges, *Labyrinth*[1]

A SHAMANIC QUEST

The identification of ancient shamanism was made possible by the identification of testimonies by nineteenth-century Bushman prisoners in Cape Town gaol, South Africa, in which explanations and interpretations of the art of the Drakensberg Mountains were imbedded. A researcher of remarkable talent and prescience, David Lewis-Williams – now Emeritus Professor in Archaeology at the University of Witwatersrand, South Africa – brought these disparate data together and developed an interpretation which was soon to develop a global impact, that of shamanism.

The study of ancient shamanism has been largely based on the interpretation of images in cave art but, in this quest for the Stone Age shaman, we will cast our net more widely. There are several reasons for this. One is that a number of studies have already been published on western European cave art with particular relevance to possible shamanic interpretations. We will revisit some of this data, but we believe it will be useful, as well, to look more widely at ritual practices involving not only caves but also graves and artifacts, in order to seek to distil those activities which may have been instigated, led or controlled by shamans. We will see, too, that

Palaeolithic ritual practices find resonances in the patterns both of burial of the dead in the succeeding Mesolithic and, even later, in the modes of use of Neolithic caves and megalithic tombs. Accordingly, chapters 2 and 3 are written from a perspective which seeks to draw out these commonalities. In this chapter, we will endeavour

- to set the scene at the opening of the story, in a world then peopled by both Neanderthals and modern humans
- to evaluate the various forms of interaction with the world of animals which may have been controlled by shamans
- to consider whether the series of ceremonial interments centred on 25,000 years ago – the so-called Gravettian burials – displays symbolism of a kind which could be argued to be shamanic and whether, in consequence, any of the graves could be argued to be those of actual shamans
- to integrate, with the painted and engraved art of the caves, the evidence of Palaeolithic figurines that may show scenes of shamanic transformation
- to consider the evidence of music, dance and ritual practice as evidence for the concepts of ecstasy and trance.

This use of evidence extends far more widely than arguments either pertaining to the neurology of the human brain, and its inbuilt capacity for shamanic trance, or relating to the interpretation of Stone Age cave art which, in Europe, lacks underpinning from ethnographic sources. We believe that such an approach will permit greater confidence in interpretations of the systems of belief and ritual practice of the later Palaeolithic peoples of Europe. Some of the names of the cultural assemblages may be unfamiliar to many readers and, accordingly, a simplified timeline has been provided with a detailed explanatory caption (Fig. 2).

The earliest modern humans in Europe are generally associated with cultural assemblages called Aurignacian. But we must keep in mind that the Aurignacian was a cultural assemblage, not a people. William Davies, who studied the Aurignacian for his Doctorate at Cambridge, believes that its origins lie not with colonizing anatomically modern humans moving from Africa into Europe but, rather, somewhere in the Middle Palaeolithic of western Eurasia[2] where it was probably an autochthonous development. Davies has presented a strong case for associating the Aurignacian industry with modern humans and the evidence for this is certainly compelling after around 35,000 years ago, at the start of Davies's 'Developed Aurignacian'. We must remember, however, that Neanderthals survived until 28,000 years ago not only in such geographically marginal areas as southern Iberia, but even in the European heartland of Croatia where remains from

2 Later Palaeolithic timeline, showing successive technological stages and chronology in western Europe. The Châtelperronian *(from earlier than 37,000 to 33,000 years ago) was once identified as the earliest stage of the Aurignacian, but is now recognized as the last of the Neanderthal assemblages known in western Europe. Its eponymous artifact is the curved-back Châtelperron point, of which one side is blunted to enable insertion as a spear-point, barb, or perhaps as part of a composite knife. A range of bone, antler and ivory ornaments occur at the Grotte du Renne located on the banks of the River Cure in Burgundy. A debate is currently raging as to whether these ornaments are independent Neanderthal inventions or the result of copying, by Neanderthals, of artifacts made by modern humans. The classic* Aurignacian *(35,000-27,000 years ago) is characterized by the earliest figurative art; by new complex social networks; by the abundant manufacture of jewellery in ivory, shell and other media; by new suites of weapons and tools in osseous and lithic materials; but, strangely there is a lack of evidence for houses or burial of the dead. Chauvet Cave is one of the best-known art sites of this period. The* Gravettian *(27,000-23,000 years ago) is marked by Europe's earliest ceremonial burials; by the development of houses and settlements; by new suites of tool and weapon types; by new technologies, including weaving and the firing of clay; and by very long distance social networks. The underwater Cosquer Cave near Marseilles is one of the best-known art sites of this period. The* Solutrian *(22,000-18,000 years ago) is limited largely to western France, Belgium and northern Spain. Important innovations include heat treatment of flint as preparation for pressure-flaking of spear (and possibly arrow) points; the earliest true eyed bone needles; and a device known as the spear-thrower which considerably lengthened the distance that a spear could be thrown. Solutrian art sites are not common, but Cougnac in the Lot region of France is a good example. The Solutrian is succeeded by the* Magdalenian *(18,000-11,000 years ago) which has a far wider distribution, from Poland in the east to the Atlantic coasts of Iberia and France. Most cave art has been dated to this period and there is a florescence of all types of art and symbolic expression. Once again there are new types of stone and osseous tools and weapons. Well-known sites of this period are Lascaux and Altamira.*

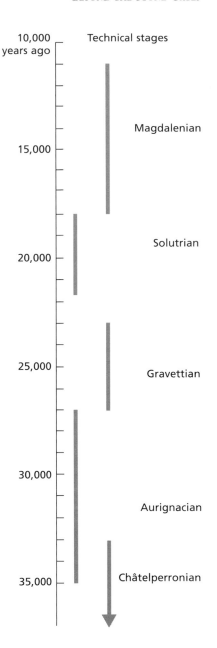

Vindija Cave have been dated to this age.[3] And the earliest dates for unequivocal remains of anatomically modern humans in Europe are actually no older than 35,000 years ago (Table 1). This leaves open the possibility that the 'pioneer' phase of the Aurignacian 'industry' – whilst generally interpreted as a proxy for modern humans – was actually made by Neanderthals. Further discoveries of fossil hominids associated with lithic industries are needed to resolve this question.

SITE / SPECIES	AGE	COMMENT
Grotte du Renne, Arcy-sur-Cure, France *Homo neanderthalensis*	33,000[4] years ago	ear bone of child associated with bone ornaments and Châtelperronian artifacts[5] in layer Xb, date on bone from same layer[6]
St Césaire rockshelter, France *Homo neanderthalensis*	36,000 33,000	burial. TL determination on burnt flint ^{14}C determination on associated charcoal[7]
Vindija cave, Croatia *Homo neanderthalensis*	29,000	mandible / from layer G, where apparently associated with Aurignacian bone tools
Peştera cu Oase, Romania *Homo sapiens*	34,000–36,000	human mandible, directly dated by [14]C
Kelsterbach, Germany *Homo sapiens*	31,000	adult calvarium no associations
Kent's Cavern, Torbay, England *Homo sapiens*	30,000	human maxilla in debris flow containing Aurignacian artifacts

Table 1. *The most reliable radiometric dates for late Neanderthals and the earliest modern humans in Europe.*[8]
A sole earlier date of 36,000 years ago, on a Homo sapiens *skull fragment from Hahnöfersand in Germany, lacked substantiation from stratigraphy or association and has now been redated as Holocene.*[9] *However, note the Peştera cu Oase date, published in September 2003.*[10]

The first appearance of the famous mobiliary and cave art of western Europe, at least, has been dated to around 33,500 radiocarbon years ago in Bavaria and 31,000 years ago in France,[11] by when Neanderthals seem to have disappeared locally. The early dating of the French cave art preserved in Chauvet Cave in the Ardèche has been contested,[12] but this challenge cannot reasonably be sustained.[13]

A way of seeing
The defining dates in the title of this chapter span both the transitional period from around 40,000 to 28,000 years ago, when Neanderthals and modern humans certainly coexisted, and the phase until the end of the Ice Age 10,000 years ago, when moderns were the sole and unchallenged occupants of Europe. The concept of stone gates in the chapter title is partly Virgilian, having the sense of portals to an underworld. But the gates evoke, for us, the story of 'The Return of Eva Peron', as told by the writer V.S. Naipaul.[14] This involves a high-status corpse and a journey both symbolic and real. For seventeen years, the exiled Argentinian General Juan Peron had resided in a suburb of Madrid known as the Iron Gate, *La Puerta de Hierro*, waiting for the call to return to power. With him was the embalmed body of his once-popular wife Eva, more commonly known now by the affectionate diminutive of her name, Evita. Eventually, in 1972, they made their return journey together

to Argentina. In Siberia, people who died in the winter were often left exposed on platforms in trees before burial in the spring – this practice may explain the many incomplete skeletons at the Mesolithic cemetery of Oleni' Ostrov in Karelia[15] (Chapter 3). Both stories indicate the importance of ancestors as a form of validation for claims relating to land, power or social status.

But there is a further site of great importance – Goat's Hole, Paviland – that will figure later in our discussion of Upper Palaeolithic high-status burials and shamanism. Once a comparable journey was evoked for the Paviland corpse, in this case not embalmed but frozen, transported for many miles to his lonely burial place in Goat's Hole Cave on what is now the southern coast of Gower, Wales. At the time of the burial, a mourner in the cave would have gazed out not on the sea but on a vast plain which was part of the mainland of Europe. It was not until the 1960s that an attempt was made to date the burial scientifically and Kenneth Oakley published a radiocarbon age determined on the actual bones of the 'Red Lady'. The result of 18,500 years ago coincided with the peak of the last Ice Age when the edge of the glacier lay only an hour's walk north of Goat's Hole. The date conjured up a picture of great charm and power, with the implication that the body might have been transported from somewhere much further south to this distant, but venerated, site at the very edge of the ice.[16] As we shall see, state-of-the-art radiocarbon dating and other scientific studies have now revealed a story of even greater complexity.[17]

Thus, our way of seeing the evidence is based on an all-encompassing approach. This involves the study of human behaviours fossilized in the archaeological evidence of settlement, use of space, systems of procurement, use of landscape and territory, ritual practice, burial and art. We doubt that it is possible to argue backwards, with confidence, from our understanding of the modern brain to infer the context of the earliest art and the nature of the belief systems of the earliest modern humans. But, as we shall see, this case has been strongly made elsewhere.

THE ORIGINS OF SHAMANISM: ISSUES OF CONSCIOUSNESS AND COSMOLOGY

Images seen within the human brain

Many scholars have seen a human divide between Neanderthals and anatomically modern humans. For the Cambridge Palaeolithic scholar Paul Mellars,[18] the evidence lies in the interpretation of the ornaments from the Grotte du Renne (Reindeer Cave) at Arcy-sur-Cure in Burgundy as copies made by Neanderthals of the work of modern humans, the hypothesis being that the Neanderthal brain could copy but lacked the ability to innovate. A similar conclusion was reached by David Lewis-Williams[19] but on quite different grounds, founded less on the evidence of archaeology than on arguments concerning the structure and evolution of the human brain.

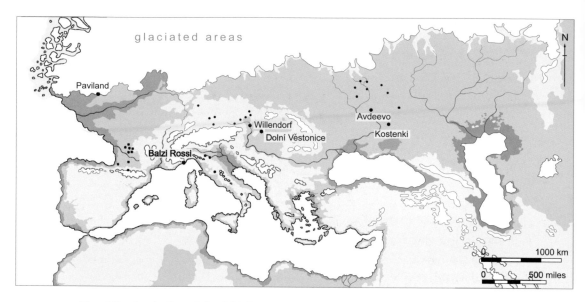

3 *'Venus' figurines in Upper Palaeolithic Europe, c. 25,000 years ago. Their wide distribution may reflect extended social networks during this period of climatic downturn. Paviland, where schematic figures were found, is also indicated. Glaciated areas are shown as at 20,000 years ago.*

Lewis-Williams's line of reasoning has two main elements: first, that both abstract and representational art were effectively absent from Neanderthal contexts, being associated only with anatomically modern humans; second, that the art did not appear as a result of copying from life but, rather, was a consequence of depicting images seen within the human brain, particularly in sleep or when the subject had achieved an altered state of consciousness. Such 'states' are widely accepted by archaeologists and anthropologists as being an integral part of shamanism.[20] Neanderthals, according to Lewis-Williams,[21] were neither able to remember their dreams nor to talk about them and so were doomed to be 'congenital atheists'. Moreover, he believes, religion was born simultaneously with art in the minds of anatomically modern humans as a consequence of the 'fixing', and subsequent interpretation, of dreamed and trance images in two- or three-dimensional form. Additional to this, the fact that the learned ability (as opposed to neurobiological capacity) to enter trances was limited to a few people meant that art and religion[22] were associated with the appearance of stratified societies.

But we must be cautious: there is no powerful evidence beyond the art itself (and therefore the reasoning is circular) to invoke social stratification during the Aurignacian. We must remember, too, that all mammals can dream and we simply cannot know whether they, or Neanderthals, can or could remember their dreams.

Mellars's arguments have been the subject of a sustained challenge, particularly by Francesco D'Errico and João Zilhão.[23] The latter would see art as appearing, apparently stochastically, in some social and ecological contexts rather than others but then, historically bounded, becoming a continuing feature of the ritual life of a number of regional communities.[24] What we have globally is the idea of ritual, of which art is but one form of expression. On a local scale, such ritual may involve rock art, including caves; portable art; the ceremonial burials of the Gravettian;[25] and, possibly linking all these themes, the enigmatic series of 'Venus' figurines (Fig. 3) which seem to provide a currency of identity and belief across the collapsing climate of the Eurasian 'Mammoth Steppe'.[26] The historical context was important for, without continuity of ritual and religious practice, systems of art and belief cannot be sustained.[27] The colder, open-environment, phases of the Upper Palaeolithic provided a context in which social territories expanded in response to the need to cooperate over wider territorial ranges in order to maintain populations threatened with dwindling resources.[28]

Reading the bumps: the issue of palaeontological species
Phrenology, the behavioural interpretation of the 'bumps' on the external surface of the skull, was often seen as a science during Victorian times. The practice lasted well into the first half of the twentieth century and holidaymakers used to 'have their bumps read', just as we might now have our fortunes told. Such activities were part of the social life of the English working classes, documented by Richard Hoggart in *The Uses of Literacy*, where he speaks of the world 'of the trams and buses … of the chain-stores, the picture palaces, the trips to the seaside'.[29]

Stephen's mother[30] told him of her encounters with phrenology during his 1950s childhood but, thereafter, the term passed out of currency until the Australian winter of July 1999 when we found ourselves at a very convivial dinner party in Canberra. One of the guests was the late Professor Rhys Jones, one of the world's great archaeologists, whose career had been devoted – with huge success – to unravelling the antiquity of the earliest human settlement of Australia. The conversation turned to the exciting discovery in November 1998 of a ceremonial burial at the Lagar Velho rockshelter in Portugal. The extended burial of a four-year-old child had been found (Fig. 11), covered with red ochre, wearing a sea-shell pendant, and accompanied by animal bones including red deer and rabbit. What was news, however, was the belief of the anthropologists involved that the child was a Neanderthal/modern human hybrid.[31] Dated to 24,500 years ago, this child would have lived at least 4,000 years after the last Neanderthal had died out in Iberia.[32] Moreover, DNA evidence from both the original Neanderthal skeleton,[33] and from the remains of a Neanderthal infant dated to 29,000 years ago and found in excavations at Mezmaiskaya Cave in the northern Caucasus, had shown that the genetic makeup of Neanderthals and modern humans was totally different.[34] It seemed highly unlikely that the two species had interbred; indeed, as separate biological species, many had wondered whether they could have mated successfully and produced fertile offspring. Yet here it seemed was the evidence and the story it told was of substantial and successful interbreeding, at least in Iberia, with the conse-quences still visible thousands of years after the last pure-blooded Neanderthal had succumbed to extinction.

Rhys's commanding voice suddenly dominated the room: 'Do not believe a word of it,' he said. 'Physical anthropology is just like phrenology: they read the bumps.' It was a combination of this event and Bristol's exciting 'Human Roots' conference the next year[35] that led one of us (SAG) to enquire just how relevant to the human story was the division, into species, of the fossil record of the last half million years in particular, when all that survived was evidence for palaeontological, not biologi-cal, species – not brains, nor tissue, and certainly not people.[36] We cannot know what artistic heights the Neanderthals might have reached given time and social context. And we certainly cannot argue evidence of absence from absence of evi-dence. Accordingly, we will not consider the issue further here.

Death and the Neanderthals

The 130,000-year-old site of Krapina in Croatia – a lofty rockshelter, 12 m (39 ft) in height – was excavated between 1899 and 1905 by Karl Gorjanović-Kramberger. The stratigraphic sequence[37] consists of over 9 m (29 ft) of sediment, divided by Gorjanović into nine layers.[38] Remains of over forty Neanderthals came from a single horizon. The extent of disarticulation of the skeletal remains, with evidence of the smashing of long bones for marrow and even the charring of some bones, led to the widespread conclusion that cannibalism had taken place.[39] In 1985, Erik Trinkaus – Professor of Anthropology at Washington University, St Louis, USA – reviewed the evidence in a paper entitled 'Cannibalism and burial at Krapina'. He concluded that the condition of the Neanderthal remains could be accounted for by natural processes (sediment pressure, roof collapse and biological disturbance) but that the pattern of skeletal part preservation showed clearly that the corpses must once have been buried by relatives or rockfall. Given the implausibility of multiple collapse events burying newly dead Neanderthals before the locally active carnivores could intercept them, deliberate burial by fellow hominids seems the most likely explanation. A study by Mary Russell[40] suggested that cut-marks at Krapina were 'consistent with *post mortem* processing of corpses with stone tools, probably in preparation for the burial of cleaned bones', a process designed to admit them into the realms of the ancestors.[41]

Tim Taylor, in his book *The Buried Soul: How Humans Invented Death*,[42] uses his dis-cussion of the Neanderthal mortuary rituals at Krapina to pose a fundamental question about the purpose of defleshing, namely 'where the 60 or more kilos of prime meat ended up '. Taylor is clear that cannibalism was consistently practised by both Neanderthals and modern humans. Indeed, the evidence from several recently excavated sites seems unimpeachable. These include the Neanderthal site of Moula-Guercy in the Ardèche, dated to *c.* 120,000–100,000 years ago. There, excavations by Alban Defleur and Tim White[43] revealed a butchered fauna, including five red deer, ibex, and the partial remains of six Neanderthals comprising two adults, two adolescents, and two children aged six to seven years in age. Both animal and Neanderthal species had been similarly treated: marrow bones were smashed, brains extracted from crania. Also, the tongue – a delicacy – was removed from at least one Neanderthal. Here, the hominids were clearly food. We cannot say with total confidence whether this arose from survival, hunting, status or insult cannibalism (Table 2), but the similarity of treatment accorded to both the butchered herbivores and the Neanderthals suggests survival or hunting as the mechanisms involved. By contrast, ritual treatment of the dead may be implied at the French Neanderthal site of La Chaise, Charente.[44] There, separate cave-chambers seem to have been chosen for adults and juveniles. Moreover, the juveniles alone seem to have been butchered, as cut-marks attest. Cannibalism has been claimed from perhaps fewer than half-a-dozen Neanderthal sites spread over 50,000 years or more. It is not clear how frequent the practice actually was.

Types of cannibalism	*Context*
survival	starvation
hunting	hunting fellow humans for food, not necessarily in the context of starvation
honour or status	endo-cannibalism; consumption of deceased relatives as a mark of respect, involving recycling and remembrance
insult	exo-cannibalism; eating one's enemies

Table 2. *Some types of cannibalism.*[45] *The terms endo-cannibalism and exo-cannibalism refer, respectively, to the practice of cannibalism* within *or* outside *the social or family group.*

Gough's Cave, Somerset, dated to *c.* 12,000 years ago,[46] has produced powerful evidence for cannibalism. Moreover, analysis of the stable isotopes of carbon and nitrogen, preserved in the bones of the fauna and humans alike at Gough's, has yielded important and startling dietary evidence.[47] The commonest, and frequently butchered, animals at the site are horse – an animal of open country – followed by red deer. The butchered humans lived, however, on a high-protein diet composed mainly of the woodland species, wild cattle and red deer, with only rare horse. The implication is that these humans were prey, not predator, and that they were not local to Cheddar Gorge. There is a terrifying possibility that they were captives, brought alive to the Gorge and 'stored' in the cave until a 'bad hunting day' moved them to the top of the menu. The fact that the top of one skull had been made into a 'fruit bowl' – and was found upside down filled with the bones of butchered red deer – is perhaps resonant of the level of disregard shown for the butchered humans.[48]

Looking at the treatment of the earliest burials, Tim Taylor[49] believes that they represent a 'fetishization of the body' and suggests that the individuals involved, far from being revered ancestors, were actually people who, being somehow apart from society, were assigned the role of scapegoats. Selecting an individual in this way and then excluding them through ritual banishment or murder, served the purpose of defusing inter- or intra-societal conflict. Such scapegoats were often actually chosen by virtue of their being vulnerable or through offering themselves as volunteers. Taylor's discussion of a Neanderthal burial from Shanidar in Iraq is chilling. The skull of this Neanderthal (Shanidar 1) displayed evidence of a severe impact to one side of his face leading to brain damage, paralysis of his right side, and to the withering of his right arm (Fig. 4). As a seriously disabled individual, he could not have sustained himself without the support of a caring community – a support all the more remarkable when we understand that Neanderthals may have provisioned themselves individually when on the move.[50] But perhaps Shanidar 1 was not a revered and beloved uncle. Perhaps – and this is a thought not without contemporary resonance – he was a low-status disabled person, a curiosity, kept alive as an apotropaic symbol, protecting against evil until the day of his natural death or his sacrifice as a scapegoat. We are reminded of the ruthlessly efficient hunting strategies once practised by some Australian Aboriginal groups. A kangaroo would be hunted and captured; its legs would then be broken and it would be brought back to camp and, there, kept alive until required.[51]

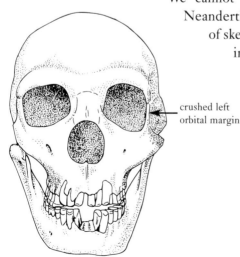

crushed left orbital margin

We cannot invoke this precise practice in the case of Neanderthals, but the latter do possess a remarkable level of skeletal injuries. These traumas, interpreted as arising from close-encounter hunting,[52] would have yielded disabled individuals whose fate lay in the hands of the community and its traditions. We probably see very few of these liminal people, just those who died or who were, perhaps, put to death in caves. Most elderly

4 *Shanidar, Iraq. This skull of a male Neanderthal, known as Shanidar I, shows evidence of a severe blow on one side of the head which led to brain damage and paralysis. He could not have lived without support from his community.*

Neanderthals probably died in the open,[53] like the elderly of the nomadic Bakhtiari of Iran who encountered the Bazuft River, swollen with melt water, during their spring migration:

> What happens to the old when they cannot cross the last river? Nothing. They stay behind to die. Only the dog is puzzled to see a man abandoned. The man accepts the nomad custom; he has come to the end of his journey, and there is no place at the end.[54]

In Europe, we see very early disposal of the dead to the chthonic realms at the Sima de los Huesos site at Atapuerca, Spain, and at Pontnewydd Cave, Wales, sites dated respectively to perhaps 400,000 and 225,000 years ago. This is followed later by special treatment of the dead at last interglacial sites, *c.* 120,000 years ago, perhaps defleshing and burial at Krapina in Croatia and cannibalism at Moula Guercy in France – and finally by more formal deposition of the Neanderthal dead during the last glaciation. Of these latter interments, Kebara Cave in Israel is of especial interest. Here, an adult male had been buried 60,000 years ago in a shallow pit, with his cranium and legs largely removed, perhaps for use as ancestral relics.[55] We may note that, where Neanderthals are concerned, only cave deposition is known. And caves were liminal places where the underworld, a place of spirits and ancestors, could be accessed. In other words, the development of mortuary rites by Neanderthals, combined with their apparently heightened interest in caves,[56] is suggestive of a latent and burgeoning cosmological perception. The concept of a universe with ouranic,[57] territorial and underworld elements came later, maybe 35,000 years ago, to form part of the cosmovision[58] that was to underpin shamanic activity.

SHAMANISM IN THE LATER PALAEOLITHIC

Neurological determinism

We introduced, in Chapter 1, the broad principles of shamanism and listed their potential archaeological manifestations. The later Palaeolithic was peopled by hunter-gatherer societies living in diverse Ice Age environments and climates. Shamanism is widely regarded as having been endemic in many recent hunter-gatherer societies and so, by analogy, may have been similarly widespread among ancient hunter-gatherers. The form of interaction between people and the Palaeolithic spirit-world is, of course, unknown to us and some would prefer to use the term 'palaeo-shamanism'.[59] One mantra of late twentieth-century studies has been the identification in abstract art of entoptics (or phosphenes), symbols (Fig. 5) generated by the brain of the shaman as he or she entered an altered state of

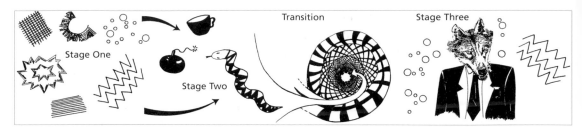

5 *People entering altered states of consciousness are said to go through the three stages illustrated here. The geometric signs called 'entoptics' are seen in the first stage. Therianthropes appear only in the final stage.*

consciousness.[60] Symbols that may be depictions of phosphenes occur in European Palaeolithic cave art[61] where dots, zig-zags, grids, meandering lines, and festoons may all be so recognized. Even so, tectiforms ('house-shapes'), claviforms ('club-shapes') and spear-like shapes are all abstract forms which similarly appear in cave art but are not phosphenes. A case clearly has to be made before the 'entoptic' representations of the European caves can be accepted as indicative of the practice of palaeo-shamanism. Piers Vitebsky[62] considered the recognition of prehistoric shamanism by reference to the practice of altered states of consciousness to be unwise because of the intangibility of the trance state. Currently, the neuropsychological model is facing scientific challenge by Patricia Helvenston and Paul Bahn,[63] with David Lewis-Williams mounting a stern defence.[64] The archaeological community has yet to reach a definitive view on this issue. The problem is that archaeologists generally lack the expertise fully to appraise the neurological arguments, with the consequence that differences of view may not be objectively based.

Colour and light
Even so, entoptics may represent only part of the story for, in a review of Amerindian shamanism, the anthropologist Nicholas Saunders[65] identifies the concepts of colour, brilliance and sacred glow as being of more relevance. Thus, as an example, there are 'light' shamans among the Warao of Venezuela for whom:

> the shapes, colors and motions of natural reptiles converge with the dynamic and chromatic forms of hallucination, evoking a nearly universal serpent symbolism that unlocks the gates of intuitive reality.[66]

The Warao shamans experience tobacco-induced trances in which their visions are both synaesthetic and multisensorial. Saunders[67] argues that the importance of entoptics has been overstressed in the Americas, leading to a 'neurological determinism' which has done violence to our understanding of shamanism. Moreover, in seeing these depictions as the involuntary products of altered states of consciousness, we are in danger of devoiding them of socially embedded meaning.[68] In Europe, images involving colour and symbols link ceremonial burials with figurines and cave art in a way that dramatically extends our ability to interrogate the data.

The use of ochre, for purposes unknown, is attested by 250,000 years ago in Africa and Europe respectively.[69] Its earliest application in these continents for the creation of art would seem to be *c.* 70,000 years ago at Blombos Cave in South Africa, where abstract designs were produced on small pieces of bone and ochre[70] and *c.* 33,500 years ago at Geissenklösterle Cave in Bavaria[71] and perhaps *c.* 31,000 years ago at Chauvet Cave in France. The true antiquity of both parietal and mobiliary art in Europe is given by the thermoluminescence (TL) age of *c.* 37,000, equivalent to a radiocarbon age of about 33,000 years ago, for the Aurignacian layer in the cave of Geissenklösterle, where both art-forms occur.

The use of ochre in ritual can be seen to be earlier, perhaps *c.* 105,000 years ago – if the date reflects the true age of the burial – for the ochred child burial at Border Cave in South Africa.[72] Large-scale mining for ochre in Africa took place in the Middle Stone Age before 100,000 years ago[73] and the use of pigments in Africa thus long pre-dates the appearance of cave art in Europe. Even so, we should remember that art, once painted on cave walls older than 30,000 years ago, generally now survives only as collapsed fragments.

All humans – and there seems no reason to differentiate archaic and modern humans here – can perceive the full range of the colour spectrum. Even so, Brent Berlin and Paul Kay's classic study[74] seemed to show that only black, white and red are universally distinguished, followed by yellow or green. Such perception is likely, however, to be culturally bounded and it is probable that the three recurring primary colours are based on the human body and so possess a universal resonance.[75] Indeed, the use of red and white to symbolize, respectively, blood and semen is regarded as 'non-arbitrary'.[76] Notwithstanding broad cross-cultural commonalities in the classification and interpretation of colours, we must acknowledge that we cannot know their precise meanings in pre-literate societies. However, clues may be offered by both the context and complexity of the use of ochre.[77] Thus, the placing of ochre on the heads of male burials, but in the groin area of females, at the Serbian Mesolithic cemetery of Vlasac,[78] may compare with the much earlier Gravettian (see below) triple burial from Dolní Věstonice in Moravia. Again, an expansion of the range of colours in use may reflect increased social complexity, as might be seen in the Bulgarian Neolithic/Copper Age cemeteries of Varna and Durankulak.[79] However, the Palaeolithic use of colour in cave art is quite restricted, with red, black, brown and yellow common, but with occasional use of white.[80] Such a bounded colour range is not suggestive of high levels of social complexity in the later Palaeolithic. This may, perhaps, tell us why very dense occurrences of rock art seem to be limited to only a few regions in Europe which may correspond to such nodes of complexity.

THE GRAVETTIAN BURIALS (27,000–23,000 years ago)

> Poor people's memory is less nourished than that of the rich … it has fewer reference points in time throughout lives that are grey and featureless … Remembrance of things past is just for the rich. For the poor it marks only the faint traces on the path to death.
>
> Albert Camus, *Le Premier Homme (The First Man)* [81]

Shamans and shamanic helpers: beyond the grave

Albert Camus, with his powerful contrast of the lives of rich and poor – the latter with their impoverished lives in which remembrance has little to focus on beyond 'les traces vagues du chemin de la mort'[82] – highlights for us the fact that the diversity of event and ritual in complex societies is likely to be mirrored in a correspondingly greater range of archaeological evidence. We see this in the form of the well-known series of Gravettian burials which span at least the period 27,000–23,000 years ago. Some of these interments have been considered to be those of shamans, or to give special treatment to the remains of certain animals which may have been shamanic helpers.

The graves are frequently closely dated through radiocarbon determinations either on the bones of the skeletons, or from specimens that were unquestionably associated with the body (Table 3). They are a pan-European affair and stretch from Wales and Portugal in the west, to central Italy, the Czech Republic, and Russia (Fig. 6). Overall, they are broadly comparable in distribution, and coeval in age, with the so-called 'Venus figurines' discussed below. Together, they tell us a great deal about the role of the individual in Gravettian society. They speak also of a special status accorded to the dead, whether as shamans, children of princely families, scapegoats, or as human sacrifices. Indeed, to borrow words written in the context of Inca society, we may perhaps see these burials as 'definitive statements of social prestige and as "real time" statements of political power'.[83] But the Gravettian ceremonial interments speak not only of power but also of belief, for the artifacts found with the burials are likely to embody myth and ritualized knowledge, as well as prodigious technical skill.

The visual impact of these burials is so considerable that two red-ochred skeletons, presumably of this age, found under a church in northern Italy, were identified as Christian martyrs. Thus recognized, their relics were believed to have restored sight to a blind man and to have driven out demons from others and, in consequence, the pair became canonized as Saint Protasus and Saint Gervaise.[84] Martin Howley has given us the full story: it seems that 'the relics were discovered by St Ambrose, Bishop of Milan, their location having been revealed to him in a vision. The discovery could not have been timed better: it was the eve of the dedication of the great basilica of Milan in AD 386. Gervaise and Protasus were regarded as

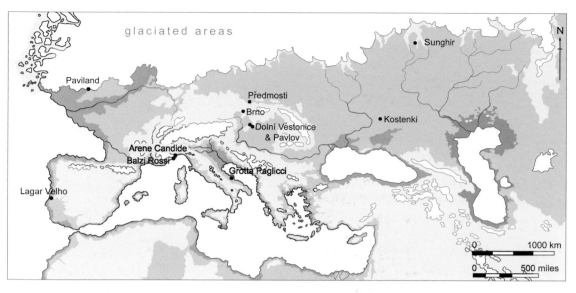

6 *Gravettian burials in Europe, 26,000 years ago. Glaciated areas are shown as at 20,000 years ago.*

protomartyrs of Milan but their burial-place had been forgotten. They were found in the cemeterial church of Saints Nabor and Felix from which they were brought in solemn procession into the new basilica.'[85]

SITE	BURIAL	DATE (years ago)
Paviland, Wales	'Red Lady' (adult male, 25-30 years old)	25,000–26,000
Lagar Velho, Portugal	4-year-old child	associated finds from grave: 24,000 – charcoal and red deer bone immediately overlying skeleton: 24,000 – rabbit bone
Sunghir, Russia	double children's burial	24,000 – ?female child 23,800 – ?male child
Brno 2, Czech Republic	adult male ('shaman')	23,000
Arene Candide, Liguria, Italy	'Il Principe' (adolescent male)	23,000
Sunghir, Russia	adult male	23,000

Table 3. *Gravettian ceremonial burials: radiocarbon determinations in dates years ago. The results quoted here are based on samples of the bone of the skeletons, with the exception of Lagar Velho, where charcoal and bone accompanying the burial have been dated.[86]*

The human remains found in Gravettian graves are not always in the form of complete skeletons. Bodies may be headless or, at times, represented only by heads or by individual bones. The Palaeolithic scholar Paul Pettitt[87] suggests that these individual bones and skulls were – like our Italian saints – sacred relics, acquired through the ritual defleshing of corpses. One such Palaeolithic relic, an adult human femur from Sunghir near Moscow, was found filled with red ochre – perhaps in mimicry of bone marrow. There is a variety of practice, too, where disposal of the dead is concerned. For example, in Moravia, burials may be richly, poorly or wholly un-endowed; may be single or multiple; sometimes apparently ritually defleshed and scattered; and, maybe at other times, inserted *via* avens into underground caves.[88] 'Jewellery' was used to adorn hats worn by the corpses, as also necklaces, and other items of clothing. There are regional variations in the use of such items of jewellery but the range includes perforated teeth, typically cervid or fox; beads and pendants of mammoth ivory; and both sea shells and fossil shells. We will seek to approach an understanding of the meaning of these Gravettian graves through case studies of several individual burial sites.

A shaman's burial: Brno 2, Czech Republic

The burial of a mature adult male who had suffered from periostitis was found in AD 1891 in a grave sealed by loess (wind-blown sand) and far from any settlement site. The skeleton had been strewn with ochre, covered by a mammoth scapula, and was accompanied by other macrofaunal remains, including mammoth tusks 1.5–2.0 m (4.9–6.6 ft) in length, numerous ribs of rhinoceros or mammoth, an entire juvenile rhinoceros skull, and the ochre-stained teeth of a horse. Accompanying the body were more than 600 *Dentalium badense* shells (fossil Miocene mollusca), interpreted as decoration for head-coverings.[89]

Other mobiliary art artifacts included two large perforated slate disks and fourteen small disks variously made of haematite, soft stone, bone, mammoth molar and ivory. Most striking of all, however, was the discovery of parts of a composite male human ivory figure, the so-called 'marionette' and also the only figurine to be found with a Gravettian burial (Fig. 7). Also, again possibly linked with 'performance', was a reindeer antler with a polished end interpreted as a drumstick, interpretation of the artifact as knapping hammer having been excluded.

7 *Brno, Moravia, Czech Republic. The ivory marionette formed part of the equipment of a possible shaman's grave. c. 24,000 years ago.*

Several features, in particular, may suggest this to be a special burial, perhaps even the grave of a shaman. Topographically, the situation of the grave away from settlement is unusual in a Moravian context. Moreover, the nature and placement of the grave goods, including the large herbivore bones, is striking: the discs are typical accoutrements of a shaman's costume; the figurine is unique; and the drumstick may relate to the sustained and rhythmic drumming often used by shamans to induce states of trance. Finally, his life of chronic pain, and perhaps related psychological trauma, might have given him social recognition as a shaman.

A place of pilgrimage: Goat's Hole, Paviland, Wales

Isolated, in much the same way as the burial from Brno, was the grave of an ochre-stained male skeleton, discovered in AD 1823 during excavations inside Goat's Hole Cave, Paviland, on the Gower peninsula of South Wales. Although almost immediately dubbed the 'Red Lady', the skeleton was actually that of a young male of some 25–30 years in age, 73 kg or 160 pounds in weight, and 'healthy, if dead' on the basis of the part of the skeleton which survived.[90] An examination of the 'Red Lady' in terms of the taphonomy of the burial (Table 4) suggests half-a-dozen separate events in the 'life' of the corpse between death and final interment. One of these events, the funeral ceremony, may well have been an important social and spiritual occasion, with the 'performance' taking place outside the cave because of the size of the audience (Plate 7). But how much can we safely infer about the 'Red Lady'?

A question-and-answer approach may help here. If we ask whether the 'Red Lady' is important, the answer is 'yes'. This is because of the status of the burial, reflected in or afforded by the act of burial itself, the use of ochre, and the provision of grave goods of mammoth ivory and marine shell. There is no simple answer to a second question as to whether this importance lay in life or death – in other words, was the 'Red Lady' an important leader or a human sacrifice? There is no forensic evidence to resolve the question of the context and mode of death of this incomplete skeleton. A third question – was the 'Red Lady' a shaman? – is almost impossible even to approach. The mammoth skull found near the burial, if once part of the grave furniture, may relate to the shaman's animal helper or may perhaps, as the Palaeolithic scholar Derek Roe has suggested, have been an osteophone or biodrum, positioned to make music at the funeral feast. Perhaps the ivory rods were once part of artifacts designed to divine the will of the spirit world (Fig. 8). One thinks, here, of the 'medicine bundles' of the North American Indians: collections, often of seemingly worthless objects, perceived by their owners as items imbued with sacred power. This might make sense of the heap of 'scrap', or perhaps ritually broken, ivory rod and bracelet fragments placed on the chest of the 'Red Lady' of Paviland.[91] The heap of perforated sea shells found on the thigh may have been collected in, or ornamented, a 'medicine bag'. These shells speak not only of journeys to the coast, but perhaps also of journeys to the underwater world of spirits.

EVENT	COMMENT
1 death	place unknown – it need not have been local
2 transport of the corpse to the cave	if the body was brought from a long distance, it may have been transported frozen; it would also imply that the burial site was in some way special
3 enrobing of the body for the burial ceremony and grave	in this instance, the body seems to have been dressed in ochre-stained leather clothing, probably comprising a shirt, trousers and moccasins
4 the funeral ceremony	if, as likely, a public event, it probably took place in the open in front of the cave; a ritual, possibly shamanic, performance is likely to have taken place
5 the grave	a grave was dug to receive the body in extended position, with small head and foot-stones placed at either end; the gravediggers chose the site for the grave carefully to lie close to, and so to appear to incorporate as part of the 'grave furniture', the skull of an adult mammoth
6 ornamenting the body	this seems to have involved placing ritually broken ivory rods and bracelets on the chest of the corpse, and placing a bag, decorated with or containing perforated sea shells, on the thigh
7 consignment to the earth	filling in the grave – perhaps the head/foot-stones were used to mark the position of the grave
8 site of grave progressively masked by natural sedimentation	formation of a talus cone
9 erosion and exposure	by the Holocene sea

Table 4. *The death, burial and discovery of the 'Red Lady' of Paviland. A taphonomic analysis.*

As part of the interpretation of the Paviland radiocarbon programme, one of us (SAG) considered – with our colleague Paul Pettitt – the implications of the full pattern of dates obtained in the context of the artifacts found and of other evidences of human activity. In essence, these showed a pattern of human presence looking something like this:

DATE (years ago)	EVIDENCE OF HUMAN PRESENCE
28,500	Aurignacian settlement with abundant artifacts, bone charcoal, and animal bones
27,000	tanged flint spearpoint, probably used in hunting
26,000	the 'Red Lady' burial
24,000	perforated ivory pendant
23,000	bone 'spatulae', interpreted as anthropomorphic figurines
21,000	worked ivory
21,000–13,000	no human presence: Last Glacial Maximum
13,000–11,000	rare Late Upper Palaeolithic artifacts

8 *Ivory rods found in Goat's Hole Cave, Paviland, South Wales. The rods accompanied the interment of the 'Red Lady'. They may have been used to divine the will of the spirit-world.*

These evidences of human presence attest a repeated, but punctuated, human presence at the site. Probably, had the cave been better excavated and had not the bulk of the animal bone collection been discarded by curators who deemed it to be of no value, some at least of the gaps in human presence might be filled. But, given the nature of some of the evidence from the site, it may be that the cave was a focus for visitation for reasons simultaneously sacred and profane. Indeed, it had been marked out as special by a series of events. The earliest of these, around 26,000 years ago, was the burial of the 'Red Lady'; later, 24,000 years ago, a highly unusual pendant was manufactured at the cave and William Sollas, its excavator, thought it to have been 'magical' in purpose; later again, 23,000 years ago, a group of anthropomorphic spatulae – artifacts unique in a western European context – was deposited at the site. The contextual evidence – the repeated visits to the site at a time during an, at times, savage climatic downturn, when there is otherwise precious little evidence for other than the most brief of visits to the British peninsula – likewise is evocative of the site's 'specialness'. Indeed, the locale of the cave, overhung as it is by sheer and towering cliffs, frequently overawes the modern visitor who has made his or her precarious way to the wave-cut platform beneath Goat's Hole. In prehistory – in an age of belief – it must truly have seemed to be a place of oneiric (dream-like) power where terrestrial humans could approach and even enter the very *mons sanctus*, the holy hill, and in the Stone Age darkness engage with the world of spirits.

A world elsewhere: Balzi Rossi and Arene Candide, Italy

The Balzi Rossi caves of the Ligurian coast – known also as the Grimaldi or Menton caves – lie close to the French/Italian border. These caves have yielded no fewer than ten separate Gravettian burials. Particularly noteworthy is the site of Barma Grande with its triple burial[92] of an adult male and two adolescents, probably male and female respectively. All were in extended position, strewn with ochre, and accompanied by ornaments of shell, teeth and bone. Pendants of ivory cannot be of local origin, for mammoths were probably absent from the contemporary land-scapes of the French Riviera and Liguria. Large flint knives, one of Vaucluse flint, point to contact with a 'world elsewhere'[93] and accompanied all three bodies. The centrally placed body had a bison bone 'pillow'. If the latter reflects practice in life, it is resonant of the use of head-rests in Africa – for example in ancient Nubia – to protect elaborate hairstyles during sleep.

In 1942, the burial known as 'Il Principe' was excavated from the cave known as Arene Candide. The skeleton was that of an adolescent male who lay on a bed of red ochre (Plate 2). He wore a cap decorated with hundreds of perforated shells and deer canines. Other grave goods included a flint blade 23 cm (9 in) long held in the right hand, pendants of imported mammoth ivory, and four 'perforated batons' of elk antler, three of which display geometric decoration. Such batons and, indeed, virtually any Gravettian artifacts of bone or antler, stand out as being very rare in Italy. It is clear, therefore, that the batons must have been of special symbolic importance, perhaps conveying encoded information capable of retrieval only by a privileged group of people.

The cure of souls: Dolní Věstonice, Czech Republic, site II, the triple burial

A single-phase multiple burial always begs the question of how a number of people came to die more-or-less simultaneously. But the circumstances of the Dolní Věstonice triple interment[94] have favoured a very wide range of speculation and interpretation in which the concepts of the eternal triangle and sexual misde-meanour have figured strongly. The burials (Fig. 9) comprised the extended bodies of two men placed on either side of an individual of indeterminate sex, but often interpreted as female, and so regarded here.[95] Red ochre was placed on all three skulls, both on foreheads and also forming a thick crust on top of the heads. With the ochre on the skulls were perforated teeth of fox and wolf, and ivory beads, all clearly decorating hats or forming diadems. Heads were, thus, a focus of adornment. Red ochre was also placed between the thighs of the central individual, possibly on a foetus which has not survived,[96] but in any case redolent of female symbolism seen in later European hunter-gatherer contexts.[97]

The positioning of the bodies is interesting for, whereas the right-hand male is lying face down and looking away from the group, the left-hand male is placed as if 'gazing at' the central individual. His left hand rests on her groin and he is himself

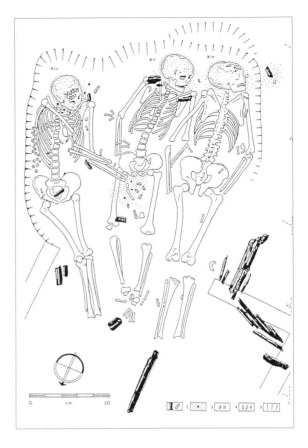

pegged to the ground by a wooden stake driven through his pelvis. This central 'female' individual was severely disabled and had died when she was between twenty and thirty years old. She had suffered serious developmental abnormalities, including deformed thigh bones, a deformed right upper arm bone, a deformed left lower arm, and there were marked differences in length of the fore-arms. Severe upper limb osteoarthritis (marked in the right shoulder and hand) was accompanied by a high level of hypertrophy in the limbs, showing sustained use. One possibility is that the woman had spent a lifetime of dragging heavy loads (perhaps sacks of mammoth bone fuel[98]). We need to ask the question whether the sustaining of this disabled individual was the act of a caring society, which valued the contribution of all members of the community and sought to occupy them with useful activity, or whether we are instead seeing the actions of a society which kept this heavily disabled individual alive in order to subject her to a life of ruthless exploitation. Finally, something never satisfactorily explained, the burials were covered by burnt spruce logs and branches. It may be that the positioning of timber over the burial was designed to serve the same purpose as the megaherbivore grave coverings – the bones and tusks of mammoths or woolly rhinos – seen elsewhere in contemporary Gravettian burials. Charcoal from that timber at Dolní Věstonice has yielded a radiocarbon age of more than 26,000 years ago, much the same age as the Paviland ceremonial burial.

9 *Dolní Věstonice burial, Moravia, Czech Republic, c. 26,000 years old. There was clear evidence for emplacement of red ochre in relation both to the head and the area of the genitals. The burnt wood shown may relate to a structure, either some kind of grave cover or, perhaps, the remains of a temporary structure used for a time to demarcate the grave. A stake apparently driven into the pelvis of burial 14 finds later resonance in later prehistoric bog burials like Windeby in Schleswig-Holstein.*

The dead might walk: Kostenki, Russia

This burial of a male aged between twenty-five and thirty years had been placed, some 25,000 years ago, very tightly bound in a flexed position (Fig. 10) and covered with red ochre.[99] The use of very tight binding may be significant and could suggest that the corpse had been so tied after a process of 'mummification' – in this case putatively via freeze-drying – had shrunk the flesh back onto the bones. Witness a comparable later prehistoric process at the Scottish site of Cladh Hallan.[100] The inferred binding of the corpse is important and may reflect fear on the part of the living that the dead might yet walk (Chapter 8). This seems to arise from a fear that the spirits of the newly deceased might be harmful to the living.

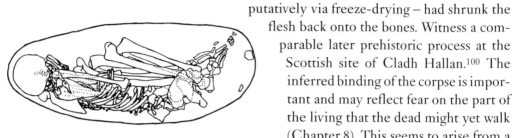

10 *Kostenki, burial 14, Russia, c. 25,000 years old. A male skeleton had been placed, very tightly bound, in a flexed position. Both head and body were covered with red ochre.*

Not shamans, but children: Sunghir, Russia

A double children's burial in a shallow grave excavated into permafrost has yielded a radiocarbon age of 24,000 years ago. The two children, aged 7–9 (?girl) and 13 years (?boy), were both in extended positions, on their backs, hands folded across hips, positioned head to head in a linear double grave. A headless adult skeleton lay extended above the bodies of the children. Patterned differences of soil colour combined with the arrangement of beads on the body are suggestive of clothing, specifically hats, jackets, shirts, trousers and footwear. The 'boy's burial' was adorned with nearly 5,000 ivory beads. He wore a cap beaded with ivory beads and fox teeth, and a belt decorated with 250 arctic fox teeth. A zoomorphic carved ivory pendant lay on his chest, an ivory pin at his throat, and a large ivory sculpture of a mammoth had been placed below his left shoulder. At his left side was the human femur, perhaps an ancestral relic with its internal cavity filled with red ochre, alluded to above. At his right side, a straightened mammoth tusk fully 2.4 m (7.9 ft) long may have been a ceremonial artifact[101] which served both to denote status and to mark out his future status as a warrior. The clothing of the 'girl's burial' was decorated with 5,274 ivory beads. She wore a beaded cap and bore an ivory pin at her throat. Interestingly, there was no use of perforated fox teeth with this burial; nor was there a pendant on the chest. At her sides, however, were two pierced antler batons, several small ivory lances, and three openwork ivory disks, of which one had been pushed onto the shaft of a lance. The presence of richly endowed children among the Gravettian burials suggests a complex society in which status could be inherited. But, for the youngest child burial, we must go far to the south and west, to the very edge of the ocean.

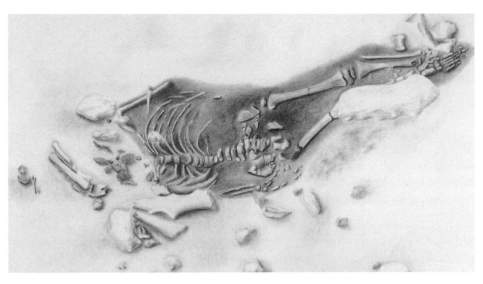

11 *The Lagar Velho, Portugal, child was probably buried in a shroud stained with red ochre. c. 24,500 years ago.*

Lagar Velho, Portugal

The extended skeleton of a four-year-old child was recovered, in 1998, from a rock-shelter in northern Portugal known as the Abrigo do Lagar Velho.[102] The skeleton and immediately surrounding sediments were heavily ochre-stained, but the ochre stopped abruptly as if the body had been wrapped in a shroud (Fig. 11). A pierced *Littorina obtusata* shell had been hung as a pendant around the neck and a headdress of red deer canines was worn. We have seen at Sunghir that these items may denote male gender. A dead rabbit and deer bones may represent offerings of food.

INTERPRETATION OF THE GRAVETTIAN BURIALS

The significance of grave-coverings

Among the Saami of northern Scandinavia, natural sites were used as places of animal sacrifice (*siejddes*), a practice which did not die out until the seventeenth or eighteenth centuries AD.[103] Animals were sacrificed to the elemental forces of thunder, wind, water and sun. The primary purpose was to guarantee a reliable future supply of food animals. Colour was important with white animals offered to the sun god and black to the powers of death. The Saami believed in the classic shamanic three-layered cosmos of sky, earth and underworld. Moreover, certain forms of *siejdde* were associated with the underworld where the dead were believed to walk upside down, their soles engaged with those of the living. These nether regions particularly included caves, marine estuaries and islands.

Saami bear graves

The Saami ritual year is centred on the bear, particularly its periods of winter hibernation followed by summer activity. Bear festivals took place during the intermediate phases. A remarkable feature of the bear burials is the frequency with which the bones – which are the residue remaining after feasting on the bear – were placed in the grave in the correct anatomical order. This practice seems to mirror the symbolic bodily dismemberment of the shaman.[104] It is useful here to summarize, from an archaeologist's perspective, the sequence of events 'from a view to a kill' based on eighteenth-century accounts.[105] They record how the bear is first roused from its hibernation, then lured from its den and killed. Some twenty-four hours later, it is brought into a specially constructed bear hut via a sacred back door. On the following day the bear is skinned, cut up, cooked and consumed to the accompaniment of 'bear songs'. Finally, the bones are buried. This animal that sometimes walks, human-like, on two legs was clearly an object of reverence,[106] whilst also a useful source of furs and meat. The literary evidence makes clear the belief that the bear, if treated respectfully, would 'rise again' and, moreover, that other bears would learn of this and allow themselves to be killed. The re-articulated skeletons were often interred under cairns or were buried in deep pits covered with logs. The purpose of these coverings is clearly stated as being to avoid disturbance by dogs.

This Saami evidence cautions us that the megaherbivore bones, stones and probably wood used as grave-coverings over some Gravettian burials – a practice focused on Moravia – may be primarily functional, whatever the symbolism of the grave itself (Table 5). Such an interpretation finds direct support from Dolní Věstonice site II, where taphonomic analysis indicated carnivore disturbance and dispersal of some human burials.[107] One must remember here, also, the reported use of ochre in graves by the twentieth-century Bushmen in order to disguise the smell of decomposing corpses and so prevent disturbance by carnivores.[108]

Site	Grave-covering
Dolní Věstonice, site 2, burials 13-15, Czech Republic	burnt spruce logs and branches
Brno 2, Czech Republic	covered by mammoth scapula
Pavlov 1, Czechoslovakia	crouched male burial covered by mammoth scapula and other bones
Předmostí, Czechoslovakia (burials 1-18, 26)	mass grave with *c.* 20 individuals in crouched positions (including 6 males, 2 females and 12 children) covered with mammoth scapulae and limestone slabs
Předmostí 21, Czech Republic	adult human mandible placed below mammoth scapula

Table 5. *Gravettian grave-coverings.*

VENUS FIGURINES

Language, whether spoken or the language of symbols, resonates with meaning and was one of the enabling mechanisms that made possible the development of extended social networks on the mammoth steppe of Eurasia during the climatic downturn of the period 27,000–20,000 years ago. Between 20,000 and 18,000 years ago conditions of severe cold were accompanied in northern Europe, and in the Alps and Pyrenees, by the growth of glaciers. Populations congregated in such favoured areas as the sheltered valleys of the Dordogne or the plains north of the Black Sea. Other regions, such as the British peninsula or Moravia, were largely or wholly abandoned. They became *terra nullius*, 'no man's land'. The pulsing climate controlled the distribution of herds of game animals, particularly reindeer, red deer, horse and bison, as also mammoth whose bones and ivory served as the raw materials for fuel for hearths in caves; and in heated houses, sometimes built of recycled mammoth skeletons; and for the manufacture of art objects. Those artifacts – as expressed by their form, composition and materiality – present an iconic grammar which offers us the possibility of approaching the thought and belief systems of the people who are the true subject of our concern.

The morphing figurines from the Balzi Rossi

The Balzi Rossi lie on the Italian Mediterranean coast with views across to the French seaside resort of Menton. The modern railway line from Marseille to Genoa passes in front of the westernmost group of caves, but the cliff then doglegs southwards and the trains run in a tunnel literally through the back of Barma Grande Cave. Nonetheless, the scene is an attractive one, with a small rocky beach below the caves as there would have been during the Upper Palaeolithic occupation.[109] Fifteen Gravettian human figurines, the largest single group in Europe, come from excavations in the 1880s and 1890s in the Grotte du Prince (Grotta del Principe) and Barma Grande.[110] Of these sites, the Grotte du Prince was largely filled with sediments before the Upper Palaeolithic, whereas Barma Grande saw intensive Gravettian settlement, plus at least three ceremonial burials, one of which was a triple interment. In spite of the importance of such Gravettian ritual activity at the Balzi Rossi caves, contemporary parietal art is absent (with the exception of engraved but undated art in the Grotta de Florestano). This is true also of European cave sites with Gravettian ceremonial burials, save only for the Grotta Paglicci in Apulia.[111]

Margherita Mussi, Jacques Cinq-Mars and Pierre Bolduc[112] have conducted a study of the Balzi Rossi figurines, examining them both as individual pieces and as members of the European series of 'Venus' figurines (Fig. 3). They demonstrated, from the presence of perforations and surfaces polished from use, that some figures had probably been worn or mounted for display. Moreover, several figurines depicted double representations of what are, with little doubt, dynamic scenes of transformation.

The authors have identified comparanda, from Pech Merle in the west to Avdeevo in the east, of representations of 'shape-shifting' on figurines that may be double or polyiconic. These pieces, that seem to display liminal beings migrating between two forms of reality (Fig. 12), are not *sui generis* but rather, relate to a wider European scene, with affinities identified with three styles of representation: figurines of Kostenki-Lespugue type, generally made of ivory and stone and widely distributed across Europe; circular masks of ivory and stone, a rare type; and 'Western-type' abstract human figurines found in western Europe and made of coloured stone. Among the Balzi Rossi figurines, two are made of ivory and ten are of steatite.

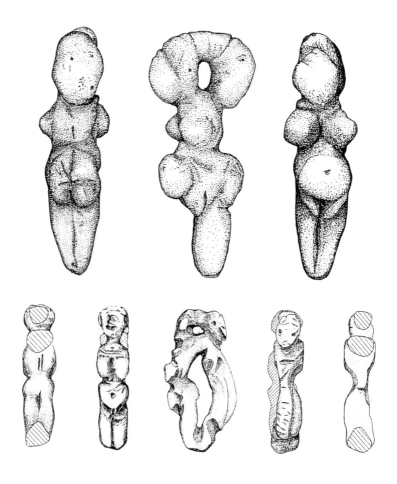

12 *These figurines from the Balzi Rossi caves seem to display beings in a state of transformation. This evidence of shape-shifting suggests a link with shamanism.*

The evidence of style and materiality suggests that the use of these figurines was imbued with meaning and value. Mussi and her colleagues[113] would see these artifacts as representing 'the expression of a sophisticated set of beliefs or a world view'. In short, they see the cosmology of these icons as reflective of the practice of a form of palaeo-shamanism. Their interpretation has far-reaching implications, for it links the art of the figurines with some, at least, of the Gravettian ceremonial burials and with Palaeolithic cave art. It is useful here to identify a further instance of a composition that may represent a further example of palaeo-morphing. We refer here to the limestone block sculpted in bas-relief recovered, with others, from the Gravettian occupation levels at Laussel in southwestern France. The image, known as 'les deux personnages', seems to show two people (or could it be just one?) with the upright individual apparently holding a second inverted person by the foot.[114] Sadly, the image lacks detail and cannot be decoded.

Exploding figurines

Dolní Věstonice is pivotal to our understanding of the Gravettian, but no story is stranger than that of its exploding figurines.[115] The basis of the story is the precocious development of ceramic technology in the lowlands of Moravia before 25,000 years ago. The two richest sites involved are the open-air settlement complexes of Dolní Věstonice I and Pavlov. Together they have produced more than 10,000 pieces, mostly animal figurines but with some human representations which include the famous Dolní Věstonice Venus (Plate 3). All were made from the local loess, were fired in hearths or kilns, but few survive other than as fragments. What seems to have happened was that the figurines were shaped, allowed to dry and then rewetted and placed in a hearth or kiln. The rewetting was intentional and the result was a loud explosion. It seems clear that the activity involved was 'performance art' rather than manufacture. Bohuslav Klíma, one of the excavators of Dolní Věstonice, believed that the principal purpose of exploding the animal figurines was that of ensuring success in the hunt, the latter notably being one of the concerns of a shaman. Klíma even believed he had identified a shaman's hut, although this has been recently called into question by Paul Bahn[116] in a review of recent research by Alexander Verpoorte. This work reveals that the human figurines found at the site include eight female, two male, and five of neutral gender. It is, therefore, clear that the interpretation of the significance of these figurines is unlikely to lie with simplistic gender-based explanations. Whatever the purpose of this art, we can reasonably argue that public performances of this kind, at aggregation sites in the Pavlov hills, are likely to have been led by a ritual practitioner.[117]

THE SHAMAN IN THE CAVE

> *Now I am ready to tell how bodies are changed*
> *Into different bodies.*
>
> Ovid, *Metamorphoses*[118]

The content and history of interpretation of European rock art has been comprehensively addressed on a number of occasions[119] and will be revisited here only in relation to practices and concepts that may be related to shamanism.

The cave as a 'monde autre'

Caves have been widely seen as special places, as other worlds. In particular, in shamanic cosmology, caves have often been viewed as places that gave access to the underworld. As far as Europe is concerned, it is possible to identify a number of ways in which ritual mediators – who may often have been shamans – may have made use of caves. These include:

- the cave as a place of sensory deprivation where altered states of consciousness could be induced with a view to gaining access to the world of spirits, which lay on the other side of the cave-wall
- journeys deep underground were conducted throughout the Upper Palaeolithic, but especially during the Middle and Upper Magdalenian (late phases of the Upper Palaeolithic). Shamans may have been involved in some journeys, but the presence on some occasions of groups of children is more suggestive of conventional initiation rites, as postulated for the later prehistoric Italian cult-caves (Chapter 3)
- engaging with the cave-wall gave access to the otherworld (the 'monde autre'). The rock was not to be seen as solid but as a veil; beyond the veil lay the chthonic realms. We may wonder, however, whether the hands depicted were reaching out to or from the world of spirits
- thus, fragments of bone, teeth of animals including bear, antler and flints, were sometimes placed in cracks in the rock wall as offerings to the spirits[120]
- human hands, both painted (positive) and in silhouette (negative) are known from some twenty sites and sometimes the hands appear to have been mutilated (Fig. 108). Of those at Gargas in the Hautes-Pyrenées, the author Sigfried Giedion[121] wrote that 'the cloud of mutilated hands at Gargas stands there like a tragic chorus eternally crying out for help and mercy'. Detailed study at that site has revealed actual hand-prints and finger-holes in clay, where fingers apparently lack phalanges.[122] The investigator's conclusion is that pathological conditions, including frostbite and Reynaud's syndrome, are most likely to have been responsible. But, whatever the

interpretation of the 'mutilations' – and it would be fair to say that most people now regard the deformed hands as a product of the way in which the hand was held before the paint was blown past it – the application of hands to the cave-walls suggests contact between the terrestrial and chthonic realms

- the apparent emergence, in cave art, of animals from cracks and fissures in the walls suggests that the artists did, indeed, perceive a chthonic realm beyond the rock face. In historic western Iberia, Christian saints are recorded as having appeared from fissures in just this way and such hierophanies have led there to the Christianization of prehistoric rock-art sites
- finally, we must point out that not much more than 50 per cent of Palaeolithic rock art occurs in the darkness zone of caves.[123] The remainder is depicted on open rock surfaces, in shallow rockshelters, or in the daylight zone of caves. Such depictions would have lent themselves much more readily to shamanic performances in such open-air situations.

An overview of African rock art[124] identifies some key issues for prehistoric European art. A key point is that art may be seen both as a store of, sometimes codified, knowledge and as a means of its communication within particular functional and social contexts. The theme of the role of Upper Palaeolithic art as a store of information about the whereabouts and condition of large game has been expounded by Steven Mithen of the University of Reading.[125] But rock art should be seen as one element in an artistic tradition embracing such diverse strands as tattooing, costume, painted and shaped artifacts, and even the planning of houses and settlements. The locales where art occurs are not random and suites of images may vary in technique or theme. Thus, rock-art galleries or displays in Europe may be in accessible places ideal for group viewing, such as the Salon Noir at Niaux, or may be deep underground in very remote and difficult-to-reach parts of cave systems. Depictions in such areas seem often to have been hasty affairs[126] but, besides the art, there is evidence for visits by adults and children alike, and some of these seem to have been dancing.[127] Perhaps a combination of song, dance, story and pictures were used to help children learn how to function and survive as hunters – the cave as classroom.[128]

Where we can approach the social context of art, it is important to note that modern and post-modern art are typically innovatory and challenging.[129] By contrast, ancient art is likely to have lain within a tradition constrained by the rubric of its social and cultural consensus. Depiction in rock art enabled the sharing of experience, whether arising from belief, instruction or record of achievement. Art gave access to knowledge and, so, potentially to power.

The geographical distribution of later Palaeolithic images

Here is a paradox. Recent shamans, of the last few centuries, have only rarely created images of their rituals. Thus, the rock art of the Drakensberg Mountains of South

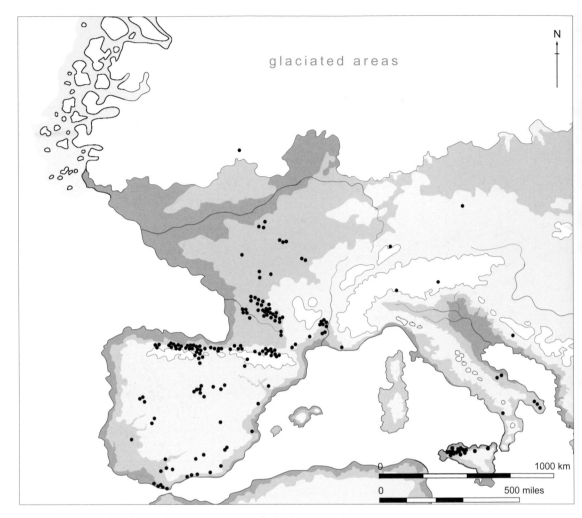

13 *The distribution of cave art in Europe. Glaciated areas are shown as at 20,000 years ago.*

Africa is highly unusual for its depiction of shamanic representations.[130] A map of the distribution of cave art shows that, although widespread, it is concentrated into relatively few areas, and that there are definite foci. Noteworthy among these are the regions – from east to west – of the Ardèche, Dordogne, the Pyrenees, and Cantabrian Spain (Fig. 13). Long and deep 'sanctuary caves' are characteristic of the Magdalenian in these areas. However, deep caves occur also in Italy, Switzerland, Austria, Croatia and Slovenia, but were seemingly not exploited for cave art, as in the Franco-Cantabrian region.[131]

1 *Yup'ik mask, Alaska, representing a half-human, half-animal spirit. The masks were used in religious ceremonies in which drumming, dancing and song were important. The ceremonies were designed to drive away illness.*

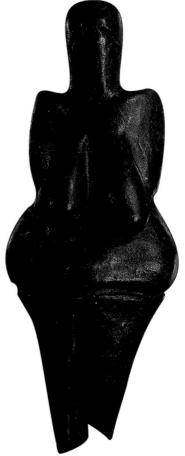

2 ABOVE *The burial known as 'Il Principe' was excavated from the cave of Arene Candide, northern Italy. It has been radiocarbon-dated to c. 23,500 year ago.*

3 RIGHT *Dolní Věstonice site 1: a 'Venus' figurine which has been ritually stabbed. It is made of fired loess. Most of the fired-clay figurines from the site are of animals. Research suggests that the prehistoric ceramic technologists could manage the firing process so that figurines could be made to explode at will and, perhaps, thereby suggest that the practitioners possessed magical powers. c. 25,000 years ago.*

OPPOSITE PAGE
4 ABOVE *A bear skull was deliberately placed on a rock in the Skull Chamber at Chauvet Cave.*

5 BELOW LEFT *Therianthrope from Höhlenstein-Stadel, Bavaria. The ivory figure has the head of a lion and a human body.*

6 BELOW RIGHT *Chauvet Cave, End Chamber. Composite bison/human image associated with and partially erasing the representation of a human female. The generous proportions of the latter recall some Gravettian 'Venus' figurines.*

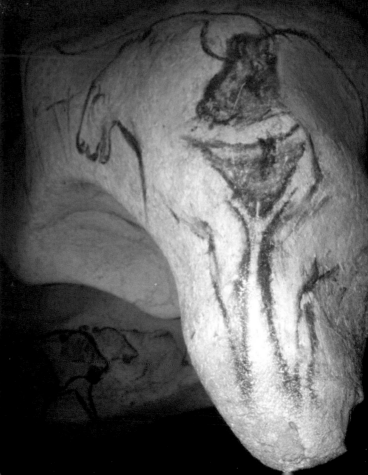

7 *The 'Red Lady' of Paviland is likely to have been a person of high status in life and his funeral ceremony, 26,000 years ago, was probably an important public event. The corpse has been laid out at the entrance to the cave and is the focus of shamanic ritual. Some participants dance around the body, whilst others play the flute or drum. Wands and bracelets of ivory have been placed on the ground and, once ritually broken, will be deposited as grave goods. The grave pit was eventually dug adjacent to a complete mammoth skull, possibly reflecting an especial reverence in which the mammoth was held. Cave art may once have existed at Paviland, although none now survives. Negative hand stencils, dots and bison are shown. The landscape beyond the cave was one of tundra, but with small stands of trees in the sheltered environment of the Severn Valley. The hills of Exmoor are seen in the distance. The coast probably then lay 100 kilometres (60 miles) to the west. The scene is set in a milder period in the Ice Age known as the 'GRIP interstadial 4'.*

8 OPPOSITE *Reconstruction of southern Scandinavian late Mesolithic burial. A dead mother and baby are surrounded by grieving relatives. At the top of the picture a shaman wearing an antler headdress, like those found at Star Carr in northern England (Fig. 1), is shown leading the mourning. Such headdresses have also been interpreted as hunting disguises.*

9 OPPOSITE *Newgrange is the most famous of the passage graves of the Boyne Valley, Ireland. Systematic analysis by Jeremy Dronfield of the typology and distribution of the art on the walls of the tomb suggests an association between lozenge motifs and the emplacement of human remains. Concentric motifs such as the spirals shown here on the left have been interpreted as entry points into the world of the dead.*

THIS PAGE
10 *'Big Man', Kalleby, Bohuslän, Sweden. Figures like these are clearly images of power, perhaps sacred power. They may depict priest-rulers.*

11 *Disc-men, Fossum, Tanum, Bohuslän. These figures may represent shamans: their disc-bodies seem to depict either the sun or a shaman's drum.*

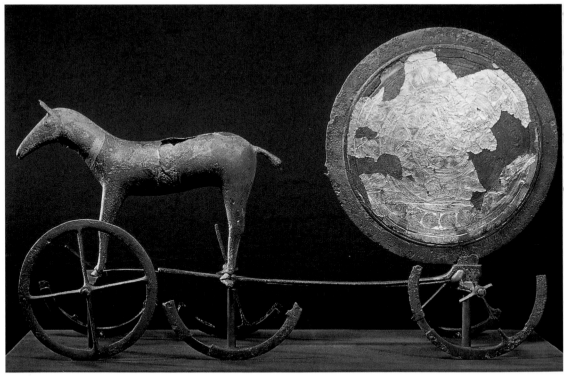

12 *Tree and disc on rock, Solberg, Bohuslän, Sweden. The rock may represent an otherworld journey, or a tiered cosmos, with trees and ships depicting different levels of being.*

13 *Trundholm solar chariot, Denmark. This unique object depicts the noon-day sun (gilded side) and the sunset, with the horse pulling the sun across the sky.*

Music and dance – the magic flute

Lovers of opera will know the story of Mozart's *Die Zauberflöte*: how Tamino possesses an enchanted flute which gives him power to charm wild animals and how, having survived ordeals of fire and water in mountain caverns, he wins his bride Pamina. With both ordeals and music, the story could be shamanic. A Middle Palaeolithic bone flute – consisting of a juvenile cave-bear femur with two perforations – has been claimed from the site of Divje Babe in Slovenia.[132] However, the 'instrument' has been comprehensively discounted, with the perforations interpreted as damage from carnivores, plausibly adult cave-bears who viewed a cub as a useful snack.[133] The earliest undoubted Palaeolithic musical instrument is the Aurignacian flute made of swan's bone from Geissenklösterle in Bavaria, from a level radiocarbon-dated to 33,500 years ago.[134] The context, here, recalls the story of the opera for, in the same layer as the flute, was found a series of figurines of mammoth, bear, bison and feline, together with an ivory plaquette depicting, in bas relief, a human figure.[135] A comparable bestiary of figurines was found in Vogelherd Cave (Fig. 14). Of thirty pipes from Isturitz in the Pyrenees, one is thought to be Aurignacian and the remainder later Gravettian.[136] All of these pipes were played end-on or obliquely, not sideways as with the classic modern flute. A further pipe, of developed Aurignacian age and made from a bear femur, is known from the Hungarian site of Istallóskó.[137]

Claims have been made for the 'playing' of resonant calcite draperies (lithophones) in caves

14 *Vogelherd Cave is situated in the Lone Valley near Ulm in Bavaria. A number of ivory statuettes of animals are known from the site including four representations of mammoth of which the finest was designed to be worn as a pendant. Other animals include lion, horse and bison. The animals illustrated here are (top to bottom): wild horse, felid and cave-lion.*

where art is present.[138] Studies have been conducted at a number of sites where such speleothems have either been damaged or identified with red ochre marks. The surprising result was a clear correlation between the positioning of the art and areas with resonant stalactites and draperies. Sometimes 80 per cent of the art was located in such 'lieux sonores'.[139] There has even been a claim for a whole orchestra of animal bones (osteophones).[140] Music – and one should include bullroarers here which, whirled round on a thread, emit a constant hum[141] – is likely to have been accompanied by dancing, or other special forms of movement, and possible evidence for this exists at the cave site of Le Tuc d'Audoubert, situated around 50 km (30 miles) from Niaux. There, several footprint trails were identified as having been made by children walking only on their heels, perhaps in the context of initiation rites. These discoveries were made fully 500 m (1,640 ft) underground, at virtually the end of the cave system and in the so-called 'salle des talons'. Feet have great symbolic importance because of their positioning at the cosmological boundary of earth and underworld. It is not surprising, therefore, that dancing should figure strongly as a key part of the development of altered states of awareness, but the explanation may, more plausibly, lie with rites of initiation. Dancing may be inferred also from Aurignacian figurines from Geissenklösterle and Galgenberg, interpreted as dancers. The female figures of Magdalenian age from Gönnersdorf and Andernach in western Germany are very schematic, but with strongly emphasized bottoms which appear to be thrust out vigorously as if dancing some kind of palaeo-'Can-Can'. Paul Pettitt has recently proposed a similar interpretation for some elements of the cave engravings discovered in AD 2003 at Creswell Crags in Derbyshire.[142]

Footprints, activity and ritual in the caves

As we have seen, footprints are sometimes preserved in the clays and sands which may naturally cover cave-floors. In most cases the prints are difficult to date and may sometimes, as probably in the Réseau René Clastres, belong to the early post-Palaeolithic period. Even there, they suggest continuation of the ritual use of caves, perhaps by people using if not creating the art. The prints studied here were all made by people walking barefoot, except for an isolated instance at Fontanet, where moccasins seem to have been worn. The distances travelled underground were prodigious and the presence of quite small children, as young as three, seemingly too young to have played a part in shamanic or initiation rituals, suggests that the purpose of certain visits may elude us. Such journeys may have been undertaken for adventure, but they would not have been entered upon lightly. The (happily usually momentary) feeling of blind terror experienced when lighting fails is known to all cavers. Long journeys into darkness would have involved careful planning with guides, wooden torches and oil lamps all being part of the equation. We can see evidence of this in the use of fossil bones as markers for a pathway in the

Tuc d'Audoubert or at Chauvet where, above a track 70 m (230 ft) long made by a solitary child, torch-wipes dated to *c.* 26,000 years ago seem to have been placed on the cave roof to mark the way back. Again, at the same site, a block of stalagmite was used to create a step at an awkward spot.[143]

It may be valuable to look in a little more detail at the sites of Chauvet Cave, the Tuc d'Audoubert, and El Juyo in order to identify forms of ritual activity not expressed through art. At Chauvet, we see:[144]

- hearths, for illumination and to produce charcoal as pigment for the parietal art
- in areas of the cave, deposits of branches and twigs on the cave floor, perhaps residual from stockpiles for fires, inferred from impressions in calcite or in the clay of the floor
- slabs from deliberately smashed stalagmitic floors used to create steps, a drawing platform or a small area of hardstanding
- two bear humeri (upper arm bones) set vertically into the cave floor in the Chamber of the Bear Hollows
- a bear skull deliberately placed on a rock in the Skull Chamber (Plate 4)
- another bear's skull marked with black lines.

The significance of bears for shamanic interpretations will become clearer in the next chapter. For now we will note both instances of bear remains or representations in ritual or art and we will show also, from the evidence of Chauvet, just how important caves were as places where bears and humans interacted. Bears solved the problem of moving deep into the darkness of the cave by scent-marking, by moving along the bases of the cave walls, and by touching the walls.[145] Bear was the commonest species of the Pleistocene cave fauna at Chauvet, with some 170 skulls and 2,500 bones. Bears marked the cave walls with their claws and paws, sometimes defacing the art in so doing, and excavated hollows in the cave floor for hibernation. Deaths occurred during this period of winter sleep, particularly of the old and young. These deaths in turn attracted carnivores into the cave in search of carrion. The presence of wolves is attested by both bones and paw-prints in the cave floor. There is paw-print evidence also of what may well be the world's earliest dog.[146] Of the herbivores, ibex certainly entered the cave, for both hoofprints and skeletal remains are known. The very few remains of horse may have been introduced by vultures.

The evidence from the Tuc d'Audoubert is likewise varied. Thus, in the 'galerie supérieure'

- fossil bones were used as markers for a pathway
- canine teeth were removed from bear skulls (for pendants?)

- stalagmites were broken and piled in heaps
- various deposits were found – a headless adder, a large flint blade, and three perforated teeth placed near an ochre-stained niche.

The 'salle des talons' (the gallery with the heel-prints), in virtually the furthest extremity of the cave system, yielded

- a crude circle of stalagmite fragments stuck into the ground
- two bas-reliefs and a small statuette of bison, all in clay
- a block of clay (?raw material for a sculptured bison) levered out of the ground with a broken piece of stalagmite
- clay fashioned into possible phallic symbols (or possibly just the clay-modeller 'testing' the clay).

Three suggestions have been made regarding the interpretation of the activities in the Tuc d'Audoubert.[147] First, exploitation of the cave (path-markers, extraction of bear canines and clay); second, vandalism (breaking of stalagmite); and, third, ritual (deposits). These categories make broad sense, although it is clear at both sites that pieces of smashed cave formation were often put to practical or ritual use. Another remarkable instance of cave ritual is afforded by the 'sanctuary' in the cave of El Juyo in Cantabrian Spain. Here, a complex structure was found in which patterned settings of different coloured clays, stone slabs and bone spear points were deliberately placed over deposits of animal bones, interpreted as sacrificial.[148] A complex ritual seems to have been conducted over a number of weeks.

The minotaur in the cave – therianthropes

> I know that hidden in the shadows there lurks another
> *Sé que en la sombra hay Otro*
>
> J. L. Borges, *Labyrinth* [149]

The interpretation of Palaeolithic cave art as shamanic is based upon a number of ideas and strands of evidence. Two stand out as being pivotal; first, the selection of geometric shapes that are judged to reflect patterns seen when entering an altered state of consciousness; second, the conflated human/animal figures usually called therianthropes and believed to represent images seen in a later stage of trance. Regarding the first set of phenomena, little can usefully be said. Clear entoptics are rare in Upper Palaeolithic art.[150] Therianthropes are seen in portable art as well, for example the 30,000-year-old composite lion/human figures from the Höhlenstein-Stadel and Höhle Fels[151] caves in southwestern Germany (Plate 5). The association at the latter site of the carving of a water bird, with its implications both of shamanic

15   The 'Death of Actaeon'. Oil painting by the artist, Titian, c. AD 1565-76. The painting depicts the death of Actaeon, shown on the right as a composite being with human body and deer's head in the act of being torn to death by his own hounds. The cause of his fate is shown left in the form of the huntress Diana whom he had impiously encountered naked in the forest.

flight and the crossing of cosmological boundaries, strongly supports a shamanic purpose for these representations. At Chauvet, equally early in date, a wall-art therianthrope nicknamed 'the sorcerer' consists of a human-handed bison, whose depiction incidentally obliterates much of a female 'Venus' (Plate 6). The idea of the depiction of therianthropes seen in trance is compelling, but is trance-imagery the only interpretation? We may recall how the Roman poet Ovid collected together and retold, in his *Metamorphoses,* some 250 stories from the Greek myths of how the petulant deities of the Olympian pantheon changed humans into animal form, generally as retribution for some real or imagined slight. Thus, Diana turned Actaeon into a stag in revenge for seeing her naked. Eventually, he was devoured by his own hounds, a scene immortalized by the artist Titian (Fig. 15). These myths are rooted in the oral poetry of preliterate Greek societies where, as we shall see, such transformations are integral to the bardic tradition.

This belief in fluidity between human and animal forms – usually at some unspecified time in the past – is characteristic of early hunter-gatherer societies.

Thus, the Inuit have a creation period when animals and humans both lived together and were able to shape-shift into each other. Accordingly, a therianthrope of a bear/human composite figure might, if part of a cosmogonic mythology, represent either a bear → human *or* a human → bear transformation. Because of the perceived similarities of its standing upright, ranging widely, using comparable hunting strategies, and building winter shelters 'strangely like the Inuit igloo', the polar bear enjoyed a continuing relationship with humans, particularly in age rituals of Inuit boys.[152] We may recall here the children's footprints in the Tuc d'Audoubert cave, and the fact that the children would have made their journey underground along a route littered with the bones of bears who had once used the cave for hibernation and had died naturally there.[153] Synergy between bear and humans, according to Inuit belief, in part underlay the turning of the 'ice-bear' into a shamanic spirit-helper. Thus, the invention of shamanism marked the end of the 'mythological world' and its replacement by a structured system of interaction between the worlds of humans and spirits. The bear played a key role in this through its ability both to grant shamanic power and, metamorphosed into a human, to become a helper. Parts of the bear's body likewise were possessed with a tangible power. For example, its penis was eaten by barren women because of its perceived reproductive capacity. Again, the making of an amulet from a bear's molar was believed to enable its owner to travel directly to the celestial realm after death.

Thus, therianthropes may relate to the shape-shifting that is part of shamanism. They may also simply be mythological characters or form part of a shamanic mythology. If myth, they may have been created through a tradition of oral poetry in which the creation of monstrous or larger-than-life figures was an important aid in the memorization of stories (Chapter 3). Finally, some figures may simply be depictions of humans wearing hunting disguises to enable them to approach game undetected.

CONCLUSION

We have looked at the evidence regarding the origins of shamanism in the context of the issues of consciousness and cosmology. We believe that the 'human capacity' is something that has developed over a prodigiously long period of time, probably in response to a range of external stimuli. These stimuli are likely to include population movements arising from both environmental and demographic pressures.[154] We are certainly doubtful as to whether the differentiation of the cognitive functions of Neanderthals and anatomically modern humans is useful or even demonstrable. What is beyond doubt, however, is that the first clear evidence for shamanic activity does appear with modern humans towards 30,000 years ago and that, in their mortuary practices, both species demonstrate a burgeoning cosmological belief at a considerably earlier date.

Specialists in the field of shamanism have used the concept of the development of altered states of consciousness as a *sine qua non* of shamanic practice. This has proved an imperfect tool, since the demonstration of the existence of such states within the prehistoric human mind has had to depend upon the proxy evidence of the inclusion within the Palaeolithic art repertoire of images said to have been produced within the human brain as it underwent its journey from consciousness to trance via what is known as the three-stage model of altered consciousness. Archaeologists have been uncomfortable with this scenario, in part because of their lack of expertise, in most cases, in understanding the neuropsychological evidence but, in part also, because they are wary of universal interpretations for Upper Palaeolithic art as a whole. The subject has suffered from this single-model approach in the past and archaeologists are simply not comfortable with a model of interpretation which assumes that many images were created or applied not in reflection of their socially embedded meanings but, rather, were the rubber stamps of the prehistoric world, speaking of conformity and vacuity.

Study of the Gravettian burials of 27,000–23,000 years ago illustrates the kind of variation which must logically be present in the art also. Thus, analysis suggests that the Brno II burial was very probably that of a shaman and that Goat's Hole, Paviland, was a special – plausibly sacred – site and so, at least, appropriate for the grave of a shaman. A powerful case has been made for the practice of a form of palaeo-shamanism from the scenes of shape-shifting witnessed on some of the figurines from the Balzi Rossi caves of Liguria and elsewhere. It is not clear whether we can safely move from these discoveries to a precise interpretation of the interment of the bodies of high-status people at Barma Grande and Arene Candide. Burials from other sites have interesting stories to tell, for example of the position of the disabled within society, as seen at Dolní Věstonice, or of fear that the dead might return (Kostenki). Finally the late burials of children at Sunghir and Lagar Velho suggest that complex, even dynastic, social groupings were now coming into being.

A range of materials was used to cover graves. The use of the bones of such mega-herbivores as mammoth and woolly rhinoceros has sometimes been seen as a reflection of the status of these mammals as animal helpers. Assessment of the significance of grave-coverings calls for careful excavation of new discoveries as they arise. However, our review here of the evidence would seem to suggest that the role of the range of grave-covering materials known relates primarily to a desire both to protect the dead from disturbance by carnivores and to protect the living from spirits wishing to return to the terrestrial world where they might be a danger to the living. This latter may indicate that the dead so treated were regarded as dangerous holy people. A comparable practice to the use of materials to cover Gravettian burials is seen in the Saami bear graves of historical times where the protection of the remains of the bears from disturbance is paramount. Interpretation of the distinctive series of 'Venus' figurines, which are broadly coeval with the Gravettian burials, is problematic. Some are arguably related to shamanism but others seem to relate to childbirth. Probably, here again, a single explanation cannot work.

The evidence of the cave art is perhaps the most compelling in respect of shamanism, in particular the depiction of images which can be related to stages of trance. Thus, the use of the topography of the cave wall to suggest not only the shapes of animals but also their emergence from cracks and fissures links naturally with the idea of the rock wall as a permeable membrane through which access might be gained to the chthonic realms. Perhaps the handprints symbolize that contact, whether representing the reaching out to the souls of the dead or, even, the outstretched hands of the ancestors reaching back into the world of the living. The therianthrope figures plausibly relate to shamanic shape-shifting, although other interpretations are possible such as the representation of people in hunting disguises or characters in a non-shamanic mythology.

Our overall conclusion broadly concurs with a recent overview of Palaeolithic art by Randall White[155] who suggests that no more than 10 per cent of images are susceptible of a shamanic interpretation, potentially leaving 90 per cent to be accounted for in other ways. Ronald Hutton makes the point[156] that the shamanic interpretation 'seems to account for certain forms of Palaeolithic art better than others' whilst noting that Jean Clottes and David Lewis-Williams in their book *The Shamans of Prehistory* made no claim that this paradigm could be the only explanation of the art. In an extended appendix to a new edition of their book,[157] which contains a set of robust and often moving responses to the – often very extreme – critiques which have appeared of the shamanic model, these authors have provided a comprehensive review of their intellectual position. We are confident that shamanism is likely to have played a significant role in the life of hunter-gatherer communities living in the later stages of the Palaeolithic and thereafter. It was almost certainly not the whole story and, maybe, only a small part of the story. Even so, of its importance for the belief systems and religious practices of early prehistory we have no doubt.

3 SWANS' WINGS AND CHAMBER TOMBS

Searching for Shamans in the Mesolithic and Neolithic

*T**he idea that primitive man is by nature deeply religious is nonsense.*
The truth is that all the varieties of scepticism, materialism and
spiritual fervour are to be found in the range of tribal societies.

Mary Douglas, *Natural Symbols* [1]

INTRODUCTION

This chapter looks at the postglacial European communities of last hunters and
first farmers, often referred to as Mesolithic and Neolithic respectively. The
Mesolithic began at the end of the last Ice Age, when changes in climate and environment, combined with population movements, provoked huge discontinuities in
the daily lives of the contemporary populations.[2] Even so, it is the differences
between the hunter-gatherer groups of the Palaeolithic/Mesolithic on the one
hand, and the farmers of the Neolithic on the other, that have been perceived as too
great to admit of any meaningful kind of continuities between the populations concerned. Our approach, however, has been to look at several case studies relating, for
the most part, to caves and burials. In these instances there is some possibility of
identifying commonalities which may arise from 'continuity' over time or which
may be situational and arise from a similarity of context. The first case study deals
with the issue of prehistoric cult caves in Italy and succeeds in bridging both this
chronological and cultural gulf, thereby aiding our understanding of Upper
Palaeolithic and later ritual practice. Finally, we close with a consideration of the
role of narcotics as trance-inducing substances in the European Neolithic.

CULT CAVES IN ITALY

A magisterial study by Ruth Whitehouse,[3] entitled *Underground Religion: Cult and Culture in Prehistoric Italy*, examines a hitherto little-known body of evidence – the caves and rockshelters of Italy. The research focuses on the period from the fifth to the third millennia BC, but sets the Neolithic and Copper Age sites firmly in their Palaeolithic and Mesolithic contexts. The quotation at the head of this chapter conveys a fundamental truth: that it is unwise to make generalizations concerning the degree of 'religiosity', whether innate or imposed, of communities disposed in time or space. Whitehouse, an admirer of Douglas, nonetheless found that the huge time depth that archaeology provides enabled her to draw conclusions regarding the possibility or reality of apparent continuity over as much as twenty millennia.

Three types of site were recognized: first, large natural caves, but generally inaccessible, tortuous and damp – the least common type; second, small natural caves, crevices or rockshelters – often in remote or hidden situations, but with easy interior access; and third, rock-cut underground tombs ('hypogea') whose entrances were perhaps once hidden.

There was evidence at some sites of special attention being paid to stalagmites and stalactites, including collection of drip water. Five to ten sites contained Holocene wall paintings. The content of the latter varied from site to site but, broadly, most figures are either of schematic humans (male and female); or of animals including deer, wild boar and dog; or, finally, may comprise abstract symbols including 'odd blobs', lines, serpentiform and S-shaped designs.

Some caves contained dug graves, but virtually all sites were used for the deposition of human remains. The latter were sometimes disarticulated. The presence of burnt human bone at a couple of sites has led to speculation concerning the possibility of human sacrifice or cannibalism. Several caves also have caches of animal bones, either in crevices in the rock wall or in pits, and it is noteworthy here that the species present are those of game animals, in contradistinction to the bones of domesticated species characteristically excavated from contemporary settlements. There are several reminders here of the Upper Palaeolithic: first, the insertion of bone into crevices in the rock of the cave wall was practised in both periods and, second, there is a parallel discrepancy in the frequencies of fauna depicted in parietal art compared with those recovered as bones in settlement contexts.

Artifacts, potentially ritual in purpose, are found in the caves and Whitehouse[4] gives useful definitions of such 'ritual artifacts' as either representing the *sacra* and, so, possibly objects of worship or, alternatively, the artifacts may be grave goods, equipment used in ritual, or comprise offerings to deities.

Some individual artifact types are worthy of comment:

stone axes One example of a ritual artifact is the stone axe. Types of axe associated with cult caves may be made of unusual or soft, non-functional raw materials; are sometimes small, or perforated, or highly finished; and are likely to be green in colour.[5] Axes of soft rocks occur in ritual contexts elsewhere in Europe. Here, the two miniature chalk axes from the later Neolithic ritual monument of Woodhenge on Salisbury Plain are particularly well-known examples.[6] Again, axes of green rock are important in Europe; examples found in the British Isles, for example, may be of jadeite, a raw material whose origin lies 1200 km (750 miles) distant in the French and Italian Alps. One such jadeite axe seems to have been placed as a ritual offering adjacent to the Sweet Track in Somerset. Here, the trackway – dated to around 3880 BC[7] – led through a marsh to a small, perhaps sacred, island where access to rituals could easily have been controlled.

bird bone Bone was sometimes given special treatment, as at the Grotta Piccioni where nine humeri of wild duck (*Anas boscas*), plus one each of coot and dove, had their lower ends encrusted with red ochre and clay. Birds, of course, may symbolize shamanic flight.

pebbles Both incised and painted pebbles are known. Incised examples first appear in the Upper Palaeolithic, at sites like the Grotta Paglicci, and mostly belong to this period, although stray Neolithic examples do occur. Painted pebbles occur equally in the Mesolithic and Neolithic. What is interesting is that, regardless of age, virtually all decorated pebbles come from caves. Perhaps the best known of the European occurrences of painted pebbles are the Azilian examples from the end of the French Palaeolithic. Here, study by Francesco d'Errico[8] has interpreted them as human schematizations.

The evidence for the cult use of caves is complex but includes burials, wall paintings, ritual deposition of food and artifacts, deposition of special items, and special treatment of cave formations. The Grotta di Porto Badisco is worthy of special consideration because of its wall paintings. In plan, it includes three connecting passages naturally segmented into chambers, like strings of sausages (Fig. 16). Here, cult activity has extended from the Upper Palaeolithic until the fifth millennium BC. In the later periods, pots were positioned to catch water dripping from stalactites, but the site is important because of its Neolithic / Copper Age wall paintings. The art is composed of nearly 1,000 motifs, both abstract and figurative and arranged in patterns or scenes (the latter often of hunting), distributed through twelve different zones of the cave. Red ochre and brown bat guano were the pigments used. Ruth Whitehouse[9] argues that groups of zones show structured sequences of depiction (II-I, IV-VI, VII-IX, X-XII), with larger numbers of images in the entry zones and fewer but special, and therefore perhaps 'secret and sacred', images in the end zones. It would seem, too, that the most sacred images were the most schematic and abstract. Analysis of gendered images shows a concentration of

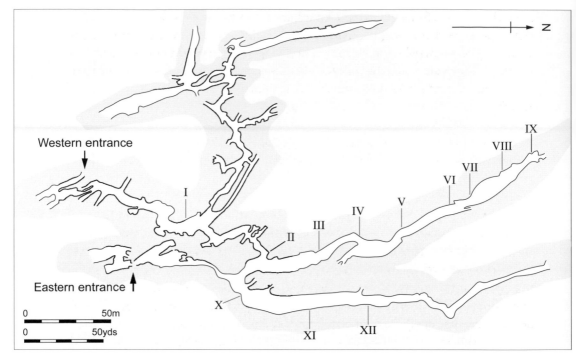

16 *The Neolithic cult-cave known as the Grotta di Porto Badisco is of special importance because of its wall paintings. In plan, it includes three connecting passages naturally segmented into chambers. The distribution and content of art in the cave suggests that only males had access to the most sacred areas.*

females in entry zones, contrasting with ubiquitous males. Finally, so-called 'mediator figures', therianthropes by any other name, occur. These horned and beaked figures always appear in hunting scenes.

In overview, the main features of the cult caves are their being underground, hidden, hard of access, constricted and dark. These, together, form a first interpretative theme – secrecy. Hunting represents a second theme, and this activity provided a pregnant source of ritual symbolism for what were now farming societies. Apart from two depictions of fish in the Grotta dei Cervi at Levanzo, all representations on the cave walls are those of large mammals. By contrast, such smaller mammals as hare, birds, wild cat and marten appear in deposits within the cult caves. One interesting example comes from the Grotta Patrizi where three hare bones had been placed under the head of a male burial. A third theme is that of abnormal water: from stalactites, in still ponds, steam (spa water) or naturally sparkling or bubbling.

The secretive human groups using such secluded sites must have been small in size. Ruth Whitehouse[10] argues that the best interpretation may be that the caves were the venues for *rites de passage,* whether of life stages or initiation into secret societies. Indeed, she argues that ritual specialists will have possessed secret cosmological knowledge which contemporary society may have perceived as dangerous and, therefore, in need of specialist control. Such a mediator was a liminal being and is well described in a quotation from the social anthropologist Edmund Leach:

> The mediator, whether he is a 'real' human being (e.g. a shaman) or a mythological god-man, then takes on liminal attributes – he is both mortal and immortal, human and animal, tame and wild.[11]

One inference is that one might expect to find representations of 'human and animal' beings (or therianthropes) associated with such liminal places as caves, where shamans might mediate between the living and the dead *or* between the living and the world of spirits. The Grotta di Porto Badisco has a scene with six humanoid figures of whom one is horned, one beaked and a third has forked feet like a bird (Fig. 17). Whitehouse,[12] noting Upper Palaeolithic parallels at the Grotta dell'Addaura and, beyond Italy, at Lascaux, speculates on the possibility of continuity.

It is clear that these secluded caves were centres where ritual practices took place, conducted by mediators or shamans. These latter had the power to access the world of spirits and possessed arcane cosmological knowledge. Both factors offered the shaman sources of power and, so, of control of a society where cult and ritual were manifestly important. The evidence of the wall art suggests that the rituals were male-centred and served to reinforce male dominance within society – probably over both women and younger men. Consistent with this is the importance accorded to hunting in the art and ritual of the cult caves, hunting being a typically male activity on the evidence of ethnography. In sum, the evidence of the Italian sites suggests a remarkable degree of continuity (or perhaps repetition) of ritual practice, though not necessarily

17 *The Grotta di Porto Badisco has a scene with six humanoid figures, including one horned, one beaked, and a third with forked feet like a bird. One of the humanoids is clearly visible, top left, and inset, in this photograph of the scene.*

of belief or meaning. This is attested by such time-transcending features as cave burial, parietal art, painted pebbles, and bird-headed humanoids. All are found within the Upper Palaeolithic.

MESOLITHIC CEMETERIES: CASE STUDIES FROM SCANDINAVIA AND BEYOND

> Today both Marxism and communism are unfashionable terms. Such systems have supposedly failed … The ideology of the capitalist marketplace now dominates … Today we are so used to hierarchy, to inequality, domination and exploitation that they have become almost norms, so that we are unable to think beyond such a situation to a society that was totally different.
>
> Christopher Tilley, *An Ethnography of the Neolithic*[13]

Readers new to archaeology will have realized by now that both the belief systems and the structures of ancient societies differed from our own. Christopher Tilley makes this arrestingly clear, in his analysis of early prehistoric societies in southern Scandinavia, seeing late Mesolithic societies there as practising a form of 'primitive communism' and set in 'a kind of Garden of Eden'.[14]

Cemeteries are a feature of the Mesolithic (8000–4000 BC), the earliest known being that from Aveline's Hole Cave in Burrington Coombe, Mendip, Somerset.[15] Here, over a period of around two centuries around 7000 BC, the remains of at least twenty-one people – and perhaps four or five times that number – were buried in the cave. Excavations by the University of Bristol yielded a double burial furnished with offerings which included perforated animal teeth, probably part of a necklace, and seven ammonite body cases.[16]

The late Mesolithic cemeteries date mostly from after *c.* 5000 BC.[17] They are distributed from Russia in the northeast to Portugal in the southwest and seem to be located for the most part in resource-rich, often aquatic, environments in coastal situations (Fig. 18). Aveline's Hole is marginal to the Bristol Channel plain and, in that regard, mirrors the situation of the later sites. It may be that the development of cemeteries relates to the invocation of ancestors to protect and validate territory. Certainly, a number of skeletons, excavated at the sites of Bøgebakken and Skateholm, had met with violent deaths from arrows or spears. Burials took various forms and, at Uleberg, Bohuslän, Sweden, a stone-lined chamber contained two skeletons of which one had been disarticulated with the skull placed on two parallel thigh bones.[18] The grave, dated to *c.* 4940 BC, recalls the virtual disarticulation experienced by the shaman, as also do the partially re-articulated bear burials of Scandinavia.

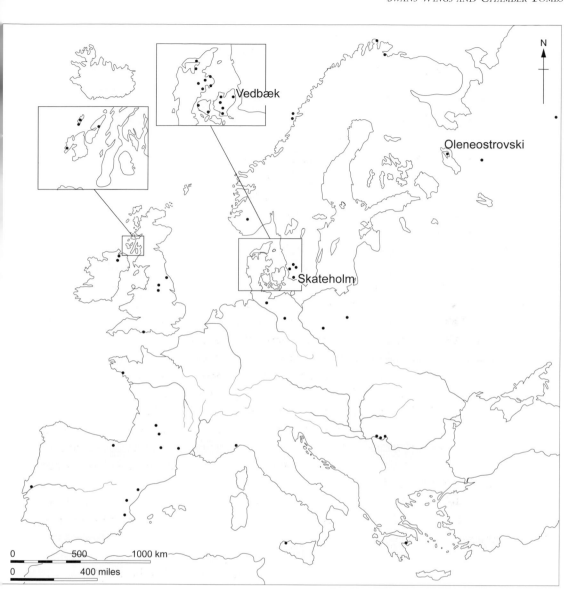

18 Cemeteries of the late Mesolithic are distributed from Russia in the northeast to Portugal in the southwest and seem to be located, for the most part, in resource-rich environments in, or close to, coastal situations.

In our quest for shamans, we will look at the evidence from three burial sites, situated in northwestern Eurasia. It is important, first, to set the context: this area is part of a continuous landmass, which once extended from the British Isles to Siberia. The latter was, as we have seen, the homeland of the term shamanism and there has been a general scholarly recognition that the traditions and belief-systems of the circumpolar regions of Eurasia – from the Saami to Siberia, as it were – are, and probably were, interlinked. The latest specialist to articulate this view is Marek Zvelebil, of the University of Sheffield.[19] He bases his views on ethnographic analogy, normative assumptions and a recognition that slight regional variations were more a reflection of an underlying unity than of division.

The hunter-gatherers of northern Eurasia were the inheritors of deep traditions which together constituted an ideology whose structure involved the perception of the natural environment as 'giving'. There was an integral belief, too, in the principle of sharing in general and in the recycling of animals in particular. Indeed, it was believed that animals had a physical self and two souls that were controlled and managed by human and animal masters. Zvelebil cleverly weaves together the evidence of the ethnohistorical present with the past encompassing both sites (rock art, burials and holy places) and the principle of historical continuity. Such continuity he argues to have been derived from a sharing both of historical trajectory and geographical region. Zvelebil's study looks at areas of northern temperate Europe and western Siberia, contiguous regions with long-term histories of contact and exchange, similar natural environments and patterns of landscape exploitation, and similar material culture. Certain symbols regularly recurred, particularly the key Eurasian animals pertaining to hunter-gatherer societies and recorded in regional ethnographies.[20] Of these, the elk has been seen as a symbol of wealth and prosperity, with a central role in myths of revival and regeneration, a mediator between the human and spirit worlds, and so acting as a guide in the heavens.

The bear's role was as a guardian of wild animals and mediator between animal and humans. The bear[21] was often not directly addressed, there being no word for bear in Slavic, Finnic, Ob-Ugrian and Germanic languages. Accordingly, the bear is called honey-eater or honey-paw ('medved') in Russian or Czech, the 'brown one' ('björn') in Scandinavian Germanic languages or 'grandfather in a fur coat' (by the Khanty of Siberia). Also, among northern hunter-gatherers, sculpted bear axes, bear-headed effigies (also called terminals because they are shown mounted on poles in rock art), and representations of bears in rock art are common. Ritual treatment of animal bones has likewise been common among northern hunter-gatherers. This relates to concepts of the 'resurrection and revival' of the animals. Bears have often been singled out for such treatment. For instance, the skull and bones of the bear may be buried together under a barrow or, again, the skull may be interred separately for use for other rituals. In the East Balkans, between the fifth and second millennia BC, there is a relative lack of bear crania and mandibles compared with other elements, suggestive of their retention in ritual.[22] Note also a Mesolithic find from La Grande-Rivoire (Isère, France), where a bear skull and mandible were found with evidence of tethering and taming.[23]

Water birds were especially important, not least for their association with myths of revival and regeneration. They are recorded ethnographically as acting as messengers between the otherworld and the earth; as guides to the 'burial beyond the water'; and as guardians of the entrance to the chthonic regions. It is scarcely surprising, therefore, that images of water birds are common as lakeside petroglyphs. Symbolically, the seasonal appearance of the water bird signalled the arrival of spring and, so, of regeneration. At this time, dancers among the Ob-Ugrians of western Siberia wore bird-masks and costumes to mimic their mythical water-bird ancestor. Thus, the symbolism was multidimensional, being based on the migratory life-cycle of water birds, with autumn equating with disappearance and so representing death. Conversely, spring marked the re-appearance of the water bird and, thus, symbolized regeneration. This ethnohistorical perspective, with its embedded mythological concepts, seems likely to be reflected in such archaeological artifacts as the 'duck-handled ladles' found both in the East Baltic (4000–2500 BC) and in Western Siberia (500–300 BC).

Oleoneostrovski Mogilnik

The full name of the site is *Yuzhny' Oleni' Ostrov* or Southern Deer Island, in Karelia, Russia.[24] It was also *hautisuolo*, the island of the dead, and seems to have served as a ritual focus for dispersed foraging groups over perhaps half a millennium.[25] Here, a cemetery of more than 170 excavated graves, from a total of perhaps 500, dates from 5000 BC. The society was clearly complex with great disparities in the 'wealth' of individual graves, sharp gender differences reflected in artifact types, and rare child burials. Status was evidently mostly achieved in life, rather than inherited, and wealth was expressed through the possession of pierced tooth pendants of bear, elk and beaver. Some special burials were, however, accompanied by carvings of elks, snakes or humans (Fig. 19). There were also four shaft graves originally described as containing bodies buried upright, which have been interpreted as the graves of shamans.[26] The graves[27] have a westerly orientation whilst others face east. Thus, the shaft graves may face the entrance to the lower world, where the souls both of shamans and the rulers of the lower world dwelt. By contrast, the souls of other people inhabit the upper world. Although perforated beaver incisors occur typically in female graves, they are associated with male and female burials alike in the shamans' shaft graves. Indeed, the robes of a shaman might contain symbols of both genders, because the shaman acted on behalf of both men and women in his/her dealings with the underworld. But Oleni' Ostrov is not alone. Thus, the burial of a young man in a seated position in grave 15 at Skateholm II, wearing an elaborate headdress, can also be viewed as a shaman.[28] Again, seated burials also occur at both

Skateholm (4500–4000 BC) and earlier at Kams on Gotland (two burials dated to 6000 BC) and, again, in the case of an 'exceptionally rich' burial at Jasnislawice (4500 BC).

There is evidence from Oleoneostrovski Mogilnik that animal effigies – which could, if not simply totemic, have represented shamanic animal helpers – might be identified with clan areas of the cemetery. Portable art was important in Scandinavia but normally took the form of geometric patterns, with only rare engravings or carvings of animals. Accordingly, even if the animal carvings from Oleoneostrovski Mogilnik represented clans, they are likely to have been imbued also with mythological meaning. The site was certainly a special place, as islands often are. Artifacts include zoomorphic figurines and elk-headed terminals (like those depicted at Nämforsen 1000 years later and 1000 kilometres away). There are rock carvings on the shores of Lake Onega, especially of elk, deer, fish and water birds (notably swan). Humans are shown hunting, harpooning, skiing and having sexual intercourse with deer (probably reindeer). This latter may be a symbolic act, reflecting the return of the animal soul to its animal master – an act leading to physical reproduction of the deer.

Skateholm

Skateholm lies on the south Baltic coast. During the later Mesolithic, between 4500 and 4000 BC, the settlements and cemeteries of Skateholm II and I (in that order) were established on islands in a lagoon cut off from the sea by sand-bars. Skateholm II had twenty-two graves, contrasting with sixty-five at the later site. The evidence from the excavation of the cemeteries[29] has been comprehensively reviewed by Christopher Tilley[30] and set in wider context.

Skateholm II The humans were buried with 'elaborate ceremonial', but with considerable variation in orientation, body position, use of ochre and grave goods. The latter included red deer antlers, perforated teeth (beads), bone harpoons, transverse arrowheads and flint blades. Males and females were equally common in death, probably reflecting status in life. Rare burials of children suggest that status was more often earned than inherited. Two double graves contained, respectively, two children and two young men.

Remarkably, the richest of the Skateholm II burials was that of a dog, equipped for the afterlife with three flint blades placed on its hip, a red deer antler along the spine, and with a decorated antler on its chest. By contrast, in another grave (VIII), a

19 *At the late Mesolithic site of Oleoneostrovski Mogilnik in Russia, special burials were accompanied by carvings of elks, snakes or humans. An elk is shown here.*

female had been buried with a decapitated dog across her legs, probably as a form of retainer sacrifice. The rich dog-burial is harder to read: was it a sacrifice, perhaps in place of a human being, or simply the special burial of a much-loved dog who had met a natural death? As Marek Zvelebil suggests,[31] being the only Mesolithic domesticate, and thereby enjoying a special status, dogs would have been regarded as different from other animals and, indeed, more akin to humans. Thus, dogs may have been interred as surrogates for masters/mistresses lost at sea or perhaps drowned in bogs and not recovered.

What does seem unlikely is that the dog was some kind of shamanic helper, for the latter is characteristically wild, herbivore and prey. We may note, however, John Lubbock's nineteenth-century record[32] of practices of the Greenland indigenous peoples, that a dog's head would be placed, at burial, with the body of a dead child to guide it to the underworld. Sometimes answers and certainties elude us, but stories reflecting the importance of dogs to human society occur widely in literature. Here, one is irresistibly reminded of Odysseus's meeting with his old and faithful hound, Argos, on his return to Ithaca after ten years of wandering.[33] Again, we should remember Ibsen's play *Little Eyolf.* Here we meet the dog Mopsemann as the helper of the 'Rottejomfruen', the Rat Maiden, who rids houses of rats. She charms the rats, first out of the houses with dog and pipes, then down to and into the fjord. Then, the Rat Maiden rows out and Mopsemann swims behind, enticing the rats to their death. Here, animal helper, music and water representing the world of the dead, all converge in a Nordic story with a clear shamanic *Leitmotiv.*

Skateholm I Of sixty-five burials, males and females were equally represented; children numbered only six; and eight burials were of dogs. In two cases bones had been removed from skeletons before burial, perhaps for use in an ancestor cult. In another case, the burial of red deer antlers may have been in place of a human, perhaps lost at sea.

Skateholm I and II: overview The two cemeteries were only 150 m (500 ft) apart and overlapped in date. Resemblances are therefore to be expected. Wooden structures were erected over some grave pits, only to be burnt down as part of the funerary ritual, a practice perhaps seen twenty millennia earlier at Dolní Věstonice. At Skateholm II, a timber structure 4 x 4 m (13 x 13 ft) square was interpreted as a corpse rotting platform, with evidence of associated feasting deposits, and with a taboo area marked out in red ochre. The feasting menu featured wild pig, red and roe deer, and pine marten among the list of animals. Birds and fish were also important. It may be significant that all three parts of the cosmos were represented at the feasts. Red deer occurred both at the feasts and in the graves, but aurochs and elk were present almost entirely in the form of perforated teeth.

Lars Larsson,[34] an archaeologist in the University of Lund, Sweden, has reviewed the evidence for diet, food offerings to the dead, and their interpretation at Skateholm cemeteries I and II. He begins by issuing a warning that there is likely to be only the weakest of correlations between animals used regularly for food and those of cosmological importance. He notes also the evidence that the jaws of species favoured and used for food generally display no evidence of tooth extraction, suggesting that teeth made into ornaments had been extracted from animals, particularly red deer, hunted elsewhere for this purpose alone. A caveat was likewise issued in respect of the settlement site of Slettnes in northern Norway. The site was on an island and the diet was likely to have been heavily biased towards marine resources, but carved stone representations are those of woodland animals, elk and bear, which are unlikely to have been living locally. Returning to Skateholm, diet is known to have involved both marine and terrestrial food, based on the evidence of bone chemistry studies. Food traces in graves could be interpreted in various ways:

- food eaten shortly before an unexpected death (i.e., a 'typical' meal)
- a 'last meal' eaten by the individual before an expected death from natural causes (i.e., a typical invalid meal)
- a 'last meal' eaten by the individual before an expected death from such unnatural causes as sacrifice or execution (i.e., a special, perhaps ritual, meal)
- food offerings placed with the corpse
- food offerings placed in the infill of the grave – a process often taking a number of days
- finally, the placing with the corpse of hunting equipment (harpoons, bows, arrows or dogs) as provision for the hunt in the 'metaphysical world' of the dead.[35]

Larsson looked briefly[36] at the notion – based essentially on the fact that the cemeteries were too small to have accommodated entire communities – that the burials were those of shamans, or of other people who were in some way set apart from society. Clearly, many people received other forms of burial but the social/species mix of men, women, children and dogs can scarcely support an interpretation that the cemeteries held only one kind of specialist. One might expect the eating of fish to have been a symbolic activity relating to the hunter-gatherer perception of the layered cosmos. In fact, where fish were concerned, analysis showed that there were no special or ritual meals. Larsson concluded that a shamanic interpretation was 'extreme'. This may be so, when argued from site evidence alone, but Zvelebil's much wider perspective set out above would suggest otherwise.

Bøgebakken, Vedbaek, Jutland

It is fitting to close this consideration of Mesolithic cemeteries with a reference to a site which has produced what is perhaps one of the most evocative discoveries known. At the Mesolithic settlement site of Bøgebakken, close to Vedbaek railway station in Jutland, seventeen graves were excavated in 1975 from a cemetery which lasted from *c.* 4,300 to 3,800 years ago.[37] The bodies were placed usually in single, but occasionally multiple graves – the latter being those of women with babies or children. With one exception, young people below the age of eighteen years were not equipped with grave goods. One grave contained artifacts but no body, the latter having been removed soon after burial. Nearly all the bodies had been sprinkled with red ochre, particularly on the head and pelvis. Most lay in extended position, arms by sides with hands turned in to the pelvic area. The male burials generally contained large flint blades and other grave goods. The number of grave goods increased with the age and, presumably, also with the status of the man. By contrast, only the younger females were adorned with large numbers of perforated teeth, perhaps once fastened to clothing.

It is interesting to examine the evidence of a few of the burials. Two unusual graves (respectively numbers 10 and 22) contained male and female individuals who were evidently deemed special: the graves were unusually deep and the skeletons were those of older people (aged forty to fifty years) resting on red deer antlers. In an unusual burial rite, the legs of the male were weighted down with stones. Were these burials those of people of spiritual power, perhaps shamans, from whom the living required protection? In Grave 6 a male burial, with an antler axe and three flint blades, had been interred in a pit which cut through a pre-existing grave (15) containing the very disturbed remains of a mother and baby. Another 'family' grave (19) contained a one-year-old child positioned between two adults of uncertain gender, but one skeleton with 'decidedly female grave goods' was plausibly that of the

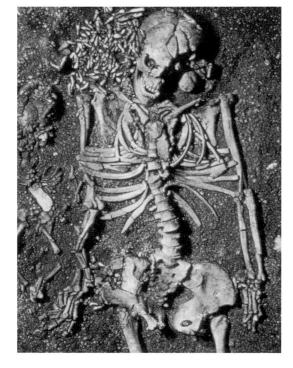

20 *Bøgebakken late Mesolithic cemetery, Vedbaek, Jutland. Grave 8 contained the remains of a woman aged about eighteen years old. Nearly 200 tooth-pendants of red deer and wild boar had been placed near her head and were covered with red ochre. Her pelvis was similarly ochred and was underlain by more perforated teeth of red deer, elk and seal. The ochred body of a baby lay at her side and had been placed on a swan's wing.*

child's mother. The second adult skeleton was that of an individual who had been murdered – a bone arrowhead was found wedged between two of the thoracic vertebrae – and who lacked, presumably for that reason, the characteristic grave goods. One wonders here if the remains may not represent the murder of an entire family. Indeed, a flint blade positioned by the woman's throat may have been the agent of her dispatch. Finally, Grave 8 (Fig. 20) yielded the evocative discovery of the remains of a woman aged about eighteen years old, her head resting on a folded-up dress, ornamented with nearly 200 tooth-pendants of red deer and wild boar, as well as a number of perforated snail shells. Red ochre was placed around the head, on the pelvis and shin bones. Her pelvis was underlain by fifty perforated teeth of red deer, elk and seal, which may have decorated a dress worn in death. The similarly ochred body of a baby lay at her side and a clue to its sex, a boy, is given by the flint blade placed at his waist. As if to give added reverence, the child had been placed on a swan's wing as if the bird were charged with escorting the baby to the afterlife.

A brief comment on Scandinavian Mesolithic art provides a degree of social context for the burials and offers a wider perspective. Apart from rock paintings, known on the shores of Oslo Fjord, the art takes the form of decorated artifacts of bone, antler, amber, stone and flint, and wood. Of 400 pieces of portable art, only three were found in graves, a pattern seen earlier in the Upper Palaeolithic. In the late Ertebølle, c. 3700 BC, pottery became the medium for art.[38] Depiction was characteristically abstract, except for two groups of material: first, naturalistic representations of animals including red deer, bear, elk, water bird and fish; and, second, human depictions. The latter number about twelve, all from bogs and so, perhaps, are votive depositions. They fall into two groups: first, schematic figures of uncertain gender and, second, squatting figures which may show scenes of childbirth, rather like the much earlier Gravettian figurines from Avdeevo in Russia[39] and perhaps those from the Balzi Rossi caves.[40] In the rock paintings, the humans appear schematically and so contrast with naturalistic depictions of the animals, a pattern reminiscent of the Upper Palaeolithic.

SHAMANS, ISLANDS AND THE BRETON COAST

> *Aquí en la isla*   Here, surrounding the island,
> *el mar*   there's sea
>
> from *Oda al mar* / Ode to the sea
> from *Love Poems*
> by Pablo Neruda, translation by Ken Krabbenhoft

Neruda's great love poem reflects the awe in which the sea is held. Accordingly, the coast is often viewed not only as a liminal place where land and sea meet, but also as a place of transformation and power.[41] Among the Saami, in particular, water was seen as the underworld zone of a triple cosmos of sky, land and water. Islands, rapids and places where rivers meet the sea, were believed to afford access to the land of the dead. Accordingly, shamans visited such locales in order to gain entry to the world of spirits. The Cambridge archaeologist Chris Scarre[42] has looked at the cosmological meaning of the extraordinary concentration of passage graves along the Breton coasts and has interpreted this choice of location:

- first, as a dramatic region where the mystery and power of the boundary between life and death was manifested *magna cum voce* through the sound of the waves, the howl of the wind and, perhaps above all, through the visual impact of the huge daily Atlantic tidal range
- second, as a place where the dead were returned to the realm of the ancestors through tomb burial, enhanced by the power of the sea-edge location.

Important proxy evidence has emerged in recent years of a widespread taboo on the eating of fish in the Neolithic – at least in Portugal, Denmark, southern Britain and probably Brittany – in contradistinction to its widespread Mesolithic exploitation.[43] Such a taboo may relate to a belief – which accords well with the shamanic concept of a tiered cosmos – that the sea was the abode of the dead.[44] If the siting of chamber tombs in coastal locations in Brittany can be related to shamanic beliefs, then the selection of similar topographical contexts elsewhere in Europe may have arisen for comparable reasons. One could cite here such diverse regions as Scandinavia[45] or southwest Wales.[46]

As far as Brittany is concerned, there is a useful rule of thumb regarding sea level: namely, that the highest tides of 5000 BC equate to the lowest present-day tides. Accordingly, sites now on islands were probably once on the low hills of a coastal plain. Detailed analysis of a number of passage graves has shown orientations involving the sea. Thus, at Barnenez, 'in entering the passages, and advancing to the chambers where the dead were interred, one was moving towards the open sea'.[47] Again, on the Île Guennoc, where a group of passage graves similarly backs onto views of the open sea, beach materials were selected for use. These included pebbles in the cairn façades and sand in the infill of the chamber of one of the tombs.[48] Scarre[49] makes a powerful case for the deliberate siting of some passage graves in coastal regions, where he sees the dramatic tidal regime as a 'metaphor for the transition between life and death'.

PASSAGE GRAVES IN IRELAND

Jeremy Dronfield,[50] when engaged in research for his Doctorate at Cambridge, developed the hypothesis that Irish megalithic art may be interpreted as shamanic.

In essence the tombs afforded a cave-type environment, in which altered states of consciousness might have been induced by such agencies as hallucinogenic substances, light flicker or migraine. Dronfield's diagnostic analyses yielded the conclusion that 'Irish passage-tomb art has fundamental characteristics in common with arts based on endogenous visual phenomena, i.e. those produced in the eyes and the brain rather than by direct sight'.[51] The idea that chamber tombs afforded a world of darkness where secret rituals could take place is difficult to dismiss. The arcane geometric designs engraved on the walls of the passage graves of the western European seaways are, thus, likely to embody hidden meanings which the archaeologist can begin to interpret.

Detailed analysis by Dronfield of the distribution and intensity of art motifs revealed a pattern suggestive of a link between curvilinear designs, perhaps symbolizing vortices and tunnels, and the passages of the tombs (Plate 9). A paper published subsequently[52] developed the concept of the 'tunnel experience', which may be linked both to altered states of consciousness and to visions of the dead. Tunnels certainly figure in some shamanic cosmologies. Among the Saami, for instance, just such a 'hole of the spirit' runs through the *axis mundi*, enabling the shaman to reach the world of the dead.[53] Of course, the passage graves were a 'world of the dead' in microcosm. They were not, however, family vaults. Rather, they were places wherein corpses were disarticulated and fragmented, and from where body-parts and bones were abstracted. The question of a possible link also between art and mortuary practice was explored through analysis of the placement of the principal motifs – the spiral, circle and arc – and other motifs, such as the dot, filigree, lattice, meander, parallel line, fortification and zigzag. The evidence was complex, but there seemed to be a relationship between the lattice pattern and the placement of the bones of the dead. There is, however, no universal meaning of the lattice symbol or of its component shape, the lozenge or diamond. Thus, among the Colombian Tukano, it stands for the structure of certain social relationships whereas, among the African Dogon, the symbol may be used to define images of ancestors.

Dronfield was able to make use of the richest database of Neolithic passage grave art in western Europe. There have been doubters, but his analysis remains highly original and challenging. If the 'darkness, isolation, cold and silence' of the Palaeolithic caves of Europe were an appropriate environment for shamanic trances, a parallel interpretation seems possible, if not compelling, for the Irish tombs.

CLUES FROM THE ROCK ART OF WESTERN IBERIA

A paper by Lara Bacelar Alves[54] has looked at so-called 'schematic art' in western Iberia from the contexted landscape perspective, rather than from the traditional art history viewpoints of the content, style and technique of the depiction. Because of the remarkable survival of collective memories within peasant societies in parts of western Iberia, we know that art sites were located in places in the landscape that were already of symbolic significance. In local cosmology, specific sites and places in the landscape are home to 'spirits and fantastic creatures'. Moreover, many places – including caves and rockshelters – are seen as portals to the spirit-world. Occasionally, such sites have been Christianized following the 'appearance' of a saint from a cleft in the cave wall. Schematic art is probably of Late Neolithic to earlier Bronze Age date and is found most commonly on the walls of rockshelters and small caves. It is sometimes associated with chamber tombs also. The art is generally monochrome, with a preference for red ochre. Human figures are common, but so are geometric shapes. Only rarely does the art display composition.

Within the landscape, the art sites may lie in conspicuous rock outcrops – preferentially geological formations of, or containing, large amounts of white quartz – but the entrances tend to be locally concealed. Compared with other caves, those with schematic art usually lack evidence of human settlement, as if reserved as places for ritual only. Also, the positioning of the art varies: normally near the entrance, it is found also in deep recesses. The experient will thus be drawn on a journey through a cave or chamber tomb, in darkness or with a flickering hand-held light, along a passage to a natural or artificial chamber. In other words, he or she moves on a journey *into* the rock. In passage graves, representations of humans are normally situated not near the entrance, but much further into the tomb. One particular schematic art site, El Pedroso, is a cave which resembles a 'natural megalith', both in terms of its geological formations and in the patterning of art within the cave. Schematic art is thus involved not only with ritual activity, but with burial also. This is manifest in the case of chamber tombs, but it occurs also with Late Neolithic cave burials.

Lara Bacelar Alves[55] has shown brilliantly how the depth of human memory in western Iberia enables us to see schematic rock art as a cultural coat of paint whose content once provided a code, even a grammar, of a cosmology embedded in the natural world. What do the sites tell us? These small sites seem to speak perhaps of correspondingly small groups of initiates receiving sacred knowledge, rather than being places for public shamanic performances involving larger groups of people. The materiality of the caves, combined with social memory, reveals to us that the very landscape was sacred. Of special interest, too, is the evidence for a parallelism in the function of some caves and chamber tombs. The origins of schematic art have been reviewed by Primitiva Bueno Ramirez and Rodrigo de Balbín Behrmann[56] who see it as rooted in the European Palaeolithic. Moreover, they see megalithic art as a version of schematic art. With the latter, they favour a survival of symbolic meanings 'in spite of cultural and material changes'.

Art, Ritual and Pilgrimage – Issues of Continuity

Continuity in oral societies

The issue of the continuity of artistic practice and, thereby, implicitly and probably, of systems of ritual expression and belief is a serious one for the archaeology of
pre-farming societies, and continues to be a problem in later prehistory. We are
dealing here not just with centuries or even millennia, but with a period of perhaps
as long as 20,000–30,000 years. However, we have to remember here that a language
is reported as becoming unintelligible after 1000 years and that, after 10,000 years, it
is likely to have suffered total replacement.[57] Jean Clottes[58] has offered two explanations for continuity in Upper Palaeolithic art, which he described as 'little
changed' over such 'an immensity of time'. First, that the continuity took place
within the framework of a 'strict educational system'. Second, that shamanism
offers the 'best-fit theory' to explain the apparent continuity of beliefs and behaviour. Other examples of apparent continuity over millennia, even decamillennia,
can be given: for example, more than 30,000 years of ochre extraction at the Karrku
mine, Australia; or verifiable events recorded in the oral histories, the 'folk memories', of some Australian Aboriginal groups extending in excess of 10,000 years;[59]
and, in the Mojave Desert of the USA, archaeological and scientific evidence for
vision questing associated with shamanism, extending back in time around
10,000–12,000 years.[60]

Folk memory

We have seen how folk memory, millennia deep, affords a context for rock art in
western Iberia. In Britain, a possible instance of folk memory is recorded in a story
told by the twelfth-century AD writer, Geoffrey of Monmouth. He related a tale
told by the local population around Stonehenge that the stone monument had been
transported by sea from Ireland and then re-erected on Salisbury Plain.[61] Given
that the bluestones – which clearly form part of a re-erected monument – origi-
nated geologically from Pembrokeshire on the southeastern shore of the Irish Sea,
this may be considered as a possible instance of such memory over more than 3,000
years. A more tangible example is the annual folk gathering and dance at Abbots
Bromley in Staffordshire. Here, a radiocarbon date on reindeer antlers used in the
dance produced the surprising result of an age in the eleventh century AD.[62]
However, this is a custom of comparatively recent origin when set against the three
millennia of recutting the Uffington White Horse high on the northern scarp face
of the Oxfordshire chalk downs.[63] In historic times, until AD 1865, the villagers of
Uffington cleaned the horse regularly and its environs were a focus for such annual
frolics as the cheese-rolling in Dragon Coombe below the chalk figure. There was
even a song:

The owl white horse wants zettin to rights,
and the squire hev promised good cheer,
zo, we'll gee un a scrape to kip un in zhape,
and a'll last for many a year.[64]

The sacredness of White Horse Hill, and its status as a place of ritualized action, was clearly underpinned by the myth of the horse. Whatever that myth may have been, it was later metamorphosed by Christianity into the story of St George and the Dragon. The sanctity, or at least the special-ness, of the hill survived. Ritualized activity often underpins continuity. We see this among the Australian Aborigines, where the 'performance arts' of song, dance and painting all serve not only as nodal points in the social engagement of an often highly dispersed people, but as a means of revisiting social memories embedded in the landscape.[65] Thus, issues of place and memory link with seasonal social aggregations which could have provided a context and platform for the activities of shamans.

The bardic world

As archaeologists whose backgrounds lay originally in the Classical world, the authors have always had a particular interest in the role of memory in early, preliterate, societies and how such communities were able to transmit knowledge and traditions. We can look at this in the context of Homer's *Iliad*. The Greeks developed the alphabet *c.* 720–700 BC and, two centuries later, had mastered the art of writing. Yet the accounts of the Homeric world refer to events that were at least semi-historical and which took place close to 1200 BC, 500 years before the development of writing. The explanation generally offered is that the poems were preserved through becoming part of the repertoire of itinerant bards. Such people were deemed capable of prodigious feats of memory.

A study by Walter Ong,[66] Professor Emeritus at Saint Louis University, is particularly helpful here, for it focuses on pure oral traditions in societies that were preliterate or non-literate. It may seem surprising but, of the approximately 6,700 languages that exist today, only 78 have a literature. Indeed, writing is not a complement to oral speech but, rather, transforms its nature. Thus, 'standard English' has more than one-and-a-half million words, whereas oral dialects typically have a few thousand words only.[67] In literate societies, there is a considerable reliance on written instruction, whereas in oral cultures people learn by apprenticeship – by observing or listening, then by copying. Thus, the very poverty of language and the need to transmit skills through face-to-face teaching, combined with very small group and population size, must have acted as a constraint on changes in belief, ritual and the use of symbols.

The nineteenth century saw the recognition of Homer as a great poet, but it was not until the 1920s that Milman Parry recognized the works as originally oral and only later written down. Such oral poetry Parry showed to be characterized by the use of standardized formulae (or clichés) and by standardized themes, limited in number,[68] such as 'the council, the gathering of the army, the challenge, the despoiling of the vanquished, the hero's shield' etc. In other words, the *Iliad* and *Odyssey* consist to a large extent of predictable formulae.[69] But could Homer be great poetry if it was composed merely of a string of clichés? This question was resolved by Eric Havelock in 1963.

> Homeric Greeks valued clichés because not only the poets but the entire oral noetic … or thought world relied on the formulaic constitution of thought. In an oral culture, knowledge, once acquired, had to be constantly repeated or it would be lost: fixed, formulaic thought patterns were essential for wisdom and effective administration.[70]

In understanding the processes involved in the transmission of stories in bardic societies, it is useful to look at research by Lord and Parry on the epic singers of Croatia and Serbia.[71] They found that the singers performed oral epic narratives that, like Homer, were presented in poems that were metric and formulaic. Study of the recordings in the Parry Collection at Harvard University shows that songs were never repeated word for word and it is clear, from interviews with twentieth-century Yugoslav bards, that poems were learnt through listening to the performances of other bards for months or even years. What was remembered was not a precise story but, rather, a set of themes and formulae.

Walter Ong[72] was able to document diachronic changes in other societies: thus, the myths of the Gonja of Ghana can be shown to have changed over some fifty years to accommodate changing political realities. Similar oral traditions existed in the mid-twentieth-century British working class societies recorded by Richard Hoggart.[73] Patterns of speech here might approach 'the elemental quality of Anglo-Saxon poetry' and, characteristically, aphorism was 'bolted on' to aphorism in a style which might not be wholly unfamiliar to the bards of the great poetic traditions. Hoggart's description of the life of his northern communities[74] will have resonance for scholars of the later Palaeolithic and Mesolithic: 'living intuitively, habitually, verbally, drawing on myth, aphorism, and ritual'.

We can be sure that oral societies had mechanisms for the transmission of stories that embodied mythologies and cosmic visions. Here, larger-than-life characters and beings – such as the one-eyed Cyclops and the many-headed Cerberus – are easier to recall in the oral poetic tradition, and so may shape the content of myth.[75] We can be equally confident of the likelihood that the detail, at least, of these stories shifted over time. This still leaves, however, a real possibility of continuities based on ritual practice[76] and reinforced by the oral traditions of the often complex societies of the later Palaeolithic and Mesolithic.

THE ROLE OF PSYCHOACTIVE SUBSTANCES

A paper by the Oxford archaeologist Andrew Sherratt, written for the proceedings of the 'Sacred and Profane' conference held in Oxford in 1989, has proved to be one of those seminal pieces of work which has had an enduring impact on our understanding of 'narcotic archaeology'.[77] Whilst occasionally outlawed by some states and religions, the truth is that mind-altering substances – most commonly, but by no means always, of the milder variety characterized at the present day by alcohol and cannabis – are hugely popular with *Homo sapiens.* If our own life experiences do not give us an entrée into this world, we can read Graham Greene's haunting accounts[78] of his experiences with opium in Vietnam: its smell 'like the first sight of a beautiful woman'; the *fumerie* with its ambience of hard couch and leather pillow, speaking of 'austerity [and] pleasure'. And, in case these might seem romantic (as they do), his description of the impact of a lifetime of smoking opium on the indigenous people is correspondingly shocking. In our own culture, the Bert Jansch song 'Needle of Death' conveys both the attraction 'to free [the] mind, to release [the] very soul' and the horror of drug addiction: 'one grain of pure white snow, dissolved in blood, spread quickly to the brain. In peace your mind withdraws, your death so near.'[79]

Our starting point with Sherratt's analysis is his observation of how bereft of sensual stimuli – whether of noise, colour, taste or smell – life in temperate Neolithic Europe must have been. Even so, there is likely to have been trade with the more richly endowed shores of the Mediterranean. A deep herbal knowledge is also to be expected. We think, at the present day, of 'smoke-filled rooms' in the context of politics. Smoke is, however, used in a variety of ways to cleanse or to perfume (literally *par fume,* 'by smoke'). One of us once saw a small charcoal-filled pit dug into the floor of the male house in an encampment of desert Arabs in the northern Sudan.[80] Upon enquiry, it transpired that the wife (there were several) invited for sexual intercourse would first of all fragrance her body through the burning of aromatic woods. Archaeological charcoals may thus have a variety of functions including heat, cooking and feasting, security against wild animals, perfuming for a variety of purposes including cleansing and sexual engagement, and 'tripping' on the powerful aroma of cannabis. The latter was a practice greatly enjoyed by the Scythians, as Herodotus tells us (see Chapter 5). Sherratt would see the inhaling of smoke as an earlier Neolithic practice. Thus the burning of narcotics seems to have preceded their ingestion in solid or liquid form. We must remember, too, that such usage of burnt botanical products may also have been medicinal in purpose. The latter was a primary activity of shamans, who engaged with the world of spirits in order to effect bodily cures.

Sherratt would see much of the smoking as relating to the opium poppy (*Papaver somniferum)* and the hemp plant (*Cannabis sativa*). Indeed, he would actually liken the form of the Central European Neolithic *Trichterbecherkultur* (TRB) pots to opium poppy heads. Poppy seeds were recovered as early as AD 1878 from the Swiss

Neolithic lake villages. They have been recovered also from the Cueva de los Murciélagos ('cave of the bats') in southern Spain, where a large number of burials was accompanied by what can only be described as esparto grass handbags which contained *inter alia* numerous opium poppy capsules. Their purpose is unknown but a clear understanding of the function of the opium is implied and may relate to its sleep-inducing properties, as well perhaps as providing an opportunity for the mourners to have a jolly good 'dope party'. Hemp is attested from the third millennium BC in eastern Europe. Again, its function was probably multifactorial. Its capacity to induce pleasure is well known (and thus often frowned upon), but it has been widely used medically for the control of pain. One of us saw such medicinal usage in the Third World forty years ago and the First World is now coming cautiously to appreciate its benefits.

In the later Neolithic, feasting and drinking seem to have come to the fore and archaeologists have both the possibility and challenge of seeking to decode the culinary syntax preserved in the form of ceramics. Later in prehistory, from the start of the later Bronze Age, the existence of large sheet-metal buckets and cauldrons leaves little room for doubt of widespread heroic feasting. Before this, however, the very complexity and rapid pace of change of ceramic styles are seen as reflecting the activities of competing 'religious' groups. Indeed, the rise of the Corded Ware beaker in parts of Neolithic western and central Europe (the cord being hemp) may relate not only to cannabis but also to the drinking of alcohol. There can be little doubt of the likelihood – as opposed to the mere possibility[81] – of Neolithic usage of mind-altering substances, with their obvious potential for use in shamanism.

We will close this section with an account of the death-pit of Nitrianski-Zámeček in Slovakia. A chamber, marked by a widening out of an area close to the base of a bell-shaped pit 4 m (13 ft) in depth, housed a remarkable death scene. Ten skeletons were found kneeling, facing the centre of the pit, hands raised as if in prayer. With little doubt, they had been asphyxiated as the pit was infilled. With equally little doubt, they had gone voluntarily to their deaths in what may have been a mass 'murder-suicide' comparable, on a vastly smaller scale, to the 900 deaths – mostly from a draught of self-administered cyanide punch – in 1978 at Jonestown in Guyana.

CONCLUSION

This chapter has sought evidence for shamanism in hunter-gatherer and early farming societies. In so doing, it has focused on the themes of caves, tombs and coasts as access points to the subterranean world of spirits; memory, repetition and 'continuity'; and what might be termed 'sharing a spliff'.

Study of Mesolithic cemeteries admits us to a world of ritual and belief. In the case of the British site of Aveline's Hole, the selection of a site in an upland valley carries with it the idea of the journey of the dead to a distant cave which gave access to the world of spirits, the world of ancestors. We see, too, that the cemeteries – as at Skateholm and Slettnes – were on islands which, like caves, were liminal places where the shaman could enter the chthonic realms. The cemeteries seem likely to have housed the graves of a small percentage of the community, of people who were in some way special. These included high-status young mothers who were deposited in the grave with some style. A male murder victim may, by contrast, have been assigned to the darkness with no symbols of earthly power. Yet others may have been equipped in death for the hunt.

Feasting and public affirmation of the life or death of the corpse evokes a world in which religious practitioners, shamans by another name, may have officiated over curing ceremonies, rites of passage, and the hunt whether located firmly in this or the metaphysical world. The dynamic societies, of which the graves were but a proxy, were ritually complex with elements that may be shamanic. Thus, the symbolism of the swan's wing in Grave 8 at Bøgebakken speaks of the flight of the shaman to the world of spirits, and recalls the crane dancers depicted on the walls of the village of Çatalhöyük in Turkey.[82] At the latter site, there was evidence that crane-wings may have been cut off and made into costumes for use in ritual dances, possibly in connection with fertility or marriage ceremonials. We will meet cranes later in this book where they are identified as highly symbolic, multi-vocal, birds associated with seasonality and possessing human characteristics. Swans embody cosmological significance: as waterfowl that feed below the surface of the water, yet also move on land and fly in the air. Again, they are monogamous for life and so symbolize marriage. Finally, they may be highly vocal and thus seem to communicate messages from another world. The cemeteries tell us a great deal about their contemporary societies and we have seen how Marek Zvelebil was able to weave together the evidence of the ethnohistorical present with the archaeological past – through a study embracing the evidence of history, ethnography, rock art, burials, artifacts and holy places – to demonstrate the deep continuity of shamanic ritual and belief that has been embedded in northern Eurasia. We can only note that the complex stratified societies that seem to be indicated throughout this period would have offered an attractive power base for a shaman.

It is clear from modern surveys of shamanism that trances were induced by various means which, sometimes, included the use of drugs. There is no evidence for their use in the European Palaeolithic or Mesolithic but it seems very likely that they were exploited from Neolithic times onwards. The archaeological evidence for their use only becomes compelling in later prehistory and we will, accordingly, explore this in later chapters.

Jeremy Dronfield's conclusions from his study of Irish passage graves were tightly drawn. First, there was the dark passage, a place where 'subjective visual experience' might take place. Second, engraved concentric motifs were significant in various ways. Thus, they may have been perceived as 'passages' through which other worlds could be entered, rather like Alice and her looking glass. Some concentrics may have been positioned for 'fixated viewing', rather like the point that the patient fastens his or her eye upon at the start of a session of hypnosis. We are tempted, indeed, to see these Neolithic concentrics as the eyes of the owls that were both the guardians of the tomb and the access to the world of spirits. Just such an owl image is dramatically seen at Knowth in Ireland. Third, the lattice decorations 'would have been used didactically by the shamans to inform or remind their audience of the network of relationships which existed between the ancestors, and how that related to the living'.[83] Finally, the passage graves were far more than structures to house the bones of the dead. Rather, they were spaces where – using ritual practices, mythology and trance – shamans could travel between layers of the cosmos, and meet ancestors and other spirits.

The coastal distribution and individual orientations of the Breton passage graves reflect an interest in the sea. It seems very likely that the topographical situation of the sites was related to the concept that islands, or the places where estuary and sea meet, were sacred liminal spaces where the shaman could enter the underworld and encounter the shades of the departed. Just as the conjunction of coast and tomb in Brittany links two modes of access to the underworld – the liminal zone of the coast and the tomb itself, so the study of schematic art in western Iberia affords a series of bridges between art, caves, tombs and folk memory. We know from this folk memory that caves were seen as portals to the underworld; as the haunt of fantastic creatures; and as places where people might emerge from cracks in the rock. The caves were generally secret places where the polarized distribution of the art – in the daylight zone and dark recesses – indicates the importance of the torch-lit journey to the world of the dead. The continuity implied by the relationship between the Iberian schematic and megalithic art and their Palaeolithic roots is seen again in the evidence of the Neolithic cult caves in Italy. The content of that art – with its focus on special rather than food animals; naturalistic representations of animals compared with schematic treatment of humans; and with abstract designs well represented – is likewise suggestive of an origin within the field of Palaeolithic systems of practice and belief. Elements of ritual practice, particularly the insertion of fragments of bone into cracks in the rock wall, again refer back to Palaeolithic practices. It is clear, from studies of the transmission of knowledge in preliterate societies, that such continuities would not have involved unchanging patterns of practice and belief. Perhaps there were just a limited number of things you could do with caves, and that is why some practices recur, but the autochthonous origins of the art seem clear enough. If we are willing to believe in a broad continuity of tradition for the twenty millennia of the Upper Palaeolithic, then it should be feasible for us to believe in some continuation of that tradition for a further period of less than an additional 10,000 years.

4 ROCKS AND GOLD

Bronze Age Shamanism?

He heard the deep behind him, and a cry
Before. His own thought drove him like a goad.
Dry clash'd his harness in the icy caves
And barren chasms, and all to left and right
The bare black cliffs clanged around him, as he based
His feet on juts of slippery crag that rang
Sharp-smitten with the dint of arméd heels –
And on a sudden, lo! the level lake,
And the long glories of the winter moon.

Alfred Lord Tennyson, *The Passing of Arthur*

CARVING COSMOLOGIES

A growing body of scholarship is concerned with the recognition of a close association between ancient rock art and shamanism. Such an acknowledgment is based in
part upon study of communities producing rupestrine[1] art in areas of the world –
southern Africa and northern Australia, for instance – which belong to a long-lived
tradition of carving the rocks, sometimes traced back from the present thousands of
years into the past.[2] Carving rocks was clearly a highly significant act for the
societies that produced and consumed the images produced, whether or not the
imagery should always be perceived as religious or even symbolic. In any case, as
argued by the archaeologist and rock-art scholar Richard Bradley,[3] it is probably a
mistake to try to divorce secular from sacred function for rock imagery. Indeed, it
may be appropriate to regard certain rock-art sites as sanctuaries and that natural

locations, 'places that were left entirely unmodified might be among the most significant to the people who visited them',[4] because the imagery carved or painted on
the rock surfaces interacted with physical space that was untouched, virginal and
therefore belonged entirely to the spirit forces residing within, around and, perhaps, created by them. What is of fundamental importance is the recognition that
context is a crucial factor in considering the significance of rock art: the art belongs
to the landscape in which it is situated,[5] and it is clear that the image-makers produced their iconography within the framework of what surrounded it, whether sea,
woodland, mountains or open country. This means that it is futile to attempt interpretations of the art unless its context is treated as part and parcel of the 'package'.

Whilst it would rightly be regarded as academically unacceptable to try to prove
close, meaningful linkages between the art of one society or time-frame and
another, it is nonetheless possible to identify certain repetitive patterns or 'gram-
mars' of imagery that recur so insistently over time and space that, as David
Lewis-Williams has observed,[6] they may be expressing perceptions or experiences,
some produced by out-of-body experience, emanating from common wiring in the
human brain. Lewis-Williams and others[7] have suggested that the unifying factor
expressed in these recurrent 'packages' of rock imagery is its production and use
within the framework of shamanistic practice and expression. It is against such a
backdrop that it is possible to begin to understand some of the apparently unrealis-
tic images that occur on Bronze/Iron Age rock carvings: the half-human,
half-animal creatures (Fig. 21), the exaggerated antlers on stags, the geometric shapes, such as nets, labyrinths and collections of
dots, the beings that disappear into or emerge from cracks
in the rock surface, that merge into circles or that
appear as dismembered or skeletonized bodies and
the images that appear to be stacked one on top of the
other. All these, together with other shapes and forms,
can be identified in regions as far apart as Namibia and
Arnhem Land in northern Australia and from southern
France to Central Asia. Some date to the remote
past, others (particularly in North America, northern and central Asia and Australia) to living
memory.[8] Lewis-Williams[9] has argued with conviction that the 'dream-images' on the rocks may have been
created by the same people who experienced them.

21 *Half-human, half-bird figure with a beak, an exaggerated
phallus and a sword with a chape, perhaps representing
someone in a bird-mask or a shape-shifting shaman.
Boglösa, Uppland, Sweden.*

This chapter focuses upon Bronze Age European rock art in two regions: southern Scandinavia, specifically Uppland and Bohuslän in Sweden, and Camonica Valley in northern Italy. This is not to dismiss the prolific and highly significant carvings of other places, such as Mont Bégo in the French Alps and Galícia in northwest Spain, but the two areas selected provide a rich variety and concentration of images, giving sufficiently large groups of 'canvases' to enable a meaningful interrogation of the art and its context. Furthermore, the two regions offer a stark environmental contrast one to the other, in terms of differing landscapes and terrains: the Scandinavian art was produced on gently sloping rock faces, by people living within sight and sound of the sea,[10] whilst the Camunians chose a location for their art far away from water, in a steep-sided, remote and inaccessible valley surrounded by mountains.[11]

SEASCAPES AND MOON ROCKS: ROCK ART IN SOUTHERN SWEDEN

'Big men' and performing ritualists

The site lies in a small seemingly self-contained landscape and the impression given as you stand at the site is of a remoteness and an intimacy that I have not often encountered elsewhere.[12]

So wrote John Coles, one of the great experts in the field of Scandinavian rock art, in a paper concerned with a Bronze Age rock-carving of a huge, apparently dancing human figure from Järrestad in Scania, southern Sweden (Fig. 22).[13] The image is not alone but it dominates the carvings around it, including those of other people on foot and on horseback, and Coles draws attention to its position, carefully chosen for maximum visible impact on viewers looking upwards from the rock base.[14] The Dancer is tall and willowy, its arms held out, hands raised, its knees bent to its left, standing on tiptoe like a ballet-dancer, the whole figure evocative of movement; its tiny head is 'bird-like and pugnacious' and it is equipped with a dagger in its sheath, hung from the waist and a sword in its scabbard juts out from its right hip,[15]

22 *Järrestad dancer, Scania, Sweden. The tall, graceful figure has a bird-beak, and appears to dance before a Bronze Age tomb. The fires lit on the rock suggest that this was a sacred place, and the dancer might be the presiding spirit or shaman.*

91

the form of the chape serving to date the image to the early/mid first millennium BC. The figure shares the 'canvas' not only with other, simply executed human images but also with boats, some upright, some inverted, and symbols such as 'wheel-crosses'; most enigmatic – though common in Scandinavian and other ancient rock art – are the associated carvings of bare feet and 'footsoles' (shod feet with a horizontal bar between heel and instep), some single, others in pairs, executed as though drawn round actual living feet,[16] depicted in their densest clusters around the figure of the Dancer. He or she is the only being represented as an individual here and, of all the humans depicted on the entire site, only this figure has weapons.[17]

The rock at Järrestad was indeed a special place; associated with it and visible from it were burial mounds, including an enormous tumulus at Kvegshög; the great human figure appears to gaze at the tomb as s/he dances. The environment was boggy and, at the time when the carvings were made, there was probably a pool fed by a spring;[18] the representations of boats emphasize the aquatic significance of the place. Interestingly, there is evidence that fire as well as water may have been important to the rock-engravers: investigation revealed a burnt area of the rock in a position where the pool would have been visible,[19] suggesting that celebrations or ritual activity at the site may have involved lighting bonfires in the vicinity of the carvings. What is more, the images themselves would have looked particularly dramatic at night, especially by torchlight, when they would flicker and shimmer and, perhaps, the dancing figure would really appear to sway and move in time to chants, drumbeats or songs. The contribution of fire to dramatic, performance-rich ceremonies is attested at other Scandinavian sites: excavations at the base of some carved rock surfaces have revealed that fires were lit on laid stone floors and traces of human action involving the hurling of pottery and stones against the rock,[20] behaviour that would not only have been visually spectacular but noisy and, maybe, quite frightening, especially at night. Some carved rocks in Uppland clearly had fires lit on them, although it is uncertain as to whether this represents contemporary ritual or subsequent desecration.[21] The association of fire and water could be highly symbolic, in terms of transformatory rituals, perhaps associated with discourse between people and the spirits or with initiation rites, involving ordeals and purification ceremonies.[22]

The rock at Järrestad was clearly carefully chosen as a canvas in so far as it commands views not only over water but a varying landscape, embracing untamed woodland, utilized (but perhaps little-modified) pasture and cultivated arable, a signifier of human order and management of the world. The figure of the Dancer, surrounded by the feet that may have represented his or her community, perhaps presided over this landscape; the relationship between the Dancer and the huge grave-mound at Kvegshög must be highly meaningful, and John Coles has hinted that the tomb may have been that of the individual whose dancing image was carved on the rock.[23] But what of the Dancer's identity? It is interesting that its gender is uncertain: the image bears weapons and has the well-developed calf muscles generally associated with male rupestrine depictions, but the wide hips suggest femininity, and it may be that the dancer transcends biological gender: unlike many human images on the northern rock carvings, this figure has no discernible phallus. The bird-like head likewise disturbs notions of realism and gives the image a restless ambiguity between human and animal.

The Järrestad image needs to be considered alongside analogous figures elsewhere on Bronze Age rock art in southern Sweden, such as the great horned (or leaf-crowned) and sword-bearing human image, arms upraised in a similar manner to the Järrestad dancer, from Bro Utmark, Bohuslän.[24] Unlike these two images, several horned human representations (Fig. 23), once again with well-developed leg muscles – from Kasen Lövåsen in the same region[25] and from Boglösa in Uppland – exhibit enormous erect phalluses (or penis-sheaths). Both, like the Järrestad dancer, have beaked heads[26] and, indeed, the upraised arms of the figures from Boglösa and Järrestad may represent wings in flight. Other 'big men', human images that dominate contiguous carvings (Plate 10), may be compared to the Dancer at Järrestad: a figure at Smörsten in Bohuslän is horned rather than beaked, but his arms are upraised and he dances, with one leg flung out in a skipping pose;[27] another rock, at Kallsängen in the same region, displays a bird-headed person with wings and an erect phallus. The great burial chamber at Kivik in Scania contains a 'narrative' scene[28] in which a man dances at the head of a group of robed figures, as if leading souls to the underworld beyond the tomb. Such images are clearly special; they dominate the figures around them and seem to be focuses of attention. The wings, beaks or horns worn by some of them suggest either that they are spirit-creatures or, perhaps, that they are shamans, dressed up in animal costume and engaged in ritual dancing, perhaps in a trance state: Ekaterina Devlet, of the Institute of Archaeology, Russian Academy of Sciences in Moscow,[29] amongst others, has drawn attention to the importance of wearing animal costume for Siberian shamans wishing to assume the persona of an animal spirit-helper. Indeed, some 'horned' men are depicted blowing lurer (Fig. 24),[30] the beautiful long sinuous

23 *Warrior with horns, scabbard and spear. The figure appears to be dancing rather than fighting, and he may represent a ritualist performing at a ceremony. Karlslund, Bohuslän, Sweden.*

bronze trumpets of which the vast majority of the real instruments come from Denmark. The association between horned beings and music may suggest the use of sound to induce trance and the visionary state of the shaman.

Whilst it would be wholly inappropriate to interpret the majority of human images on these rocks as shamanic, some of them – apart from the 'big men' already considered – are depicted in a manner that resonates within such a framework. It is possible to cite several examples of opposed pairs, as if mirror-images of each other: one panel from Skjuleröd in Bohuslän depicts paired bird-headed, big-calved people each with a hammer and wielding lacrosse-like nets weighted with 'bolas', as if in mimicry of bird-catching;[31] a variation on this theme is perhaps represented on a carving from Kallsängen in the same region (Fig. 25), where the artist depicted a group of winged, bird-beaked warriors armed with swords, of whom one is Janus-headed.[32] It is possible that such double-figures represent a shamanic being as a two-spirit person, belonging both to earthworld and the realm of the supernatural.

Other human images show elements of fantasy or distortion that fit into a possibly shamanic context. In northern Bohuslän, a number of humans are represented with enormous hands.[33] Certain figures are represented without arms: at Boglösa in Uppland, armless beings with long slim legs are shown, as on a rock face at Rickeby, and the legs may be asymmetrical, with the left carved longer than the right.[34] In the same area, images of exaggeratedly long-legged persons are carved across a deep crack in the rock surface, separating heads from bodies.[35] Likewise, the depiction at Enköping, Uppland (Fig. 26), of an archer pursuing a stag from which he is separated by a vertical fissure in the rock surface[36] might reflect a common shamanistic hunting motif wherein the shaman must invoke the spirit of the hunted animal in

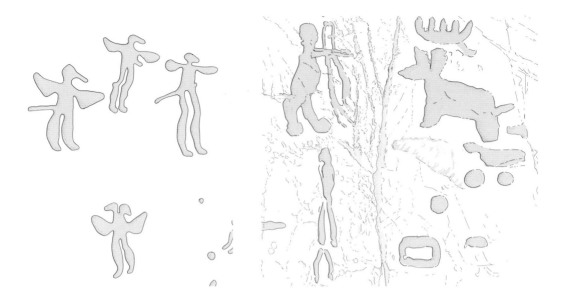

the supernatural world. The incomplete bodies, without arms or other parts, and images carved across cracks may resonate with shamanistic tradition in the ritual dismemberment and reborn reincorporation that the shaman may have to undergo as part of his or her initiation by the spirits.[37]

Perhaps oddest of all the human images are the 'disc-men' (Plate II), individuals with swords or axes, sometimes ithyphallic and bird-headed,[38] whose torsos are in the form of four-spoked wheels or concentric circles. The disc-people at Biskopskulla in Uppland are even stranger in that they consist of wheel-cross circles with legs but no heads or arms.[39] We wonder, indeed, whether it is possible to offer an alternative interpretation and suggest that such motifs (Plate 12) may represent not humans but shamans' drums complete with drumsticks: in Siberian rock art, quartered open circles depict such drums with cross-handles.[40] Percussion, specifically drum-beats, have been identified as central to many shamanistic rituals because the resonance enables the shaman's receptivity to the spirits.[41] (In certain Japanese rituals, for instance, the resonating drum plays a spectacular role, in which a huge barrel-shaped drum, carried through the streets on a great platform, acts in retribution, lurching from side to side and injuring persons inimical to the community such as corrupt traders or mean landlords.)[42] But 'solar'-headed images, in the context of Central

24 OPPOSITE *Lur players, Kalleby, Bohuslän, Sweden.*
25 ABOVE LEFT *Winged warriors, including Janus-figure; Kallsängen, N. Bohuslän, Sweden.*
26 ABOVE RIGHT *Archer and deer, separated by a natural crack in the rock; Enköping Vårfrukyrke, Uppland, Sweden.*

Asian rock carvings, relate to trance-induced entoptic phenomena.[43] However one interprets these 'unreal' images, it is worth noting John Coles's observation[44] that mushrooms local to northern Bohuslän contain hallucinogenic properties and these may have been instrumental in the production of transcendental art.

The tentative identification of some human images in Scandinavian rock art as ritualists is supported by the liminality of their presentation: their appearance as half-human, half-animal may be understood as shamans dressed up in animal costume in the context of performance and of enabling contact with the spirit-world; the bird-guise may have further signification in so far as shamanic trance frequently includes the sensation of flying between cosmic tiers. What is more, the dominance of these 'big men' suggests that they were significant individuals within their society and, perhaps, that they were either actually or at least symbolically responsible for the motifs with which they were surrounded. But it is time to explore some of these other motifs, to see if they, too, support an association between this northern art and shamanistic practices, as expressions of that reaching-out to the spirit-dimension that is the core of shamanic systems.

VISIONS OF OTHER WORLDS

The carvings as a whole combined the real and the imagined, the direct reflection of important elements of the visible world with the unseen world, the world beyond, which was the more powerful in times of stress and change.

John Coles, *Rock Carvings of Uppland*[45]

We have explored some anthropomorphic imagery that lends itself to its interpretation as representative of special people, perhaps those who were spiritual leaders, distinctive in their ability to move between worlds and to negotiate with supernatural forces on behalf of their community. The other important – and closely related – issue to be addressed is the possible identification of 'fantasy' motifs that may reflect the shaman's out-of-body

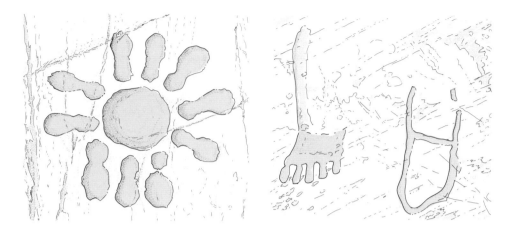

experiences while in a mind-altered trance state, whether induced naturally or by means of ingested hallucinogens. There is a 'design grammar'[46] of motifs that are not only repeated in wide-ranging areas of the prehistoric world but which may also sometimes resonate with 'modern' shamanistic expression in the repertoire of, for instance, some circumpolar, Australian and southern African rock art.

Transition, transformation and liminality are features that recur time and time again in the treatment of Swedish Bronze Age rupestrine iconography. Allusion has already been made to the presentation of humans with horns or in the guise of birds, features that may express shamans' perceptions of themselves whilst in altered states of awareness. The rock art includes other hybrid, monstrous beings, such as the curious polysemic 'antlered-tree-human' perched on a boat or sled from Litslena in Uppland[47] (Fig. 27) and the part-deer part-horse image from Kallsängen, Bohuslän,[48] surely the product of a trance-induced 'otherworld' vision. Other transitional motifs include the ubiquitous depictions of human feet, single or in pairs, sometimes bare, sometimes as sandalled 'footsoles'. Many of these are life-size or greater: at Litslena a pair of footsoles fit a (continental) size 44 foot.[49] The feet are clustered around a central image: the Järrestad Dancer is surrounded by footprints; at Boglösa in Uppland, a large disc (Fig. 28) has footsoles radiating from it like solar rays.[50] Sometimes, the positioning or treatment of foot symbols is distinctive: a pair of naked feet at Rickeby (Boglösa) shows one as an outline and the other hollow-carved into the rock;[51] on another group nearby, a bare foot and a shod foot (Fig. 29) are carved side by side, deliberately placed over a vein of quartz in the rock.[52]

27 OPPOSITE *Composite human/tree/stag figure on boat/sledge; Litslena, Uppland, Sweden.*

28 ABOVE LEFT *Footsoles grouped around a disc; Boglösa, Uppland, Sweden.*

29 ABOVE RIGHT *Bare foot and shod foot carved over a quartz vein; Boglösa, Uppland, Sweden.*

Chris Scarre, of the University of Cambridge,[53] draws attention to the persistent association between the luminescence of quartz and perceptions 'associated with shamanism and hidden power'. Such idiosyncrasies may provide clues as to the meanings perhaps associated with foot-carvings: the differential treatment suggests transition or transformation, the outlined and deeply carved foot representing a person's journey through the rock to another world. Likewise, the bare and shod foot on the quartz line may refer to different stages of being; the glittering vein of quartz might have been perceived as a gateway to that otherworld, facilitating the entry of the foot-owners. The feet on the rocks may represent the living, in process of mental transformation to unearthly layers of the cosmos; they may equally represent the dead, who cross over between worlds when their souls part from their bodies in a manner – perhaps – broadly analogous to the Indian Jain tradition of carving of footprints on stone plaques set up in sacred places to commemorate those who starve themselves to death as sacrificial offerings, a ritual that is still occasionally practised.[54] But it is noteworthy that not only human feet are represented on the rocks: northern Bohuslän contains images of paw-prints and those of cloven hooves as well;[55] perhaps animals as well as humans were walking between worlds and disappearing into the rock.

It has been suggested[56] that the 'shod' footsole motifs could represent snow shoes. If this were so, then the bare and shod feet could be associated with seasonality and transition between summer and winter. Interestingly, such imagery may be tentatively identified on other rupestrine depictions, namely the numerous boats that sail along the rock faces as though on the sea, some of which are definitely ships but others appear to be more sled-like and certain images[57] show an ambiguity that may be deliberate (Fig. 30). Again, these could be seasonal references, perhaps marking ceremonial occasions or signifiers of weather-transition, but they might also be metaphors for life and death, the light and dark worlds or the domains of earth and underworld. This idea is supported by the presentation of upside-down boats[58] which, significantly, are carved particularly deeply, suggesting either that their depth within the rock was symbolically important and/or that the images were constantly being embellished by members of the community, maybe during successive rituals. In a model of transition between worlds, the rock

30 *Ships and suns, Bohuslän, Sweden. These may represent spirit-boats sailing to other worlds.*

itself may hold a central place as the sea, the gateway between cosmic layers, just as is the case in the myths of early historical Ireland, or Classical legend, as described in Virgil's *Aeneid*,[59] where Lake Avernus provides access to Hades. Interpretation of the rock face as sometimes reflective of water is buttressed by the presence of other motifs, namely concentric circles that resemble ripples in still water, sometimes in association with boats: this occurs, for instance, at Litslena in Uppland.[60]

Apart from the boats, the most ubiquitous motifs on southern Swedish rock art consist of so-called 'cupmarks', raised circles that appear either singly or in clusters or form sinuous linear patterns. Frequently, boats and cupmarks share rock panels but, where they do appear in association, they occupy distinct areas: at Biskopskulla in Uppland, a boat occupies the lower register whilst cupmarks occupy the space above;[61] it is tempting to interpret such scenes as reflective of upper and lower worlds. The cupmarks themselves are interesting within a possibly shamanistic perspective, for 'it is not uncommon to find a row of cupmarks carved into natural cracks in the rock as if seeking an entry into the rock itself':[62] this occurs, for instance, at Enköping, also in Uppland. Modern shamans, while in trance, persistently experience the sensation of penetrating solid rock[63] or squeezing into cracks.[64] Lines of circles or cupmarks might represent entoptic phenomena, visual effects of phosphenes in the eyes, the result of neurological disturbances during mind-altered states: such designs are common occurrences in shamanistic contexts where trance is induced by hallucinogenic agents.[65] The same may be true of so-called 'net' motifs, spirals and labyrinths, all of which appear in the northern Bronze Age artists' repertoire:[66] also present are ladder-designs[67] which, albeit speculatively, might be interpretable as depictive of gateways between the layers of the cosmos – like the cosmic tree[68] accessible only to the shaman.

Pattern and meaning on the northern rocks
There is a 'grammar' within the rock-art tradition considered above that includes several recurrent patterns of treatment that were surely charged with significance for the producers and their 'patrons', and that are distinctive in their apparent surreality. Boats disappearing into crevices, cupmarks emerging from cracks, incomplete figures without limbs or heads, schematic and realistic motifs sharing canvases, half-human, half-animal creatures, curious designs, such as nets, ladders, meandering lines of circles and footprints are all repetitively produced in several regions of southern Scandinavia, as if belonging to a common currency of value and meaning. Several points of significance emerge from study of these 'signified' rocks, some of which should, perhaps, be regarded as sacred places, locations where groups of people, maybe from several communities, met regularly or at times of great moment in order to communicate with each other or with otherworldly beings: in either instance, a person in the role of a shaman, able to act as negotiator, would be of crucial importance.

John Coles rightly emphasizes[69] that the themes selected for expression in the carvings reflected what was interesting, important and to be remembered. We should not forget elements concerning the rock art apart from the designs themselves; most of them are positioned so that they would be viewed from below, suggesting that the people looking at them were deliberately placed as if the carvings formed a world above them. The sea would have been much closer to the rocks in the Bronze Age than it is today; the shore, with its numerous inlets and fjords, would have been intimately associated with the art; in speaking of Uppland, John Coles[70] draws attention to the 'flurry of activity' apparently associated with rock carvings produced as the sea retreated, the land rose and new islands emerged. Certain rocks were singled out for multiple, often superimposed carvings; sometimes cracks in the rock were avoided, at others used as foci for the art; designs might be grouped vertically or horizontally, as though structures and relationships between motifs were important. We should note, too, that when the rock was freshly carved, the motifs would stand out dramatically from the weathered rock surface around them, and sun, moon and torchlight would create varying shapes and forms.[71]

The contribution of senses other than sight should also be acknowledged, in terms of total experience: the sound of the sea would provide a constant backdrop to the production and consumption of the art; furthermore, different rocks would emit different sounds as they were worked,[72] and this factor may have been significant in the choice of canvas. This reminds us that the 'finished product' was only one stage in the evolution and use of the rocks: the act of making the images was probably at least as significant as the motifs themselves. If shamans were to have been involved, the production of the art, perhaps following trance-experience, would have been a public act of performance, perhaps in the context of large gatherings. Considerable effort would have been needed, particularly to make the deep incisions;[73] granite is difficult to work, so the designs and images were far from being the result of an idle half-hour's sketching.[74] It is clear that the artists responsible for the carvings must have enjoyed significant status within their communities,[75] whether or not we are right in suggesting their shamanic identity. Given that an important role of traditional shamans is to share the results of their soul-journeys, it is worthwhile to propose that the perpetrators of the art were either the ritualists themselves or that they at least provided the inspiration for some of the more esoteric motifs.

HIGH PLACES OF SANCTITY: ROCK ART IN THE WESTERN ALPS

People carved the rocks of Camonica Valley, near Brescia in northern Italy, from the end of the last Ice Age until medieval times. During the Neolithic, Bronze Age and Iron Age, the Camunians (until their absorption into the Roman Empire in 16 BC) carved the sandstone rocks in a manner similar to the Scandinavian communities discussed above, to signify themselves, their world and the supernatural dimension. Unlike the southern Swedish art, the Camonica carvings were situated in a remote and mountainous landscape, far away from the sea, in a valley that formed a natural corridor for the movement of game; ship-images are absent from the repertoire of motifs and animals, particularly deer, assume a prominence missing from the northern iconography. Nonetheless, there are striking similarities between the two regions, both in some motifs and in the clustering and superimposition (or stacking) of images[76] on rocks that were clearly special places, arguably foci of ritual activity. Recurrent themes include footprints, handprints, half-human, half-animal beings and 'sun-discs'; Chris Scarre[77] has suggested that the complex scene depicted on the Bedolina rock near Capo di Ponte, probably of Bronze Age date, may have served as a map, perhaps of a mental, cosmological landscape to enable ritualists to access other worlds: modern shamans possess 'maps' or charts of cosmic worlds.[78] Some carved images may have been painted: pigment-processing sites have been identified,[79] and it may be that newly added images were singled out for painting.

Camunian mindscapes: trance & ritual in stone

Jacques Briard, a Bronze Age specialist from the University of Rennes,[80] alludes to an Iron Age image of a 'smith-god' at Camonica with hammer and anvil as a transformative being, a reflection of his ability to change rock into metal. Indeed, many anthropomorphic figures on the Camunian rocks exhibit signs of ecstatic or trance-induced experience: some are depicted with their hair standing on end; at Nadro, a village south of Capo di Ponte, two pairs engage in what seems to be a ritual dance or fight (Fig. 31) (highly reminiscent of the graceful 'combat' decorating the bronze couch found in the rich tomb of an early Iron Age chieftain buried at Hochdorf in

31 *Symbolic combat scene, perhaps in the context of a funerary ceremony, between radiate-haired 'shamans', Camonica Valley, Italy.*

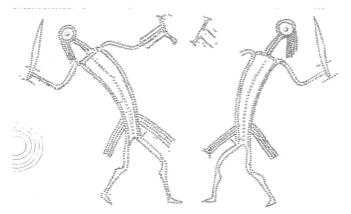

32 LEFT *The Hochdorf dancers, engaged in symbolic combat, probably in the enactment of some kind of funerary ritual; decoration on a bronze couch from the Hallstatt chieftain's burial at Hochdorf, Germany.*

33 OPPOSITE LEFT *'Shamanic sacrifice' scene, Camonica Valley.*

34 OPPOSITE RIGHT *Camonica Valley stag-man.*

35 OPPOSITE BELOW *Stags and suns; Camonica Valley.*

Germany: see p. 126) (Fig. 32) and three have spiky, upstanding hair.[81] Another figure, also at Nadro, dances on the rock face with a sword and what may be a divining rod, or a more prosaic staff of authority.[82] Other human figures not only have 'radiate' hair but appear to be dressed in spiky animal-pelts, and one adopts a 'praying' attitude, with arms upraised;[83] a striking scene shows a human with a rectangular, netlike body holding a large circular object above his head, while his two flanking companions attack him with knives and swords: significantly, the assailants wear long-haired animal skins over their heads and bodies and one has a tail (Fig. 33).[84] One interpretation of this scene is in terms of ritual performance involving initiation ceremonies and the symbolic killing and dismemberment of an apprentice shaman. (The hair 'en brosse' may be associated with the stress of out-of-body experience and symbolic death, just as – in southern African rock art – the spirit-animal shows its liminal state between life and death by raised dorsal bristles.)[85] Interestingly, in this respect, Emmanuel Anati, who pioneered Italian rock-art studies and has spent a lifetime recording and interpreting the Camonican images,[86] illustrates an image of a horse with what looks like a spiky nimboid headdress similar to those on human figures, but perhaps, instead, the erect mane of a spirit-creature is depicted.

Identification of animal costumes on some human figures on the Camonican rocks is interesting in the context of shamanic transference between person and beast, a recurrent theme noted in many traditional shamanistic societies and referred to throughout this volume. On their own, the Italian images may be understood as those of people, albeit special people, who wore fur clothes, but there is an important group of figures who seem to exhibit more genuine fusion between human and animal (usually a stag) and who also appear to function as 'big men' in

much the same way as identified in the Scandinavian art: in the north these images are often horned; here they sprout antlers. The most striking of these figures was carved on the great Naquane rock at Capo di Ponte: a huge standing figure, dressed in a long robe, antlers on his head, two torcs slung from his elbows and with a serpent nearby (Fig. 34). His (if he is correctly identified as male) attitude is that of a dancer, legs bent and arms upraised.[87] But other, similar images were drawn on the rocks here, including a very stylized antlered 'matchstick man' incised on a panel at nearby Pian Cogno,[88] and another dancer from Paspardo in the same region.[89]

It could be argued that the depictions of antlered people represent ritualists wearing antler headdresses, and this may well be so,[90] but another group of figures show entrance into a deeper and more intertwined relationship between stags and humans: thus, at Naquane and Nadro, humans merge with stags in centaur-like hybrids.[91] It may even be that the different types reflect stages of the shaman's journey to becoming an animal during deepening trance-experience. The recurrent use of stag imagery here (Fig. 35) is testament to the importance with which these animals were regarded by the Camunians: many images of stags, including those of superb alpha-males with enormous 14-branched antlers, at Cemmo, for instance,[92]

display the Camunians' preoccupation with these creatures, as does the depiction of herds of stags (unusual in life, for they tend to be solitary beasts). Images of hunted stags, with spears thrust through them,[93] may represent the daily subsistence activities of the local community, but they may also be 'spirit-animals', the souls of slain deer that had to be appeased by the shaman so that they would always return to provide food again. It is interesting that the analogous rock art of Mont Bégo in the French Alps presents similarly close associations between 'big men' and animals, but the French material emphasizes not the stag but the bull: 'bull men' with great horns or with the entire human head replaced by horns are depicted, and there are numerous images of bulls with exaggerated horns.[94]

Other anthropomorphic images resonate both with the Scandinavian repertoire and with traditional expressions of shamanic experience. The Camunians, too, represented 'bird-people' (Fig. 36), with beaks and wings,[95] as if reflective of soul-flight between worlds. Fantasy and surreality are expressed in the weird tree-like motif with human heads (alternatively interpretable as a shaman wearing a feather-cape) at Val d'Assa[96] or the human figures or faces peering out from vortex-like labyrinth-motifs (Fig. 38).[97] The symbolic 'death' of the shaman and the dissolution and the reassembly of his body in rebirth initiation rites, such as are present in certain Canadian traditions,[98] might be reflected in the 'skeleton' images[99] and the amputees, with heads, arms or legs missing.[100] Piers Vitebsky explains skeleton-imagery in the

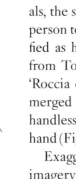

context of shamanistic healing: when engaged in curative rituals, the shaman may need to be able to 'see' through the sick person to the bones and internal organs. What may be identified as hallucinogenic distortion is expressed by the figure from Torri del Benaco, where a rock known locally as the 'Roccia della grande mano' depicts a human figure with a merged head and torso, a rod or serpent attached to the left handless wrist and the right arm terminating in an enormous hand (Fig. 37), as large as the rest of the body.[101]

Exaggeration of hands occurs elsewhere on Camunian imagery (as in Scandinavian rock art and, indeed, on some Iron Age sculpture, the figure from Pauvrelay in central

France being an example)[102] and these should perhaps be related to the numerous handprints carved out of the rock surface,[103] as though they are penetrating the stone. Handprints are known in Upper Palaeolithic cave art[104] (as we have seen in Chapter 2), and have sometimes been interpreted as expressions of movement between earthworld and the supernatural layer of the cosmos. But the exaggerated hands on some human figures are curious and, in this context, they perhaps represent the power of the shaman or of spirit-beings in shamanic dreamscapes. The motif of footprints, so common in the Scandinavian sample studied here, also occurs at Camonica, though less persistently: one striking image is that of a bird-beaked person and other anthropomorphic figures carved within a pair of large footprints.[105] Could it be that the prints were themselves agents for travel between dimensions and that the people inside them were using them as gateways? Both footprints and handprints persistently occur also in the coeval art of Mont Bégo.[106]

Other Camunian motifs, perhaps explicable in terms of entoptic phenomena, are highly reminiscent of Scandinavian depictions: spirals, labyrinths, sinuous lines, clusters of dots and concentric circles all form part of the Italian rupestrine repertoire.[107] 'Nets' and net-like human figures, too, are present (Fig. 39), as in southern Sweden[108] and, indeed at Mont Bégo.[109] The Bedolina (Capo di Ponte) rock art of the late Bronze Age includes images whose torsos are in the form of rectangular nets, sometimes filled with dots;[110] a figure at Pian Cogno is drawn as a matchstick man whose body is a network of criss-cross lines.[111] The net images present an interesting ambiguity in so far as nets are common phenomena within the visual spectrum of trance experience, but at Camonica, where hunting imagery is common, it is possible to interpret some of the nets as implements for hunting birds: indeed the two ideas need not be mutually exclusive, especially given the bird-men depicted on the Camunian rocks; after all, the ritual hunt is an important element in most traditional shamanistic systems. One curious, also ambiguous, motif at Camonica is the 'paddle', perhaps an unlikely interpretation in a

36 OPPOSITE LEFT *Bird-man, Val d'Assa, Romita, Camonica Valley.*

37 OPPOSITE RIGHT *Human figure with no head and a large hand, Torri del Benaco, Roccia delle grande mano, Camonica Valley.*

38 ABOVE *Labyrinth-phallus-face, Camonica Valley.*

39 RIGHT *Armed 'net' figure, Camonica Valley.*

landlocked context, but possibly these shapes might be better understood as mirrors, in which case they fit well within a repertoire of art that is associated with shamanism. In the European Iron Age, mirrors appear to have been highly symbolic objects, and were perhaps linked with double, two-spirit identity and the ability to see behind as well as in front, with consonant resonances of belonging to two worlds (see Chapter 5).

Stones, Shamans and Spirits

Study of the later prehistoric art within the two chosen study-areas – southern Sweden and Alpine Italy – suggests considerable cognitive linkage, in terms of the motifs, figures and treatment of images. While it would be folly to try and explain all the rupestrine iconography as shamanic, or even spiritually determined, it is valid to propose that the communities responsible embraced multi-spirit worlds, acknowledged their situation within highly numinous landscapes and may have relied on special people, shamans, to access, control and manipulate supernatural forces that were considered to be intimately associated with people's daily lives and concerns, whether hunting, farming the land or voyaging by sea. The rocks have preserved the signatures of these communities and, perhaps, something of the nature and experiences of their ritualists. It is fitting to conclude with a comment by John Coles, made in the context of his discussion of rock art in Bronze Age Uppland:[112]

> Mute signs and symbols can transmit a greater depth and freedom of variation than any spoken word and, unless they are directly and consistently consecrated by hierophantic activity, they may undergo transformation both in shape and in subtle interpretation through the passage of time.

Sacred Gold and Celestial Magic

At about the same time that Bronze Age artists were decorating living rock with symbolic, perhaps shamanic, motifs, people were expressing the sacred world in metalwork, particularly in gold. They appear to have associated this metal with celestial bodies, especially the sun, its diurnal and seasonal journeys and with the ability to make calendrical calculations, a form of knowledge that – in many ancient cultures (including those of Greece and Rome) – was associated with holy men and women.[113] It is perhaps no coincidence that solar motifs form a dominant component of Bronze Age rock art in both Scandinavian and Alpine regions, and it is possible that these rupestrine symbols relate to a broadly coeval group of gold and bronze 'celestial' objects from central and northern Europe.

'Solar' headgear?

In 1953, a curious sheet-gold cone 95 cm (37 in) high (Fig. 40) was discovered on the hill of Brentenberg between Etzelsdorf and Buch in Bavaria.[114] Decorated in repoussé with horizontal rows of circles and 'wheel-motifs', the cone has relatives in other similar pieces from Avanton (Vienne) and Schifferstadt, near Berlin,[115] this last one being found to contain traces of aromatic resins. It is unclear as to what such flamboyant gold objects may have been, but it is possible that they were worn by people or images on ceremonial occasions (the Schifferstadt one, with its broad brim, looks very hat-like), and the 'celestial' decoration, together with the choice of gold for their production suggests that they may have been associated with some kind of solar ritual, perhaps concerned with solstice festivals. When worn or carried, these fantastic objects would have glowed as they caught the sunlight, reflecting the myriad decorative relief-motifs and dazzling the eye, as if a sun's ray had been solidified in gold.

Drums and discs

> When the Pleiads, Atlas' daughters, start to rise
> Begin your harvest; plough when they go down.
> For forty days and nights they hide themselves,
> And as the year rolls round, appear again
> When you begin to sharpen sickle-blades.
>
> Hesiod, *Works and Days*[116]

The front cover of *Der Spiegel* for 25 November 2002 displays a picture of a remarkable object discovered near Nebra in Germany in that year, a bronze disc, about the size of a dinner-plate, decorated with celestial bodies in gold-inlay (Fig. 41): stars, a solar (or lunar) disc, a crescent-moon and what has been interpreted as a 'sun-boat',[117] together with two inlaid arcs on the edges (one of which was removed in antiquity) representing horizons and marking the position of the sunrise and sunset at the solstices; seven of the stars group to form the Pleiades. This unique 'sky-disc' was found with a hoard of other objects, including a pair of swords, flat axes and spiral arm-lets, and it has been suggested that the disc itself was perhaps over a hundred years old when it was deposited, after it had been subjected to deliberate acts of ritual damage. The cache was found in the middle of a circular enclosure on a commanding hill. The star-disc has been provisionally dated to *c.* 1600 BC.

40 *Gold cone/hat from Etzelsdorf, Bavaria.*

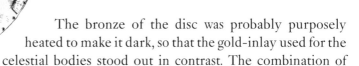

The bronze of the disc was probably purposely heated to make it dark, so that the gold-inlay used for the celestial bodies stood out in contrast. The combination of horizons, the sun or full moon and the lunar crescent, the solar boat and the Pleiades makes it more than likely that the Nebra disc was used by specialist ritualists who employed it to compute complicated calculations, linked to major seasonal events, such as sowing and reaping and the festivals associated with the farming year. As indicated by the quotation from *Works and Days* at the head of this section, the Greek writer Hesiod (eighth century BC) comments that the rising of the Pleiades signalled the time for harvest and their setting indicated the right season for ploughing. It may well be that the disc belonged to a fraternity of holy persons whose power rested in their abilities at precognition, at controlling the firmament and their curation of secret knowledge. The disc was finally interred, perhaps, when a particular dynasty of ritualists came to an end.

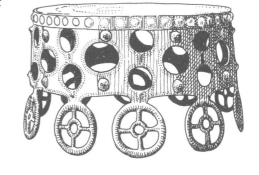

In seeking to relate the Nebra sky-disc to cognate Bronze Age material culture, the two most obvious parallels lie in northern Europe, in the bronze 'sun-drum' (Fig. 42) from

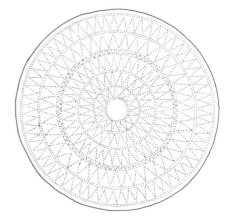

41 ABOVE *The sky-disc from Nebra, Germany.*

42 RIGHT *Bronze 'sun-drum', Balkåkra, Scania, Sweden.*

43 OPPOSITE *Close-up of solar decoration on chamfrein of the Trundholm horse.*

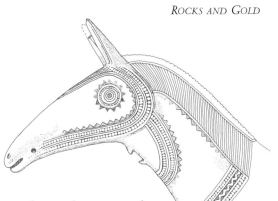

Balkåkra in Sweden and the disc mounted on a horse-drawn cart from
Trundholm, Denmark (Plate 13). The first consists of a cylindrical object,
about 40 cm (15.7 in) in diameter, supporting a flat lid-like disc decorated with
linear and circular designs, mounted on ten miniature wheels.[118] Its size and
appearance suggests that it may have been utilized as some kind of drum or table,
perhaps used in a similar manner to a shaman's drum, both as a percussive device
and as a means of plotting the future, maybe in conjunction with rods, counters or
other items that could be cast 'at random' on its surface. Traces of wear around the
holes under the rim suggest that the drum may have been hung up when not in use.

The Trundholm disc (actually a pair of discs joined by a cast bronze ring) is also
bronze but gilded on one side; it is mounted vertically on a six-wheeled wagon
drawn by a slender horse, which wears a chamfrein (a headdress) (Fig. 43) decorated
with what may be interpreted as celestial motifs. The surfaces of the disc are similarly ornamented with rays, circles and spirals.[119] Like the Nebra sky-disc, the
Trundholm wagon was subjected to deliberate damage before its careful deposition, this time not in a dry hoard but in a peat bog. Before its interment, itself a
highly ritualized act arguably performed by professional clergy, the cart may have
been used in dramatic ceremonies associated with the veneration of the sun and its
diurnal and seasonal journeys across the skies. The bright, golden surface may have
represented the full noonday summer sun, while the duller side symbolized the sun
at sunset or in winter. It is not too fanciful to suppose that the community's shamans
or religious practitioners were responsible for orchestrating ceremonial events and
the manipulation of the wagon in order to replicate and thereby induce the sun's
return after the dark and cold of winter when the sun deprived people of its life-
giving force. The Trundholm disc, together with cognate material culture of the
Bronze Age, needs to be set within an Indo-European context, in which the solar
chariot and solar boat were familiar cosmological *leitmotifs*.[120] The 'barque' identified on the Nebra disc may relate to the 'sun-ships' decorating the later Bronze Age
vessels from northern Europe, typified by the splendid Danish sheet-bronze urn
from Mariesminde (Fig. 44), that have tentatively but persuasively been interpreted as ritual containers associated with 'weather-magic', involved in ceremonies
connected with the supernatural control of rain and the propitiation of the sun.[121]

44 *Detail of a sheet-bronze vessel with ship and sun decoration, from Mariesminde, Denmark.*

CONCLUSION

This chapter has focused principally upon two threads of evidence: the imagery presented on rock carvings from Scandinavia and Alpine Italy, on the one hand and, on the other, on some spectacular Bronze Age metalwork from northern and central Europe. The rock art shows us a kaleidoscopic repertoire of iconography, at least some of which appears to reflect visions of other worlds and of the ritualists, perhaps shamans, who made journeys to them, on foot, by boat or with wings. Symbols on the rocks include expressions of transference between dimensions of being, particularly in the therianthropes (half-human, half-animal creatures) that can be interpreted as metaphors for transition between earth world and spirit worlds. Certain recurring motifs, like the nets, labyrinths, footprints and arrangements of dots, may be related to entoptic, trance-induced experience, and we will draw attention to their presence in the material culture of Iron Age Europe, notably on coins (Chapter 5). Other imagery, like the Dancer from Järrestad, could be interpreted as representatives of shamanic big men, controllers of the sacred. In examining other ritual objects from Bronze Age Europe, it is difficult to explain the presence of regalia, like the bizarre conical gold hats, as other than equipment linked to ritual performance. But most spectacular of all is the material that seems to refer to a sophisticated conversance with heavenly bodies and their use to predict the future and present perceptions of Bronze Age cosmologies: the 'sun-chariot' from Trundholm and the, even more dramatic, star-gazing disc from Nebra, with its map of the sky and the seasonal marker of the rising Pleiades.

5 PRIESTS, POLITICS AND POWER
Controlling the Supernatural in Iron Age Europe

Philosophers ... and men learned in religious affairs are
Unusually honoured among them [the Gauls] and are called by them
Druids. They further make use of seers, thinking them worthy of
High praise

Diodorus Siculus, *Library of History*[1]

The Iron Age in northwest Europe saw the genesis of a sophisticated repertoire of symbolic, spiritually inspired art that survives mainly in metal. It is becoming increasingly accepted that many of the fantastic, 'surreal' motifs decorating implements, jewellery, coins and other objects may have been inspired by transformatory trance experience, perhaps brought about by the ingestion of hallucinogens: drugs, alcohol or naturally induced altered states of consciousness. There exists both archaeological evidence and (for the late Iron Age) literature from the Classical world suggesting that power may have been invested in the few and that religion and political influence were closely allied. For the last few centuries BC, it appears that – in Gaul (the name given by the Romans to France, North Italy, Belgium, Switzerland and Germany on the left bank of the Rhine) and Britain at least – the Druids were mixed up in both spiritual matters and power-broking, and it is probable that at least some of their ritual activities can be identified as shamanistic behaviour. It may even be that art on metalwork was Druid-driven.

Archaeological evidence bears witness to the presence of ritualists, who were buried with special equipment, sometimes apparently wrapped in animal skins (a possible indicator of the animal personae adopted by shamans in many traditions). Some of the bodies deposited in north European peat bogs bear witness to their special nature, and to their ingestion of hallucinogens, both perhaps suggestive of

their occupation of a shamanistic role in Iron Age society. One of the most important aspects of ritualist action may have been divination, a skill closely related to
healing. It is possible to identify diviners in both material culture and literary testimony: in the mid-first century BC, Caesar and Cicero give us the name of one such
individual – Diviciacus, who was a political leader, friend of Rome, ritualist predic-
tor of the future and Druid.

DANCING MEN AND SEEING WOMEN

Danish dervishes

In about 250 BC, at remote places in Jutland – Tollund Fen in the Bjaeldskov Valley
and Nebelmose near the village of Grauballe – two men met violent deaths, each
event almost certainly hedged about with complex ceremonial and communal participation. After they had been deliberately killed, their bodies were consigned to
bogs, perhaps because of the known preservative properties of marshy graves. The
Tollund Man (Plate 14), discovered in 1950 by local men engaged in cutting peat for
fuel, was probably about forty or fifty years old when he died by hanging; the
Grauballe Man from Nebelmose (so called because his discoverers came from
Grauballe) was a younger man (Plate 15), and he had been dispatched by a savage
throat-slash; his body was discovered less than two years later than the Tollund
individual, also by peat-cutters. These two belong to a large group of Iron Age bog
bodies whose deaths may have been the result of ritual murder,[2] but that they may
have been special is suggested by their ingestion of food containing a curious, deliberately assembled, mixture of cereal grains, chaff and wild seeds and, what is more
significant, quantities of ergot were present in the gut.

Ergot is a complex and toxic alkaloid substance contaminating cereals, particularly rye, consumption of which induces 'wild hallucinations, a burning sensation
in the mouth and extremities ('St Anthony's Fire'), acute abdominal pain and con-
vulsions'.[3] Indeed, the modern psychotropic drug LSD is an ergot-derivative. The
fungus is unmistakable, giving rye grains a distinctive elongated and purplish
appearance. There is no doubt that sufferers from ergotism would have behaved in
a most peculiar manner, as if possessed, throwing themselves about and screaming
with mental and physical anguish. Ergot contamination occurs naturally in damp,
fermenting cereal and, despite its singular appearance, may sometimes have been
ingested accidentally or under conditions of famine when there may have been
little choice. However, it is conceivable that controlled quantities of ergot may have
been deliberately consumed by individuals seeking to enter an altered, hallucinogenic mental state. An interesting feature of ergotism is its ability to cause
collective delusions: thus one influential sufferer might control and share his or her
mind-bending experience with others. It is highly possible that the men interred at

Tollund and Nebelmose were shamans who consciously took ergot in order to transcend worlds and commune with the spirit-forces. Under extreme circumstances, they may have even connived at their own deaths: Mike Parker Pearson of the University of Sheffield, who has made a major contribution in the study of ancient death rituals,[4] has suggested that the amount of ergot consumed by the Grauballe Man was sufficient to send him into a coma or kill him.

The behavioural products of ergotism are spectacular and, in terms of shamanic performance, would have caused the sufferer to act in strange, contorted ways, perhaps involving weaving, dancing movements, as the discomfort of 'burning' limbs or stomach cramps took hold. Even if the Tollund and Grauballe people were not shamans, deliberately inducing a mind (and body) altering state, it may be that accidental sufferers from the contaminant behaved in such a frightening, inexplicable manner that their deviancy marked them out as polluted or blessed and as chosen by the gods for sacrifice. In acute physical and mental distress, the 'dancing men' might have flung themselves about, shouting out their delusions, thus acclaiming themselves as instruments of the supernatural world.

Ergot was not the only strange substance ingested by Iron Age bog people, though it was probably the most dramatic. The archaeobotanist Gordon Hillman[5] has pointed out that both the woman from Huldremose, found at Ramten in Djursland (Jutland) in 1879, and Lindow Man (Plate 16), discovered in a peat bog at Lindow Moss in Cheshire in 1984 (Lindow II), had eaten a final meal containing infected barley. More interestingly, Lindow Man had consumed a minute quantity (four grains) of mistletoe pollen. This might be important, for mistletoe has a long pedigree as a remedy for a range of disorders, including insomnia, cramps, vertigo, hypertension and some tumours. The type of mistletoe ingested at Lindow is *Viscum album*, precisely the western European sub-species of the plant depicted as 'leaf-crowns' on a discrete group of stone and metal anthropomorphic images from Iron Age Europe, including Pfalzfeld, Heidelberg, Glauberg and Schwarzenbach.[6] If the mistletoe ingested by Lindow Man was deliberately fed to him by others or self-administered, its purpose might have been shamanistic, perhaps a compensatory self-healing agent consumed just before he met a violent and symbolically triple-fold death, by being clubbed over the head, garrotted and his throat cut before being 'drowned' face-down in a marsh-pool.[7] But, aside from its curative properties, mistletoe may well have been a potent symbol of rebirth and fertility: it flourishes in winter, appearing as vigorous green growth upon the skeletons of 'dead' trees, with berries whose white viscosity invokes images of milk and semen. Pliny the Elder's comment[8] concerning the significance of mistletoe for Gaulish Druids specifically associates the plant with the moon and regeneration.

Apart from mistletoe, there is a body of evidence for the ingestion of special food by bog victims. Gordon Hillman and Rob Scaife[9] draw attention to the variety of weeds forming part of the porridge or griddle-loaves consumed by the people interred at Tollund, Grauballe, Lindow, Borremose and Huldremose. The inclusion of such plant material in these meals may be simple testimony to poverty or famine, but it may, instead, point to a symbolic representation of a wide range of both wild and domesticated species, perhaps in order to demonstrate the bog people's local identity. If these individuals were sacrificial victims, it may be that the purpose of their deaths was to purify their community[10] and, if this were so, it might be important to represent the land and its products as faithfully as possible.

Although belonging to a different time and space perspective, it is worth observing that an episode in the early medieval Welsh group of mythic tales known as the *Pedeir Keinc y Mabinogi* describes the use of wild plants in magic: in the Fourth Branch of the Mabinogion,[11] his mother Arianrhod's curse denies the hero Lleu a human wife, so the magician Gwydion, the youth's uncle, conjures for him a wife, Blodeuwedd, who is made of wild flowers: those of the oak, meadowsweet and broom, each of which blooms at a different time of the year in different habitats, as if deliberately to encompass all seasons and types of land. But the manner of her birth renders the 'flower-woman' unstable and amoral, as if the untamed and uncultivated nature of the plants used in her creation cause her to eschew the admired human values of constancy and chastity. Such instability may also be a feature of Iron Age shamans, special, marginal people who belonged both to the earthly and spirit-worlds but also to neither. The placement of the Tollund, Grauballe and – indeed – other human bodies in bogs, themselves marginal, unstable and dangerous places, may be interpreted as appropriate behaviour. Christian Fischer has drawn attention to the circumstances of the Tollund Man's interment, particularly the postmortem closure of his eyes and mouth and the arrangement of his body as if he were peacefully asleep: 'it is hard to imagine that they would have carried him into the bog and carefully placed him in the sleeping position in which he was found, if they had considered him a criminal'.[12]

The blind seer of Windeby

Sometime in the earlier first millennium AD a young girl, about twelve or fourteen years old, was taken to a peat bog at Windeby in Schleswig-Holstein, blindfolded with a strip of material, perhaps cut from her own brightly coloured woven belt and led out to drown in the marsh. The Windeby girl (Fig. 45) was discovered by peatcutters in the late spring of 1952. She lay on her back in a hole dug in the peat, her head turned to the right. She wore nothing but a cowskin cape, an oxhide collar and her blindfold. Although no evidence survives as to the manner of her killing, her body was weighted down with hurdles of birch and a large stone; a thick birch-branch rested in the crook of her right arm, almost in the manner of a ceremonial wand, and wild flowers were strewn around her body. The young girl's body was taken to the Schleswig-Holstein Museum in a hearse where she was subjected to a postmortem examination.[13] Forensic study of her bones revealed that she had suffered from malnutrition: the presence of Harris lines is testimony to arrested growth due to an inadequate diet. Her light-blonde hair had been shaved off with a razor on the left side of her scalp.[14] This feature, together with the presence of the collar and her poor nourishment, suggests that she may have been a person of low status, maybe even a slave.[15] But Tacitus makes specific allusion to head-shaving as a punishment for errant wives in ancient Germanic communities:

> Adultery in that populous nation is rare in the extreme, and punishment is summary and left to the husband. He shaves off his wife's hair, strips her in the presence of kinsmen, thrusts her from his house and flogs her through the whole village.[16]

The state of the Windeby girl's body, her virtual nakedness, her collar, shaven head and blindfold, might lead us to the conclusion that she was an individual of little worth to her community, and that she may have been executed for disobedience or some other form of misconduct. But we need to look again at the circumstances of her death, particularly at the blindfold. Whilst such a feature could be interpreted as analogous to the 'humanitarian' treatment of people facing executional firing-squads, the presence of the blindfold on the Windeby girl might be capable of alternative, symbolic interpretation. The band covering the girl's eyes was a highly elasticated *sprang* (a Scandinavian term describing a complex plaiting technique) 49 cm (19 in) long; it is of similar design to the waistband worn by the sixteen-year-old strangled female bog victim from Yde in the Netherlands.[17] The Windeby girl was not simply thrown into the marsh to drown, like an outcast or executed criminal; like the Tollund man, she was carefully placed there, staff in hand. It could be argued that the blindfold contributes to the image of a death surrounded with ceremony, because the victim herself held a special position within her community, a position signified by her symbolic blindness.

45 Windeby Girl, Schleswig-Holstein. This is the body of an adolescent girl, perhaps a seer, killed and placed in a North German peatbog in the first centuries AD.

A great deal of evidence suggests that prophets or 'seers' in antiquity were physically blind or visually impaired, their sensory loss serving to heighten their ability to see into the spirit-world. A prominent blind 'shaman' in ancient Athenian drama was Tiresias (see also Chapter 6), an outspoken individual presented as being a mediator between the spirit and earthly worlds and employed by the gods as their mouthpiece.[18] His state, as befits a go-between, was ambiguous: he could not see the physical world but his spiritual vision was sharp – the leader of the chorus in Sophocles' drama *Oedipus the King*, makes this clear.[19] The denial of physical vision to shamans, in order to concentrate their force inwards, to the spirit realms, finds resonance within traditional societies of modern times. Piers Vitebsky[20] illustrates Indonesian shamans in a state of trance, having covered their eyes with cloths 'in order to simulate blindness and activate their second sight'.

The tentative identification of the Windeby Girl as a prophetess or shaman, by reason of her special burial and her symbolic blindness, can only be a matter of conjecture. But a further feature of her death may be relevant in this regard, namely her age. Like many northwest European bog people, she was an adolescent, neither child nor woman and, perhaps, was perceived as being in a liminal, transformational life-state appropriate to the marginality and ambiguity of a shaman. Furthermore, pre-pubescent teenage girls may, before breasts and feminine hips develop, resemble boys giving rise, perhaps, to a perception of dual sexuality or even absence of gender. At the same time, the pre-fertile time of a female's life might make her powerful and independent of men's hegemony, just as has been argued as being the case for women, termed *femmes soles* by Roberta Gilchrist of Reading University, once their child-bearing age had past.[21] Taken altogether, there are grounds for treating the Windeby Girl as a special person within her community and it may be that the presence of the blindfold points in the direction of her identity as a shaman. In discussing shamanism among the Sora of northeast India, Piers Vitebsky[22] describes the importance of the menarche in identifying young female shamans, emphasizing the significance of puberty when the initiate will enter into marriage with an underworld spirit.

A sequestered holy woman: Veleda of the Germans

The adolescent state of the Windeby Girl leads to consideration of a prophetess named Veleda (Fig. 46) whom Tacitus describes as a powerful political figure in the great Rhenish rebellion against Rome led by the Batavian agitator Julius Civilis in AD 69–70. Veleda was a seer and, furthermore, there is specific reference to her unmarried – presumably (though not necessarily) virginal – state.

46 Veleda in her tower. The Roman writer Tacitus describes Veleda as a Germanic prophetess, kept sequestered in a tower, although her utterances earned great authority within her community.

The legionary commander Munius Lupercus was sent along with other presents to Veleda, an unmarried woman who enjoyed wide influence over the tribe of the Bructeri. The Germans traditionally regard many of the female sex as prophetic, and indeed, by an excess of superstition, as divine. This was a case in point. Veleda's prestige stood high, for she had foretold the German successes and the extermination of the legions.[23]

In one episode in this long-drawn-out conflict, Tacitus describes Veleda in interesting detail. The context was the attempt by an envoy of the Tencteri, one of the rebel tribes, to persuade the Roman citizens of Cologne to join the revolt and submit to Civilis and Veleda. Tacitus says of the seer:

... a deputation sent to Civilis and Veleda with gifts secured a decision fully satisfactory to Cologne. But any personal approach to Veleda or speech with her was forbidden. This refusal to permit the envoys to see her was intended to enhance the aura of veneration that surrounded the prophetess. She remained immured in a high tower, one of her relatives being deputed to transmit questions and answers as if he were mediating between a god and his worshippers.[24]

Several issues arise from Tacitus's narrative, not least of which is Veleda's political influence, a seeming paradox with her seclusion. She was clearly a separated, marginal being, perhaps – at one and the same time – too dangerous and too sacred to mingle with her community. It is possible to discern close similarities between this north European holy woman and the female oracles of the Classical world, notably the Cumaean Sybil, who also communicated through a 'medium' and, indeed, such traditions may well have influenced Tacitus's description of Veleda. Roberta Gilchrist suggests[25] that, in medieval England, virginity was a metaphor for a fortress and that the sequestering of noblewomen in the depths of castles expressed the idea of the female body and the castle as hidden, guarded and secret spaces, controlled and used as a resource by men. Veleda's unwed state and her albeit presumably voluntary incarceration in a high tower resonate with this medieval notion of the need jealously to protect this valuable asset who wielded power over other foreigners and enabled the future to be determined.

Veleda's unmarried state is interesting for a number of reasons. We are not told her age: she could have been young or old but, in a sense, her celibacy denied her gender and set her apart from the rest of her community. By not conforming to the general pattern of adult female behaviour, she was both genderless and – like the virgin saints of early Christianity – able to engage in 'male' activities, such as political negotiation and business. Paradoxically, her virginity perhaps conferred upon Veleda a potent sexual power because it had not been dissipated by union with men. We find a similar circumstance in the Fourth Branch of the early Welsh medieval prose tale the *Mabinogion*, in which Math, lord of Gwynedd, was compelled to rest his feet in the lap of a virgin except while at war.[26] It was from his virgin-footholder Goewin that Math received his ability to rule, and Goewin's rape challenged the kingship itself, threatening to deny Math's sovereignty and, indeed, the very fertility of the land.

Veleda's virginity, her seclusion, her political influence and, above all, her powers of prophecy, suggest that she held a marginal and special place, as a link between gods and people and as a particular resource through whom the spirit-world could be tapped. Her status as a shaman must remain a matter for conjecture, but she fulfils many of the criteria, as do the oracles of Classical antiquity. The control of her speech by a member of her family suggests that her contact with the otherworld needed a third party in order to interpret her holy words or to shield the community from the perilous nature of the spirits. Her symbolic denial of gender implies that she was, in a sense, above human sexuality and marked out as different. Although cloistered from her community, her high tower would have been clearly visible in the landscape (and she herself would have had a wide field of vision) and her prophetic, inspired utterances, perhaps in an unintelligible tongue, would have added to the dramatic nature of her performance; she seems to have been a powerful shaman, in all but name.

TOUCHING WOOD: SHAMANIC PATHFINDERS

In recent years there has been an upsurge of interest in wetland archaeology and, not least, in the steadily increasing body of evidence for prehistoric wooden anthropomorphic iconography from northwest Europe, preserved in watery and boggy contexts. A fine new temporary exhibition entitled *Mosens Guder (Immortal Images)* opened in August 2001 at the Silkeborg Museum in central Jutland: it had brought together the great majority of surviving figures from the Mesolithic to Roman periods and from as far afield as Ireland, Scotland, eastern Germany, Denmark and Finland.[27]

Two papers by the archaeologist Bryony Coles, of Exeter University and an expert on wood and wetlands,[28] have drawn attention to the possible symbolic and religious significance of ancient wooden figures, pointing to both contextual and intrinsic features that serve to distinguish them as ritually special. It may even be that the medium of wood was selected for certain representations because of its mutability and its pattern of decay, so similar to that of human bodies whilst, again like flesh, it is preserved in watery locations.[29] There is, of course, no reason to interpret such images as shamanistic simply on the grounds of the organic nature of the material used to produce them; nonetheless, certain characteristics are suggestive, notably the presentation of gender, on the one hand, and the asymmetric treatment of the faces, especially the eyes, on the other. Both features are particularly prevalent in figures of the Late Bronze and Iron Ages.

Gender-ambiguity forms part of the persona of shamans in many traditional belief systems. Genderlessness, sexual ambivalence and gender-transgression may each contribute to the image of the shaman as an unstable, marginal being, able to oscillate between the earth- and spirit-worlds, just as he/she may wander between masculinity and femininity and between human and animal form.[30] Bryony Coles has argued[31] that the selection of wood-species for carving figures may be relevant, commenting on the apparent preference for evergreens (yew and pine) in the production of the images she has studied where ambiguous gender has been observed. Thus, the Irish Bronze Age image from Ralaghan (Co. Cavan) (Fig. 47) bears a pubic hole above what might equally represent a scrotum or exaggerated pudendum: the orifice might depict either a penis-socket, a vulva or both. The genital hole on the Ralaghan figure broadens out from the opening and, moreover, contains a small deposit of white quartz,[32] as if – perhaps – to represent semen. The genitalia of the five extant pine figurines, dating to the earliest Iron Age, from Roos Carr, near Hull, are similarly treated, although they have been reconstructed for museum display as uncompromisingly male.

The second potentially significant feature of the evergreen figures from Britain and Ireland relates to the asymmetrical treatment of their faces, notably around the eyes: the left side of the face and the left eye are either deliberately damaged or carved more shallowly and (apparently) with less care.[33] Similar sinistrality has been noted on some of the wooden and stone 'pilgrim-images' from the early Gallo-Roman healing sanctuary at *Fontes Sequanae* near Dijon,[34] though the wood-species the craftspeople employed at this site was almost entirely oak.[35] In considering the combination of gender-contradiction and ocular sinistrality, there are some grounds for conjecture that certain later prehistoric wooden figures might represent not simply gods or high-status people but special holy men and women enjoying close relationships with the supernatural world. Sacred individuals with both visual defects and gender-crossing traits are documented in both Classical and Norse mythology, Tiresias and Odin[36] exemplifying such traditions.

A further link between shamans and wooden imagery concerns pathways and routes between the upper realms of the spirits and earth-world, the shamanic highways trodden by these sacred go-betweens, who sometimes

47 LEFT *Bronze Age wooden figure, from Ralaghan, Co. Cavan, Ireland.*

48 OPPOSITE *Wooden figures from Oldenburg trackway, Lower Saxony, Germany.*

exposed themselves to considerable danger in the process.[37] In Siberian Tungus tradition, wooden figures represent ancestral spirits standing guard over the sacred way along which the shaman must travel to make contact with supernatural forces:

> The search for lost reindeer, the shaman's performance before a journey, the foretelling of the future, and other analogous activities of the shaman were usually held in an ordinary tent. Performances on more important occasions were usually conducted in a special tent. On two sides of this tent stood a row of wooden figures, representations of shamanistic spirits symbolizing the mythical shamanistic clan-river. The number of spirit-figures varied according to the 'powers' of the shaman, but the type of construction was always the same.[38]

Interestingly, there is some archaeological evidence for the association between wooden figurines and trackways. One of the most striking finds, dating to the third century BC, was made in the 1960s near Oldenburg in Lower Saxony, where a plank-built 'road', 3.5 km (2.2 miles) long, crossed the Wittemoor peat bog. At one point, the track crossed a watercourse and here, at its most dangerous spot, two tall oaken figures (Fig. 48) guarded the pathway, one on each side, each image terminating in a pointed tenon driven into the peat. The crossing-place was later deliberately destroyed, the images removed from their slots and deposited flat and the smashed track and figures covered with a layer of peat. The two figures are 'gendered': the long straight statuette is interpreted as male, the shorter, rounder one – with a 'vulva slot' at its crotch – as female. Since the original excavations, other discoveries

have been made here, including more anthropomorphic images.[39] It is possible to identify other wooden figures associated with marsh trackways: incorporated into the foundations of the oak road built over the Corlea bog near Longford in central Ireland, with a tree-ring date of 148 BC, was a curious semi-anthropomorphic, semi- animal figure carved from ash; it has been suggested that the image may once have stood as a cult-figure, perhaps in an open-air shrine, and then was built into the trackway in order to protect it and its users.[40] Later in date than Oldenburg and Corlea is the figure found lying across the track – significantly at its weakest point – over waterlogged ground at the Grosses Moor, near Lake Dümmer in Lower Saxony; tree-ring analysis gives a date for the road of between AD 115 and 250.[41]

The trackway images may simply depict divinities whose role was to provide a focus of veneration for travellers, and to bless and protect wayfarers on hazardous journeys. But, particularly in the light of the quotation (above) about Siberian ritual practice, it is at least worth considering whether such figures may represent shamans guarding pathways that were perhaps perceived not only as earthly crossing-places but also as a means of ingress to the spirit-world. The trackways may even have been used as foci for ceremonies involving human rites of passage: puberty, marriage or death. The roadways themselves may have been special, ritually charged places where dry land interacted with water and where the mysterious world of bogs was penetrated and transgressed. Such marshy places were clearly perceived as spiritually potent in Bronze Age and Iron Age contexts; witness the deposition of precious metal objects and bog bodies: the early Iron Age watery site at Fiskerton, Lincolnshire, is a case-in-point.[42] If the trackways were encroaching on numinous space, it was entirely appropriate that such perilous, marginal and unstable locations, redolent with spirit presence, should be guarded by shamanic images who would intercede with sacred forces on behalf of people and act as their protectors.

DREAMWORLDS AND PSYCHOTROPES: IMAGE AND EXPERIENCE

Dope and drink

First … I must mention that hemp grows in Scythia, a plant resembling flax, but much coarser and taller. It grows wild as well as under cultivation … And now for the vapour-bath: on a framework of three sticks, meeting at the top they stretch pieces of woollen cloth, taking care to get the joins as perfect as they can, and inside this little tent they put a dish with red-hot stones in it. Then they take some hemp seed, creep into the tent, and throw the seed on to the hot stones. At once it begins to smoke, giving off a vapour unsurpassed by any vapour-bath one could find in Greece. The Scythians enjoy it so much that they howl with pleasure.

Herodotus, *Histories*[43]

Herodotus, writing in the fifth century BC, was apparently describing a glorious hallucinogenic 'trip' experienced by Scythian men inhaling cannabis vapour (Fig. 109).[44] There is a small but persistent body of archaeological testimony to the use of psychotropic drugs not in Scythia but in Iron Age Europe. The presence of ergot in the intestines of the Tollund and Grauballe bog-men has already been mentioned and, it will be argued later, such drug-use may have influenced some of the fantastic, surreal art produced and consumed in the so-called La Tène Iron Age tradition. Traces of cannabis and other hallucinogenic plants are occasionally discernible in tomb-goods: cannabis was present in the grave of the 'nobleman' interred with great ceremony at Hochdorf, Germany, in the late sixth century BC.[45] Half a millennium later, at the dawn of the Roman period (*c.* AD 50), a votive site at Frensham in Surrey, England, was the focus for the deposition of several miniature ceramic vessels, one at least of which contained cannabis.[46] Roughly synchronous with Frensham, is a man's grave at Stanway, near Colchester in Essex (Plate 23), furnished with elaborate equipment, including a set of Roman-style surgeons' tools, eight rods (four of bronze, four of iron) and a straining-bowl whose spout contained a plug of plant material identified as a variety of *artemisia*, ingestion of which can induce a psychotropic effect.[47] The combination of this substance, the medical kit and the set of rods is highly suggestive that the Stanway grave was that of a special person, perhaps a shaman-healer. Indeed, in describing Germanic customs, Tacitus refers to a divinatory practice (Fig. 49) involving the use of rods:

49 *Reconstruction of lot-casting among the Germans, as described in Tacitus's* Germania *(10).*

For auspices and the casting of lots they have the highest possible regard. Their procedure in casting lots is uniform. They break off a branch of a fruit-tree and slice it into
strips; they distinguish these by certain runes and throw them, as random chance will
have it, on to a white cloth. Then the priest of the State if the consultation is a public
one, the father of the family if it is private, after a prayer to the gods and an intent gaze
heavenward, picks up three, one at a time, and reads their meaning from the runes
scored on them . . .[48]

The discovery of mind-altering substances in a high-status burial (Stanway) and
a religious site (Frensham) dating to the mid-first century AD accords with John
Creighton's assertion[49] that hallucinogenic plants may have been deliberately
selected in Iron Age Britain. Creighton, a lecturer at Reading University, is a specialist on Iron Age coinage and, in his book *Coins and Power in Late Iron Age Britain*, he
specifically mentions mandrake, henbane and opium, citing the quantities of henbane present in late Iron Age and Roman levels at Farmoor near Oxford, and of
opium poppies mixed in with spelt wheat at Wallingford, Oxfordshire, in the earlier
first millennium BC. The so-called 'cult-tree' from Manching in Bavaria (Fig. 50),[50]
probably dating to the third century BC, may provide circumstantial evidence for
the use of mind-altering plants in ritual activity: it consists of a gilded wooden rod
adorned with gilt-bronze leaves whose form closely resembles those of the con-
volvulus family, some of which produce seeds containing hallucinogenic toxins.[51]

But trance states could have been achieved by ingesting substances other than
psychotropic plants. Wine and other liquor may have been involved in intoxicating
ceremonies involving the attainment of altered mind states: the sheer volume of
wine attested by amphorae found on Burgundian and Auvergnian Iron Age sites,

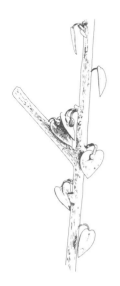

such as Bibracte and Corent,[52] seems far in excess of requirements
for 'normal' consumption. Bettina Arnold, an anthropologist at
the University of Wisconsin-Milwaukee and a specialist in early
Iron Age society,[53] reminds us that 'all alcoholic drinks are mood-
altering substances, and in many cultures are considered as a way
of communing with some form of Otherworld'. It is very probable
that the serious liquor consumption indicated by the elaborate
array of drinking equipment – amphorae, cauldrons, vats, tankards,
flagons, strainers, horns and drinking-cups – present in certain
high-ranking tombs dating both to the early and late Iron Ages carried with it considerable socio-symbolic significance.[54]

50 The 'cult-tree' from Manching, in Bavaria, western Germany.

The chieftain's burial at Hochdorf is a case in point: the forty-year-old man interred here was equipped with a dinner-service and some paraphernalia for serious drinking, including nine aurochs drinking-horns, decorated with gold, slung around the walls, of which the biggest (with a capacity for 5.5 litres) was hung above his head, as if that one belonged especially to him; a great cauldron, once containing mead, stood in a corner.[55] Mead and ale seem to have been popular beverages in Iron Age Europe, and fermented berry juice may also have been consumed. Many of the rich later Iron Age graves in Britain and Gaul contained stave-built wooden buckets bound with iron or bronze: those from the cemetery at Tartigny, Oise, Fléré-la-Rivière, Indre, both in France, and Aylesford, Kent,[56] may have held ale or mead. The Danish site of Juellinge revealed signs of a kind of alcoholic gruel – thick, sweet and rather horrible – consisting of honey, cereals, wild fruits and herbs for flavour, including meadowsweet; traces of a similar concoction were found contained in a birch-bark vessel placed in a Bronze Age oak coffin at Egtved, also in Denmark.[57]

The most important thing about Iron Age liquor consumption is that, according to the tomb evidence, drinking was closely associated with power, status and ceremony; it may well have also been linked with trance, divination and talking with the spirits. The large size of many vessels, particularly the buckets and cauldrons, may be associated with interaction between the drinkers and shared intoxication.[58] Brigitte Fischer[59] certainly regards wine as a significant trance-inducing agent in later Iron Age Gaul. Elizabeth Bott[60] discusses the symbolic significance of drinking, in the context of Polynesian kava ceremonies in Tonga, wherein not only liquor consumption but also the hierarchy of seating around the kava bowl and the cross-legged position of the participants play important roles: 'The kava ceremony is one of a series of ceremonies that clarify social principles and social roles',[61] and one of its essential aspects was its function as a 'conserving and conservative institution'.[62] A combination of wine and the drum performs a function in the attainment of ecstasy within Central Asian Dervish rituals, in an Islamic tradition related to Sufism.[63] Viewed in the context of sacred drinking, perhaps we should look with renewed interest at the bronze 'cult-wagon' found in a tomb of the seventh century BC at Strettweg in Austria (Plate 18):[64] on the four-wheeled platform are several human and animal images, including horsemen and what is probably a stag sacrifice but, towering over them all is a central female figure who holds a great cauldron aloft, as if to offer it to the gods. She could represent a goddess but she could equally be a shaman with her vat of trance-inducing liquor. In general, the symbolic prominence of vessels, such as cauldrons and buckets, in the Iron Age archaeological record[65] may be viewed from the perspective of the brewing of intoxicating substances by ritualists who, perhaps, can be seen as the distant ancestors of the witches and cauldrons of later mythology.

Of course, mind-bending can occur by means other than ingestion: sensory deprivation, hyperventilation, isolation, sleeplessness, music, chanting and dance.

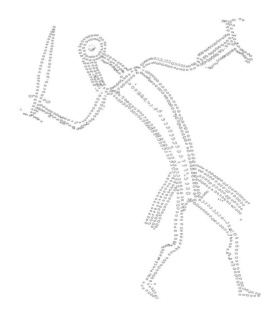

Indeed, ritual dances are occasionally discernible in iconography: the bronze dancers from the late Iron Age shrine-deposit at Neuvy-en-Sullias, Loiret, in France (Fig. 51),[66] and the figures, apparently engaged in a ceremonial fighting-dance, engraved on the back of the bronze funerary couch at Hochdorf (Fig. 52), may be cited in support of such cultic practices. Similarly, the presence of musical instruments, such as the set of four bronze trumpets from Loughnashade in Co. Antrim,[67] the figurine of a girl flute-player from Roman Silchester in Hampshire (Fig. 53),[68] and the rattle found in the Romano-British religious hoard from Felmingham Hall in Norfolk (Fig. 54),[69] attest to the use of musical instruments in ceremonial contexts. But we must remember that music and dancing may simply have been for pleasure, for entertainment, and we have to be careful not to read shamanic experience, or even ritual, into all our evidence for these activities (although the cult context of some evidence is suggestive).

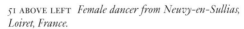

51 ABOVE LEFT *Female dancer from Neuvy-en-Sullias, Loiret, France.*

52 ABOVE RIGHT *Dancer engraved on the back of a bronze funerary couch, Hochdorf, Germany.*

53 LEFT *Flute-player from the Romano-British site of Silchester, southern England.*

54 RIGHT *Felmingham Hall rattle.*

Art and ecstasy: virtual realities & surrealities

It could be argued that imagery on Iron Age art may have been produced as a result of shamanic visions while in an altered state of consciousness. If this supposition is to have any validity, we have to assume a close and symbiotic relationship between all contributors to the visionary experience: the 'dreamer', the artist and the consumer, in whatever combination.[70] Neurological disturbances experienced during trance can cause the eye to see entoptic images, including dots, crescents, beaded ribbons, weaving lines and 'fortification' or 'basketry' patterns (Figs. 55, 56).[71] John Creighton has argued[72] that it is precisely these images that are recurrently present in Iron Age numismatic art and in some of the cross-hatched patterns decorating late Iron Age British mirrors. It is certainly possible that the weird and asymmetrically distorted human faces depicted on the backs of the mirrors at Latchmere, Hampshire,[73] Aston, Hertfordshire,[74] and Great Chesterford, Essex,[75] were produced as a result of visions while in an altered state of consciousness. Mirrors themselves, indeed, may be significant, in so far as they might evoke the notion of two-spirit people, and it is even possible that some of the Iron Age British female mirror-burials were those of ritualists. The woman interred with rich grave goods, including an iron mirror at Wetwang in East Yorkshire (Plate 17), was certainly special: facially disfigured by a growth from her youth, she was accompanied by her chariot and objects ornamented with more coral than found in any other Iron Age site in Britain.[76]

55 TOP ROW *Entoptics diagram (left), taken from images on Iron Age coins (right).*

56 RIGHT AND BELOW *Entoptic motifs at Val Camonica, northern Italy.*

It may be possible to discern images of shamans themselves in Iron Age art. Some of the naked horsewomen depicted on coins are shown galloping, with their arms flung wide, as though in a state of ecstatic frenzy (Fig. 57).[77] We wonder, too, whether the persistently cross-legged position of certain Iron Age and Gallo-Roman human images, particularly those wearing antlers,[78] might indicate a 'yogic' trance state. During out-of-body experiences, shamans sometimes assume particular facial expressions evocative of their out-of-body state, the most striking aspect of which may be staring or bulging eyes.[79] It is worth considering whether such a feature is visible in Iron Age European art. Indeed, in a survey of the way some human faces are represented, on decorated La Tène metalwork and carved stones from the fifth to first centuries BC, this trait is clearly discernible. The heads carved on cult monuments of fifth-century BC date from Pfalzfeld and Heidelberg[80] are presented with prominent, staring eyes; the same treatment is accorded the faces on the broadly contemporary bronze flagon-mount from Kleinaspergle (Fig. 58),[81] and on the fourth-century BC gold ring-jewellery from the 'princess's' grave at Reinheim,[82] all from German sites. Furthermore, there is often an animal element in such depictions: thus, the bearded Kleinaspergle head bears horns and birds of prey emerge from the female heads on the Reinheim ornaments.[83]

The presence of animal features on human imagery reinforces the interpretation of some Iron Age anthropomorphic art as possibly shamanistic. Coeval rock art from Camonica Valley in northern Italy – which we discussed in the previous chapter – depict antlered humans,[84] and similar beings appear on the late Iron Age silver cauldron from Gundestrup in Denmark (Fig. 59) and on a silver coin from the

57 ABOVE *Breton coin with ecstatic horsewoman.*

58 LEFT *Horned face on flagon-handle at Kleinaspergle, Germany.*

59 OPPOSITE ABOVE *Antlered 'shaman' surrounded by animals, detail from the Gundestrup Cauldron, Denmark.*

60 OPPOSITE BELOW LEFT *Coin with image of human-headed horse, Gaul.*

61 OPPOSITE BELOW RIGHT *Coin with multiple heads, minted by the Osismi tribe, Brittany.*

British Midlands, dated to about AD 10.[85] Human-headed horses are represented on a fourth-century BC flagon-lid from a tomb at Reinheim;[86] and the same theme occurs on a range of coins, including Breton issues.[87] John Creighton[88] has drawn attention to iconography on the reverse of gold and silver coin-issues involving close visual interaction between horses and human faces (Fig. 60), citing as a powerful example a gold issue of the Ambiani depicting a human head with a horse disappearing into one ear and emerging from the other.[89] It has been argued by Creighton and others[90] that the merging of human and animal features on coins and other Iron Age (and Roman) visual media is linked with dreamworlds, trance experiences and expression of the shaman's transitional character. Taking the coin images further, it is possible to cite other iconography possibly indicative of shamanistic transience between worlds, including horses galloping over cauldrons,[91] flying and swimming horses, a winged 'bird-man' on a North Gaulish silver issue[92] and the image on coins minted by the Breton tribe of the Osismi comprising a central severed human head attached to smaller satellite heads by thin lines (Fig. 61). This last Creighton suggests might represent the shamanic notion of departure

from the human body by the shaman who had to retain contact with it by leaving a pathway between earth- and spirit-worlds. Though Creighton explains the smaller heads as 'spirit-heads', in our opinion it is more likely that these peripheral heads represent the shaman's earth-community to which he or she is tethered whilst visiting the supernatural world of ancestral spirits. The persistent image of horses on Iron Age coins[93] might be interpreted in terms of its evocation of the spirit world: Thomas Dowson and Martin Porr, of the universities of Manchester and Southampton respectively,[94] cite shamanistic traditions in which the horse plays a crucial role in its ability to convey the shaman between worlds with great speed. Furthermore, in some traditions, the horse is credited with prognosticatory powers on account of its reputation for precognition.[95]

The vein of fantasy running through a great deal of Iron Age art seems to display resonances of early twentieth-century surrealism, in which themes based on reality are twisted out of shape to produce a dream art, a virtual world in which a new, transcendent realism replaces the naturalism of earth-world. It has been suggested elsewhere[96] that surreality may be an appropriate prism through which to view and understand some of the weird and monstrous images present in the Iron Age (and Gallo-Roman) artistic repertoire, and that the transgression of species barriers attested by horned and antlered figures (see Chapters 4, 6) may be the result of

transcendental visions: the mixing of human and animal elements[97] is a common theme in shamanistic visionary experience. The late Iron Age anthropomorphic stone figure from Euffigneix in Gaul (Fig. 62), who wears a great buffer-torc, with a huge eye carved along the side and a boar striding along his torso,[98] makes good sense within a shamanistic context. Another highly diagnostic schema is the exaggeration of animal features, particularly the dorsal ridge, a noticeable feature of the Euffigneix carving. James Blackmore, at the University of Southampton,[99] has noted such distortion in Namibian shamanic rock art, wherein the giraffe is frequently drawn as a dead or spirit animal with erect bristles along

62 *Stone image of torc-wearing being with boar carved on its torso, from Euffigneix, Gaul.*

its backbone. We see exactly this exaggeration in the treatment of wild boars on Iron Age numismatic and other imagery in Britain and Gaul.[100] A further very marked disproportion can be observed in the treatment of antlers, especially on coin stags[101] and in Camonican and Galician rock art.[102]

If Iron Age art displays themes interpreted as the products of shamanistic experience, we need to unpick the processes involved, to examine the linkages between visionary event, presentation and understanding. The visionary, the artist and the spectator would all need – to some degree – to be conversant with trance experience. John Creighton[103] makes a convincing case for the origin of some Iron Age coin art as having its genesis in shamanic vision, arguing that professional clergy – Druids, for instance – may well have been instrumental in the choice of images presented in a medium that – in its use of precious metals and its circulation – was clearly closely associated with power. But what was the relationship between Druids and art? It is possible (see below) that some metalsmiths were themselves shamans. But even were this not to be so, we have to remember that the shaman's role in society was not just that of the visionary but to engage in performance, to share his or her experience in a more-or-less public forum.

Shamans and smiths
Eastern Siberian and Mongolian religious tradition contains strong connections between shamans and smiths: Piers Vitebsky[104] comments on the spiritual power of the Siberian blacksmith:

> He had a similar mastery of esoteric techniques, but a greater mastery of fire, and he made the metal ornaments which were essential attachments to the shaman's costume. he was also the master of the shaman's initiation…smiths and shamans were nurtured in the same nest, but the smith was the shaman's elder brother. He had no fear of spirits and the shaman, being the smith's junior, could not cause his death because the smith's soul was protected by fire.

Shamans are concerned with transformation, with transference between worlds. Metalsmiths (Fig. 63) are also boundary-crossers, having charge over the alchemy that produces shiny metal from rough rock. Fire is the ultimate transformatory agent: heat changes wood to ash, flour and water to bread, clay to pots and ore to metal; fire and water (another significant agent of transformation) are the blacksmith's partners in making wrought iron. The smith has to control fire: success depends on his skill at 'reading' the fire, its colour and sound key factors in judging temperature.[105] Intimacy with fire, staring into its heart, induces weird dream images as the flames flicker, swirl and change colour.[106] The smith is involved in a complex set of cognitive processes, a 'constellation' of ideas, tools and material;[107] like the shaman, he is engaged with performance, with a 'choreographed' dance

between the forge-fire, anvil and toolkit. The smith lives a paradox: he may be a solitary, marginal, 'edge' person, like the shaman, often living on the borders of the settlement, but he is nonetheless central to the community and depends on a network of support for his power. Like shamans, smiths – working in all metals, not just iron – are associated with the ancestors and with long-term memory; they are specialists, with an awe-inspiring and arcane ritual of praxis. They can produce objects that clang, rattle and 'sing', that can reflect light, people's faces and the world and glow with colour. John Creighton has suggested[108] that goldsmiths making Iron Age coins deliberately manipulated their raw material to produce a particular yellow-gold, symbolic of the sun and the other astral bodies depicted on the coinage, citing, as comparable, the Aztec shamanic tradition in which metalsmiths sought to replicate the shimmering world of dreamscapes. Irish medieval stories make unequivocal reference to the association between blacksmithing and shamanistic Druidry, a link shown clearly in the following excerpt from the *Scéla Eogain*.

> When Cormac was born, the Druid-smith Olc Aiche put five protective circles about him, against wounding, against drowning, against fire, against enchantment, against wolves, that is to say against every evil.[109]

Other early myths make similar connections between smiths and supernatural power. The Anglo-Saxon legendary Wayland was a swordsmith who was able – like a shaman – to fly, using self-made wings,[110] a story reminiscent of the Classical mythic tale of the craftsman Daedalus, who made wings for his son Icarus, though the boy's

63 ABOVE *Castorware sherd with image of smith-god, from Sawtry, Huntingdonshire, England.*

64 OPPOSITE *Scene from the Gundestrup cauldron, showing at left a warrior being lowered head first into a vat.*

pride induced him to fly too near the sun, melt the wax fastening his wings on and perish. Wayland gave his name to Wayland's Smithy, a Neolithic chamber tomb in Berkshire; according to one of the legends associated with the tomb, if you place money on the capstone of the eastern burial chamber, Wayland's spirit will shoe your horse for you.[111]

Like the shaman, the smith is both dangerous and at risk. Both are full of supernatural power but for each, that power is steeped in peril: the shaman faces profound psychic danger in accessing the spirit-world; the smith deals with the perilous caprice of fire and hot metal. Furthermore, the blacksmith may sometimes play an essential role in the shaman's initiation in rituals wherein the latter is symbolically deconstructed and reintegrated by the spirits, sometimes cooked in a cauldron by the smith as part of the process.[112] Incidentally, this last resonates strongly with a scene on the first-century-BC silver cult-cauldron from Gundestrup in Denmark, one engraved plate of which bears a scene wherein a warrior is lowered head first into a vat (Fig. 64).[113] The First Branch of the early medieval Welsh mythic tale, the Mabinogion, contains an episode in which a magical cauldron, belonging to the powerful supernatural character Bran, has the capacity to cook and restore the dead to life.[114] (Furthermore, the story bears a strong resemblance to a Homeric scene enacted on a Greek black-figure vase depicting Circe and Odysseus in which the shaman/sorceress uses her transformational cauldron to change the hero's followers into pigs and is about to try and do the same to Odysseus.)[115] Iron, product of the blacksmith's alchemy, often maintained a power and awe even when it had passed from the craftsman's control as a finished implement. It is interesting that, among Siberian Yakut communities, it was believed that the upper, spirit-world was made of iron,[116] a perception that resonates with the iron house associated with supernatural cauldron-bearers, in the same Mabinogion story.

The sacred, magical character of iron in ancient Gaul is demonstrated by two passages in Book XXIV of Pliny the Elder's *Natural History*, each of which –

interestingly – present iron as a force inimical to the herbal craft of healing. He comments firstly that, in gathering tamarisk for the cure of stomach cramps, iron tools must not be used; secondly, he alludes to the curative powers of the selago plant only if iron were kept away:

> It is gathered without iron with the right hand, thrust through the tunic through the left armhole, as though the gatherer were thieving…The Druids of Gaul have recorded that it [the selago] should be kept on the person to ward off all fatalities, and that the smoke of it is good for all diseases of the eyes.

Both comments are interesting, not only in their references to the negative force of iron in curative craft but also to herbal lore and contact magic and, in one instance, direct association between health and the Druids. One of the shaman's principal roles in most shamanistic traditions – from Siberia to the Amazon – is as a healer. Pliny is not the only Roman author to mention the need to avoid iron in ceremonial contexts: at about the same time, Tacitus recorded the custom of locking all iron objects away during the Germanic agricultural festival held in honour of the goddess Nerthus.[117]

There is some archaeological testimony to the veneration of iron in the northwest European Iron Age. Iron objects were recurrently deposited – as votive offerings – in watery places, following a tradition in which bronze implements were 'sacrificed' during the Bronze Age, a rite continued even when iron became the usual metal for edge tools.[118] In late Iron Age Britain, sacred water sites as far apart

as Llyn Cerrig Bach on Anglesey[119] and the river Lea at Waltham Abbey, Essex,[120] were repositories for blacksmiths' equipment. Some iron objects, dedicated as sacred gifts, were themselves extremely special: the superbly crafted firedog from Capel Garmon in North Wales (Fig. 65),[121] with its conscious asymmetry and gloriously idiosyncratic animal terminals, half-horse, half-bull, with horns and manes, was carefully interred beneath a stone in a remote marsh. It has been estimated that it perhaps took as long as three person-years to produce. This highly decorated wrought-iron hearth furniture was a freehand, 'one-off' statement to the smith's mastery over his medium but it was, at the same time, spiritually inspired, perhaps dream-induced, and its investment with sacred value is attested by the ceremony of its deposition and – maybe – its subsequent biography as an ongoing line of communication between earth- and spirit-worlds.[122]

Other iron objects may have been intrinsically sacred and even associated with shamanic rites. Vincent Guichard, of the Centre de Recherches Européen du Mont Beuvray, has suggested that the massive and intricately made late Iron Age 'slave-chains' from such sites as Llyn Cerrig Bach on Anglesey[123] and Verdun-sur-le-Doubs in Central France[124] are more likely to have held a sacred significance than to have been used merely for the mundane purpose of transporting slaves or prisoners-of-war for which restraints of hemp rope or sinew would have been just as effective. The manufacture of these chains represents an enormous investment of skill, time and resources, and it is significant that they are found on ritual or funerary sites. They may have played a part in human sacrificial ceremonies,[125] but their role may equally have been associated with shamans and the symbolism of their subservience to the supernatural forces. Tacitus records the presence of a sacred grove in Germany wherein no one might venture unless bound with a cord.[126] The iron slave-chains may have been symbols of power, ownership and subjugation, all of which resonate in both social and ritual contexts.

Finally, the link between metalsmithing and the sacred becomes unequivocal during the Roman period, when images of smith-gods, modelled on the Roman Vulcan, appear on north British ceramics (Fig. 66).[127] At the close of the Gaulish Iron Age, people living in the *oppidum* (Iron Age town) of Engehalbinsel-bei-Bern in

65 OPPOSITE *Iron bull-headed fire-dog from Capel Garmon, North Wales.*

66 RIGHT *Appliqué smith-god image from Corbridge, northern England.*

Switzerland were worshipping a divinity named Gobanus, a Gaulish name cognate with Welsh Gofannon and Irish Goibnhiu, smith-deities of early medieval western myth (see Chapter 7). Devotees of Gobanus who dedicated the inscribed zinc plaque to him gave him a local soubriquet 'Dobnoredus', 'he who rules the earth'.[128]

DIVINATION AND POWER

> Divination is a means of discovering information which cannot be obtained by ordinary means or in an ordinary state of mind.
>
> Piers Vitebsky, The Shaman[129]

Divination, tapping into the consciousness of the spirit-world, is an important ingredient in the traditional shamanic 'package', although by no means exclusive to shamanism. But the close association between shamans and using supernatural force in order to tell the future is implied by the factor of trance, the need for the religious practitioner to employ some means of crossing the boundaries between profane and sacred domains. Speaking with the spirits, the ancestors and the dead would have been a special skill, given only to those with the gift of mental transference via trance:[130] good Classical examples of such individuals include the Cumaean Sybil and the Delphic Oracle, both of whom were female. Paradoxically, a person skilled in the divinatory craft would have power over time itself, having the ability to tap the ancestral past in order to tell the future. A body of literary evidence from Classical observers is testimony to the use of divination by the Gaulish Druids as a means both of exploiting and demonstrating their sacro-political powers. Diodorus Siculus comments:

> The Gauls likewise make use of diviners, accounting them worthy of high approbation, and these men foretell the future by means of the flight and cries of birds and of the slaughter of sacred animals, and they have all the multitude subservient to them. [131]

The linkage between divination and political power is made clear by other statements of Classical writers on the Druids. In the context of the Gallo-German revolt led by Civilis in AD 69–70, Tacitus[132] speaks of the Roman fear of the Druids and their prophecy that the empire would be destroyed and the world dominated by 'tribes beyond the Alps'. (Indeed, according to Piers Vitebsky,[133] shamans often act as foci of political resistance.) Much later, in the late third century AD, the peculiar set of Roman texts known as the *Augustan Histories* make repeated allusions to the prediction of future emperors – Diocletian, Alexander Severus and Aurelian – by Gaulish Druidesses.[134] Indeed, divination is closely associated with the symbolic potency of words, something to which Vitebsky[135] refers when discussing shamanic powers. He also comments on the symbolic manner in which ancestral spirits of the dead may speak backwards to shamans, in recognition that they belong to a parallel otherworld, a mirror-image of earth-world: for the Saami and the Indian Sora, the seasons are reversed in the world of the dead and Saami ancestors walk upside-down in the footsteps of the living.[136] Such inversion strikes a chord in Romano-British religious practice, where – at Bath, for instance – curse-tablets to the goddess Sulis were sometimes written backwards.[137] It may even be possible that the Iron Age woman found bound and interred at Great Houghton near Northampton, with a lead torc placed back-to-front round her neck,[138] is identifiable as a special being, in touch with the upside-down world of the spirits.

The poet Ausonius, a native of Bordeaux, commented that the whole dynasty of the Druids who presided over the Aquitanian healer-god Belenus were famous for their rhetorical skills.[139] The symbiosis between religious – especially divinatory – power and political force is aptly displayed in Roman literary descriptions of Diviciacus, pro-Roman ruler over the Burgundian tribe of the Aedui in the mid-first century BC.[140] In his *De Bello Gallico*,[141] Julius Caesar speaks of him as a friend and calls him a *vergobret*, a high-ranking Gaulish magistrate; the same word was inscribed as a graffito on a pot at Argentomagus (Indre) in the earlier first century AD.[142] Significantly, his broad contemporary, Cicero,[143] met him in Rome in 60 BC, and mentions that he was a Druid of no mean skill at divinatory pronouncements. This is praise indeed from the foremost Roman orator of his time.

The recognition of archaeological evidence for divination has to be based on conjecture. But certain objects from Iron Age or Gallo-Roman contexts suggest that their purpose may have been as instruments of prognostication. The set of rods from the 'Doctor's Grave' at Stanway, Essex (Plate 23), was mentioned earlier in connection with the presence of psychotropic substances, a combination of finds that makes the idea of a shamanic tomb an attractive proposition. There is a group of objects that appears to have been used to measure time and to predict the future by means of calendrical computation. Most sophisticated of these devices is the Coligny calendar (Fig. 67), a large, now fragmentary bronze sheet from near Bourg in central France, which probably dates to the first or second century AD. The calendar was inscribed with the names of sixty-two months, covering a five-year period, in Gaulish using Roman script; by each name the abbreviations MAT or ANMAT indicated whether the month was complete or incomplete, that is whether it had twenty-nine or thirty days.[144] Every month was divided into two halves by the word ATENOUX ('returning night'), a light and a dark, according to the fortnight of the waxing or waning moon, and pegs slotted into holes by each month-name were used for calculations of cosmic events. The Coligny calendar almost certainly belonged to Gaulish Druids and was probably a powerful piece of equipment in enabling the priesthood to make predictions concerning monthly and seasonal

67 *Fragmentary bronze calendar from Coligny in central France. It covers a five-year period and lists seasons, months and days. It may have been used by ritualists in predicting auspicious times for certain activities.*

change, a skill that would have given them considerable *dignitas* within their community.[145] In parallel with cognate calendars used in Greece and Rome, calendrical knowledge would have been, first and foremost, the preserve of the clergy and their prime function was to calculate times for religious festivals.[146] It may be that other calendrical devices can be identified in the archaeological record. Andrew Fitzpatrick[147] has suggested that this is the explanation for the presence of the inlaid astral symbols decorating certain middle Iron Age sword-blades, such as the one from Saint-André-de-Lidon,[148] with a full and crescent moon divided by a vertical median line, as if to express the mid-month ATENOUX inscribed on the Coligny calendar.

PLACES TO WORK AND PLACES TO REST

Although shrines and temples would frequently have been foci for religious activity and for communication with the supernatural world (Plate 19), shamanic trance and performance probably often took place in the open air, with maximum potential for public theatre and at significant places in the landscape. For Saami shamans,[149] specially charged access points to the otherworld were the 'edge' places: estuaries, islands, rivers and rapids (Plate 21), all contested space between land and water, or caves and mountains – liminal locations jutting into the sky or leading the way underground. Richard Bradley[150] argues that sacrificial activity involving shamans took place at these boundary-places because it is there that chaos and human-based order meet and it was essential that *humanitas* prevailed. The importance of mountains and water for ritual action was also associated, for the Saami, with the out-of-body, trance-induced shamanic experience of flying or swimming to the spirit-world.

In ancient northwest Europe, it is possible to identify holy places that are similarly connected with liminal, edgy places. Thus confluences, such as the conjoining of the great rivers Saône and Rhône at Lyon, were potent spirit-ridden locations.[151] Likewise, bogs, mountains and islands were sacred for Iron Age Europeans. The bog bodies of Denmark, Germany, the Netherlands and Britain may have been interred in these water/land spaces because both they and their burial-places were related to liminality.[152] The violent treatment often meted out to these individuals, living or dead, wherein they were systematically mutilated, dismembered and decapitated, may even be linked to traditional shamanic initiation rites in which – in order to be accepted into the spirit-world – the shaman might have to undergo symbolic deconstruction and re-integration or rebirth,[153] in a manner resembling medieval rites of passage, as described by Roberta Gilchrist.[154] We know, both from archaeology and from Classical literature, that islands were foci for ritual practice. Llyn Cerrig Bach may have been selected for votive deposition in the later first millennium BC because of Anglesey's island status; Strabo's horrific first-century description of the annual human sacrifice of a priestess by her sister clergy on a holy island off the mouth of the Loire[155] may carry all the more significance in the context of shamanistic boundary-ritual.

If Iron Age shamans worked in edgy locations, close to the borders of the spirit domain, they may also have lain in specially accoutred graves. Given the animal personae frequently adopted by traditional shamans, it is possible that the occurrence of animal skins in high-status tombs carries significance. Certain late Iron Age tombs have been noted as containing traces of bear-pelts: the rich grave, dating to *c.* 25–15 BC, found at Welwyn Garden City, Hertfordshire, in 1965 contained elaborate drinking equipment, including six Italian wine amphorae, a silver goblet and a bronze strainer. 'Burnt claws were found with the heap of human bones, suggesting

68 LEFT *Pair of spoons from Castell Nadolig, West Wales.*

69 RIGHT *Casket from the female grave at Wetwang, Yorkshire.*

that the body had been cremated wrapped in a bearskin.'[156] Similar ritual took place at a funeral in Baldock, also in Hertfordshire, where the body of the deceased appears to have been cremated in a bearskin: once again, feasting paraphernalia dominated the tomb furniture: iron firedogs, bowls, wooden buckets and an amphora.[157] The tradition was not confined to southeast Britain: in about 80 BC, a fifty-year-old man was cremated on a funeral pyre, at Clemency in Luxembourg, wearing a bearskin fastened by a brooch.[158] After fire had consumed the flesh, the calcined bone fragments were interred to the accompaniment of sacrificial ritual during which four wild boars were slaughtered and grave goods offered to the spirits of the underworld. About thirty amphorae had been placed on the pyre and the burnt sherds were then deposited in a kind of pavement at the grave-site. The inclusion of wild-animal skins in rich graves can be traced to the beginning of the Iron Age in Europe: the great Greek bronze cauldron of mead placed in the elaborate Hochdorf burial was placed on a wooden table covered with a badger-skin.

Other graves contain material that mark them out as special, perhaps those of ritualists: rich tombs at, for instance, Acy-Romance in the Ardennes, dated to the second century BC, were furnished with high-status equipment, including buckets, and one contained an axe that might have been used in human sacrifice;[159] in the Marne cemetery known as the 'Necropole du Chemin de Vadenay' at Bouy was a cremation burial dated to the second or first century BC,[160] accompanied by a curious set of six amulets, all fitted with suspension-rings, including tiny horse and wolf figurines, a miniature axe and model carnyx – this last unique, as far as we are aware. Inhumation graves, too, may contain distinctive goods, suggesting the living profession of the dead: a female burial at La Chaussée-sur-Marne, of third-century BC date, contained a set of ritual equipment, comprising a bowl and a pair of spoons, originally wrapped in a bag.[161] One spoon is lost but the other is engraved with a

cross dividing the surface into four quadrants (Fig. 68) and, on analogy with pairs from Britain,[162] the other spoon was probably drilled with a hole; Andrew Fitzpatrick has argued that spoons like this could have been used in divining rituals, wherein powder or liquid was poured through the opening in the upper spoon onto the lower, and its position on the cross-marked surface used in religious predictions. One of the female chariot-burials from Wetwang in Yorkshire contained a personal object in the form of a small sealed bronze casket (Fig. 69), decorated with La Tène designs, hanging by a chain probably from the dead woman's belt;[163] on analogy with certain early medieval tomb-furnishings,[164] the little vessel may have contained consecrated liquid, healing herbs or other symbols of the shaman's craft. Another richly furnished inhumation grave, at Saint-Georges-les-Baillargeaux (Vienne), contained a knife and three razors (Plate 20), all of bronze.[165] It is possible that the deliberate selection of copper alloy rather than iron, the more usual metal for edge-tools like knives, could have a religious meaning, perhaps because of its bright colour and that the Saint-Georges grave should be identified as that of a priest or shaman: the knife may have been used in sacrificial ceremonies, while the set of razors could be associated with rites of passage and – maybe – the ritual cutting of young men's hair as a mark of adulthood.

CONCLUSION

The archaeological record for the European Iron Age includes a great deal of circumstantial evidence for the presence of holy men and women, at least some of whom accord closely with the persona of the shaman. Some of the bog bodies from northern and central Europe (and even from Britain) seem to have been special people, interred in special ways. The blindfolded girl from Windeby may have been a seer; and some of the male bog victims ingested substances that would have caused them to experience hallucinations. There is evidence, too, that the people selected for ritual killing and consignment to marshes had physical attributes that may have led them to be regarded as marginal persons, touched by the gods. The presence of guardian spirits, in the form of wooden figures, protecting travellers crossing bogs on trackways, could be related to the identification of these watery places as entrances to the otherworld.

The testimony of Greek and Roman writers, such as Caesar, Pliny and Tacitus, suggests that professional clergy in Gaul and Britain, particularly the Druids, shared many characteristics with traditional shamans: control over access to the supernatural world, healing powers and the ability to tell the future by communicating with the spirits and consulting calendrical equipment, like the Coligny calendar, that may have been the Gaulish equivalent of the Bronze Age star-disc from Nebra (see Chapter 4). We even know some of their names: Veleda, the sequestered virgin priestess described so graphically by Tacitus, was a powerful Batavian prophetess. Some of the later Iron Age tombs from Gaul and Britain, such as Wetwang in Yorkshire, Stanway in southeast England and La Chaussée in eastern France, contained equipment suggesting that they were the grave goods of ritualists.

Perhaps the most exciting material from Iron Age Europe to suggest the activities of shamans is the increasing body of evidence for the ritual use of mind-altering substances, whether in the form of drug-residues in the graves from early Iron Age Germany (Hochdorf) and late Iron Age Britain (Stanway) or of the large quantities of liquor contained in the amphorae from the Auvergne and Burgundy (Corent and Bibracte) and in cauldrons and buckets from Britain and the Continent. Cauldrons are especially interesting, for they turn up in sacred deposits from the earliest Iron Age to the Roman period and there is strong evidence from the mythic literature of early medieval Ireland and Wales (see Chapter 7) that cauldrons were associated with healing, regeneration and transition to the spirit-world, all activities associated with the traditional repertoire of the shaman. The evidence for mind-bending agents causes us to scrutinize some of the motifs and images on Iron Age art, especially metalwork and to put forward arguments for interpretation of some of it within a shamanistic framework. It may even be possible to suggest that motifs on late Iron Age coins related to the agency of the Druids who may, like the shamans of modern societies, for example in Siberia, have been in control of both politics and religion until their power-bases were eroded and driven underground by the new authority and ideologies of *romanitas*.

6 MONSTERS, GENDER-BENDERS AND RITUALISTS IN THE ROMAN EMPIRE AND BEYOND

Now hear the rest of what I have to tell,
*   What crafts,*
What methods I devised – and you will wonder more.
First in importance: if a man fell ill, he had
No remedy, solid or liquid medicine,
Or ointment, but for lack of drugs they pined away;
Until I showed them how to mix mild healing herbs
And so protect themselves against all maladies.
Then I distinguished various modes of prophecy,
And was the first to tell from dreams what Fate ordained
Should come about; interpreted the hidden sense
Of voices, sounds, sights met by chance upon the road,
The various flights of crook-clawed vultures I defined
Exactly, those by nature favourable, and those
Sinister ... how to interpret signs in sacrifice,
Smoothness of heart and lights, what colours please the gods
In each, the mottled shapeliness of liver-lobes.

Aeschylus, *Prometheus Bound*[1]

The Greek dramatist Aeschylus was born at Eleusis near Athens, the centre of the arcane cult of the Eleusinian Mysteries, in 525 BC; he wrote this powerful play, *Prometheus Bound*, in the mid-fifth century, an examination of the strange eponymous hero, Prometheus, mythical champion of humankind, himself half-human, half-divinity. Prometheus belongs to two worlds; he is a changer of human lives, harnessing the transformational power of fire to allow mortals to warm and protect themselves, to cook meat, make bread, forge and cast metal and create pots. Furthermore, Prometheus is specifically credited as the first prophet, able to divine the will of the gods through dreams, signs and portents; he challenges the gods in the spirit-world and suffers appallingly for his patronage of humans, condemned by Zeus to lie forever chained to a rock while an eagle pecks at his vitals: he thus possesses many elements of a shamanic being.

This chapter explores the nature of the shaman in later antiquity as a 'two-spirit' being and, in particular, how the ritualist's multiple persona may have been expressed in contemporary literature, in imagery and in material culture. The focus is the western Roman empire, but the search for understanding involves visits to other ancient cosmologies and consultation of ethnographic comparanda. There is evidence, both from documentary sources – drama, myth and religious expositions – and archaeology (from imagery, in particular), that visionaries explored other worlds, through the pathways of dreams or ecstatic states and that such 'ritualists' expressed their ambiguous nature in ways that reflected their double status as human emissaries to the spirit domain. It is possible to interpret some of the 'surreal' imagery present in the later European Iron Age and the western Roman provinces as depictive of a shamanic dreamscape, where fantasy becomes the reality and the sacred mediator enters a 'virtual' world in which the real and the fantastic are both mingled and inverted. Such surreality may be expressed by images that spring ultimately from nature but are altered, distorted and rendered strange, weird and unfamiliar: hybrid forms, half-human, half-animal or dual-gendered beings and creatures with exaggerated or multiplied body-parts that may represent spirit-beings or ritualists who transcended the different tiers of the cosmos. Additionally, material culture may reveal ancient shamans to us, in the form of their toolkits, the equipment they needed in rituals designed to visit sacred worlds, negotiate on behalf of their communities and manipulate the spirit-forces to heal, prevent famine and induce prosperity and know the future.

VISIONARIES AND DREAMERS: EVIDENCE FROM THE CLASSICAL WORLD

The consideration of archaeological evidence for shamans in later European antiquity is only valid from the perspective of a context within which other indications of visionary religion are present. One such marker comprises material culture associated with narcotics,[2] an issue discussed in Chapter 5; another is the body of literary evidence from ancient Greece and Rome, some of which resonates strongly with the monstrous imagery from the western Roman provinces explored later on in this chapter.

In AD 150, the Greek Artemidorus wrote a treatise named the *Oneirocriticon* (the *Interpretation of Dreams*), in which he describes two types of dream: *oneiroi* and *enypnia*, the second only occurring during sleep. The first, the *oneiros*, is significant in so far as it was associated with the process of divination, prognostication enabled by contact with the spirit-world. Artemidorus discussed two kinds of *oneiroi*: *theoretimátikoi* (which came true clearly and immediately) and *allegorikoi* (whose understanding was more delayed and revealed itself through 'symbolic pictures').[3] Greek texts identify visionary-practitioners called *oneirokritai*, prophets possessed by particular divinities and who uttered vaticinatory (future-telling) proclamations while in an altered state of consciousness induced by the god's presence within him or her.[4] The Delphic Oracle and the Cumaean Sybil are good examples of such ecstatic ritualists.

Greek myth, as presented by dramatists such as Sophocles and Euripides, identifies religious visionaries, individuals in constant touch with the world of the spirits, and their descriptions of such persons reveal their strongly shamanistic character. This is clearly exemplified by the character of the blind seer Tiresias, who appears in several Greek dramas and in other literature. According to Pindar, a Boeotian poet born in 518 BC, Tiresias was the resident *mantis* (priest, seer) of the people of Thebes, at the time of the city's founder and first king, Cadmus; in Pindar's *Nemean Odes*, Tiresias is presented as a superlative diviner of Zeus's will.[5] Like so many prophets in many cultural traditions, Tiresias's gift for divine prediction was acquired as compensation for physical blindness. According to a very ancient version of the myth,[6] Hera robbed him of his sight because of his temerity in announcing that women enjoyed sex more than men, a proclamation that outraged the goddess's sense of womanly propriety. Tiresias's views on the subject had apparently been sought because he himself had experienced gender-change, altering from man to woman and back to man. This gender-bending is of intense interest within the context of shamanism, for it is a 'shamanic marker' found across many time- and culture-zones (see below). Other aspects of Tiresias's persona equally identify him as a ritualist whose relationship with the spirit-world is truly shamanistic, including his association with animal imagery and his role as the 'voice' of the gods. Quotations from three Greek plays clearly illustrate Tiresias's relevance to shamanism: in the first, taken from *Antigone* by Sophocles, the prophet addresses the Theban tyrant Creon:

> As I sat on the ancient seat of augury, in the sanctuary where every bird I know will hover at my hands – suddenly I heard it, a strange voice in the wingbeats, unintelligible, barbaric, a mad scream.[7]

In another play, *Oedipus the King*, the same dramatist presents Tiresias as the speaker of divine truths: in two places, the Leader of the Chorus describes him:

> I still believe
> Lord Tiresias sees with the eyes of Lord Apollo,
> Anyone searching for the Truth, my king,
> Might learn it from the prophet, clear as day.[8]
>
> ...look,
> they bring him on at last, the seer, the man of god.
> The truth lives inside him, him alone.[9]

The most powerful presentation of Tiresias's character appears in Euripides's disturbing and powerful drama, *The Bacchae*, written in the late fifth century BC, in the context of the cataclysmic social upheaval caused by the Peloponnesian War, civil conflict between the supreme states of Athens and Sparta which challenged civilization itself. The whole play is framed within the confrontation between earth- and spirit-world, a contest with the inevitable outcome of divine victory but at the cost of great human carnage. The god Dionysus (Roman name, Bacchus: Fig. 70) appears to the Theban ruler Pentheus whose power he challenges. In the passage quoted here, the prophet Tiresias – fearing what will happen if Dionysus is denied – attempts to act as a mediator between god and human, proclaiming the links between the deity and himself:

> Go, someone, say Tiresias is looking for him,
> He [Dionysus] knows why; I'm an old man, and he's older still -
> But we agreed to equip ourselves with Bacchic wands
> And fawnskin cloaks, and put on wreaths of ivy shoots.[10]

This last passage is of especial relevance in our shamanic quest, in so far as it directly associates Tiresias with the equipment and persona of a ritualist: he carries a magical, transformatory wand or staff, a headdress and dons animal apparel. Tiresias's ambivalence, as belonging half to the worlds of humans and the gods, is depicted not only by the paradox of his blindness and clear-sightedness but also by his sexual ambiguity.[11] Such a combination of visual impairment and transgenderism is witnessed elsewhere in antiquity, for instance in the presentation of the Norse shamanic god Odin, who sacrificed one of his eyes in order to gain wisdom and who was temporarily banished from the company of the gods on account of his transvestism.[12] All these features may be related to the image of the shaman as a liminal being, negotiator between worlds.

Both Greek and Roman religion made use of soothsayers, interpreters of dreams and portents, sometimes in the context of mystery cults that involved an ecstatic, out-of-body element both for the ritualists themselves and for initiates. In ancient Rome, any peculiar, unnatural phenomenon – a solar eclipse, a sweating statue, or 'the discovery of hermaphrodites' – was reported to the Senate[13] and such happenings would have been set before professional seers for their interpretation. Sometimes these people, in tune with the otherworld, would ply their craft in the temples, but – if the story of Julius Caesar's soothsayer, who besought the dictator to beware the Ides of March, has any authenticity – some may have wandered the streets, uttering prophecies as the spirits possessed them. In the temples, seers had the special role of negotiator between sacred and profane: god and pilgrim. The holy places were themselves 'embassies' of the spirits, where holy and unholy came together and the worshipper sought access to the divine force. In late Roman Britain, the great shrine to the indigenous healing-god Nodens at Lydney, overlooking the river Severn in Gloucestershire, was served by an official 'interpreter of dreams' (see below), who recorded his profession on a mosaic dedicated to the deity.[14]

The resident priests at certain sanctuaries expressed their direct linkage with this otherworld in a number of ways, one of them being the importance of going barefoot on holy ground, so as not to interrupt contact with the sacred: the great sanctuary to Zeus at Dodona is recorded as being inhabited by barefoot clergy;[15] we find similar traditions in Classical literary allusions to 'barbarian' religious traditions of the west: the Greek geographer Strabo, for instance, makes detailed reference to the elderly barefoot priestesses of the Germanic Cimbri, who presided over the ritual murder of war-prisoners.[16] Carol van Driel-Murray,[17] a specialist in Roman footwear at the University of Amsterdam, stresses the significance of feet in religious symbolism and ritual, making the point that 'feet are on the frontier and it is around frontiers that ritual accumulates'. This may, in part, be why – in many shamanistic traditions – dancing plays such a crucial role in the attainment of out-of-body experiences and transic contact with the spirit-forces.[18] The bronze figurines of male and female dancers from the Gallic religious temple-hoard found at Neuvy-en-Sullias (Loiret) (Fig. 71) may well represent ritual performance.[19]

70 OPPOSITE *Marble statue of Bacchus, from Spoonley Wood, England.*

71 RIGHT *Neuvy dancer, rear view.*

Ritualists, Material Culture and Healing

> When she had finished speaking, she [Boudica] employed a
> species of divination, letting a hare escape from the fold of
> her dress; and since it ran on what they considered the
> auspicious side, the whole multitude shouted with pleasure,
> and Boudica, raising her hand toward heaven, said:
> 'I thank thee, Andraste, and call upon thee as woman
> speaking to woman …'
>
> Dio Cassius, *Roman History*[20]

Dio's vivid account of the British freedom-fighter Queen Boudica's ritual action in the sacred grove of Andraste, the local Icenian goddess of Victory, is of interest in so far as it would seem to present the warrior-queen in the guise of a shaman, performing divinatory practice before setting out on campaign, using an animal spirit helper to make contact with the supernatural world prior to her massacre of the women in Roman London. Dio thus opens a door on a world where ritual action, theatre and performance were endemic in the desire to 'know' the spirit-world. Boudica is projected by Dio's writing as a contesting, resistant figure, calling upon her gods in her fight against Roman imperialism, in much the same way as shamans, in many societies, form a focus for political rebellion and opposition of socially dislocational change.[21] Jane Webster[22] has recently applied such a model of the Druids as a focus of political and religious subversion to the Roman-conquest period in Gaul and Britain, drawing attention to their portrayal in Roman literature as agitators, fomenters of revolt and robust opponents of colonialism. Similarly, in early medieval Britain and Europe, shamans were also marginalized members of society, a 'shadowy underclass' condemned by the Christian Church but still regarded as a force sufficiently dangerous and destabilizing to cause King Alfred to make it a capital offence for women to practise magic and cast spells.[23]

It is sometimes possible to identify ritualists' equipment in the material culture of Roman and early medieval Europe, paraphernalia that shows parallels with the toolkits and personal trappings of religious functionaries in well-documented shamanistic traditions. An evocative Romano-British find from Brough-on-Humber consists of a grave interpreted as that of a priest; if it has been correctly identified, then its archaism and its conscious harking back to Iron Age traditions, may well be associated with the kind of resistant imagery suggested as relevant to shamanism under stress from new ways. The grave, covered with thin limestone

72 OPPOSITE LEFT *Wooden wheel on shaft, Wavendon Gate, Milton Keynes, England.*

73 OPPOSITE RIGHT *Silver coin with antlered head, Midlands.*

slabs, contained two bodies; grave goods accompanying one of them included 'ritual' objects: an iron-hooped wooden bucket, and – more significantly – two iron 'sceptres'. On the bucket was a bronze handle-mount in the form of a human head; each sceptre was surmounted by a bronze helmeted head.[24] The bucket has similarities with vessels from late Iron Age tombs in southeast England and northern Gaul and these containers, like cauldrons, may have been used for brewing intoxicating substances, perhaps related to ritual, even shamanic activity (see Chapter 5).

So-called wands or sceptres are recorded in other Romano-British contexts: Willingham Fen in Cambridgeshire produced one whose terminal was elaborately decorated with religious imagery;[25] plainer examples come from shrines, such as Muntham Court in Sussex[26] and Farley Heath, Surrey,[27] the latter surviving as a thin binding-strip, once again depicting cult-scenes or figures from myth. The curious wooden wheel mounted on a shaft, from an early Romano-British waterlogged pit at Wavendon Gate, Milton Keynes (Fig. 72),[28] may also have been used on ceremonial occasions, perhaps in the invocation of the sun.

Apart from ceremonial staffs that – on analogy with the wizard's wand – may be interpreted as bodily extensions of authority and supernatural power, the remnants of ritualists' costumes, especially headdresses, sometimes survive. A significant number come from temples, a context that reinforces their interpretation as ceremonial regalia. Joanna Bird[29] has analysed the evidence for British headdresses, a survey sparked by her investigation of the finds from the Wanborough Roman temple in Surrey, which produced three chain-headdresses made for attachment to hats of leather or cloth, two of which were surmounted by wheel-shaped finials. The great interest of the Wanborough headgear lies in resemblances between these spoked-wheel terminals and the diadem worn by the antlered human head (Fig. 73) decorating the obverse of the late Iron Age silver coin from the British Midlands:[30] such a feature connects regalia like this with possible shamanic identity.

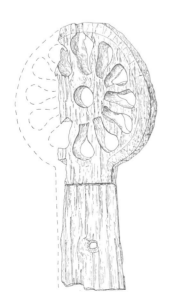

Occasionally, the archaeological record of western Europe in Roman and early medieval periods provides evidence that clearly chimes with divinatory practice. The 'Doctor's Grave' at Stanway in Essex (Plate 23) dates to about AD 50, a time when *romanitas* came into direct and large-scale contact with indigenous cultural traditions. Gilly Carr[31] has suggested that the use by Britons of imported Roman medical equipment may have imbued such individuals with powers that were both highly charged and dangerous because they lay outside the British social order. In her studies of medical toolkits used by the Roman army, Patty Baker[32] has argued that surgical instruments might be buried in tombs because, had they been used in unsuccessful treatment, they could be regarded as irretrievably polluted, particularly if such failed procedures resulted in the patient's death. But she points to Ernst Künzl's study of medical tools in Roman military tombs, and his exploration of peculiar grave-finds, such as cuttle-fish bones, bells and Neolithic stone axes, which might be interpreted as ritualists' equipment.[33]

Chris Knüsel[34] has studied archaeological and literary indicators for the presence of ritualists in early post-Roman Europe; he emphasizes the significance of symbols for shamanic identity, their significance for the shaman's performance and for his or her ability to engage with the audience. In playing on the senses, symbols – whether materially visible or not – act as the means by which shamans change minds and manipulate worlds.[35] Their ability to move between the cosmic tiers may be expressed by ambivalent symbols associated with, for instance, human/animal or female/male. In Anglo-Saxon and Norse tradition, the shaman's bag of symbolic equipment seems to have possessed special importance: a female seer named Thorbjorg is described, in the Norse saga of *Eirik the Red*,[36] as possessing a wand and a bag full of magical objects and, what is more, she used a bronze spoon and a knife with a broken tip for eating, the significance of which is revisited later in this section. Knüsel draws attention to the paraphernalia of an analogous shamanic figure

74 LEFT *Romano-British jet bear-figurine, Bootle, Lancashire, England.*

75 OPPOSITE *Gallo-Roman relief of god with birds on his shoulders, Moux, Burgundy.*

disparagingly described, by the sixth-century Christian holy man Gregory of Tours,[37] as having a bag full of animal parts deemed to have powers as 'charms' including moles' teeth, mouse-bones and bears' claws (Fig. 74).

Anglo-Saxon graves, particularly female burials, have produced similar ritual paraphernalia, including bags, metal boxes hung from chains (very similar to the one from the grave of an Iron Age woman at Wetwang (see Chapter 5)), remains of herbs, bones and other curious material.[38] The use of a shamanic bag is interesting for it is part of the toolkit of ritualists over many traditions: David Lewis-Williams,[39] for instance, points to the significance of hunting bags used by southern African San shamans and perceived as symbolic of transition between worlds, perhaps because of the two concepts of travel and the hunt (which transforms from life to death and renews life by the provision of food). In this context, some Gallo-Roman images may have relevance, in so far as they depict anthropomorphic figures clearly associated with wilderness and the hunt and carrying bags. One, from Moux in Burgundy (Fig. 75), consists of a bearded man, carrying a knotted staff and a billhook, with two birds on his shoulders and a hound at his feet, and with an open bag containing what we have interpreted as oak-apples tucked under his left arm.[40] Two images, virtually identical to each other, come from a remote sanctuary in the Vosges mountains of Alsace: each consists of a 'hunter-god' who may actually be a shaman, for the animal theme in the iconography is so strong. He, too, carries a bag of 'forest-fruits' – acorns, nuts and pine cones, along with a spear and chopper; he wears a wolfskin, on his boots are the heads of small animals and a stag stands by his side.[41]

The Norse prophetess Thorbjorg's cutlery set may carry significance for her identity as a shaman, in two respects. Firstly, her bronze spoon may appear commonplace, but the ritual nature of spoons in antiquity should not be forgotten. In late Iron Age Britain and Gaul,[42] pairs of spoons – one marked with a cross, the other perforated with a single hole - are repeatedly found in ritual contexts, sometimes in the graves of persons deemed to have been ritualists (see Chapter 5). Perforated spoons sometimes form part of the tomb-furniture of Anglo-Saxon graves, often paired with crystals: one such burial comes from Chessel Down on the

Isle of Wight where, in the sixth century AD, a special person was interred with a crystal in a silver holder, three buckets and a perforated spoon carefully placed beneath the knees.[43]

It is arguably possible to interpret such paraphernalia – spoons, crystals and buckets – as belonging to cult-practice involving purification, divination and healing: the buckets may have held pure water, the spoons would have functioned as sprinklers of the holy liquid[44] and we would suggest that the crystals may have represented, at one and the same time, solidified water and the ability of the shaman to see into and move between the two worlds of earth and spirit. It is worth mentioning the hoard of late Roman silver from Thetford in Norfolk, which included over thirty silver spoons dedicated to an obscure Italian nature-god Faunus equated with local deities with British names. Spoons like this may have been used in Roman contexts as highly charged cult objects, employed as measures for votive offerings.[45] In terms of shamanic practice, it is of considerable interest that one of the gods whose name was inscribed on a Thetford spoon was named 'Medugenus' ('Mead-Begotten'),[46] perhaps a reference to religious intoxication and trance-induced visions. The presence of cult material associated with hallucinogens is attested in Romano-British contexts, as at the Walbrook *mithraeum* in London, the silver casket and strainer from which, it has been suggested,[47] may have been designed for drug-laced wine; ceramic vessels, deliberately deposited in pits and once containing drugs such as hemlock, have been identified at Silchester.[48]

In returning to the Norse seeress Thorbjorg, a final point of interest concerns her use of a broken knife without its tip. In discussing aspects of shamanic practice among the Tungus, Peter Jordan[49] comments on the belief that sharp objects can be equated with harm, particularly the danger of piercing the shaman's shadow. Such perception resonates with two curious observations on ancient Gaulish ritual by Pliny the Elder and Tacitus:[50] in describing the gathering of the selago plant by Gaulish ritualists for healing the eyes, Pliny stresses the importance of not using iron; similarly, in recounting ceremonial behaviour associated with the Germanic agricultural goddess Nerthus, Tacitus comments that, during her festival, all objects of iron must be locked away. Both writers perhaps bear witness to a shamanic tradition related to healing, fertility and purification in which contamination with implements that could symbolize harm had to be avoided; the singling out of iron as a metal to be shunned in this context could be associated with its usual choice for weapon production, but it may also relate to the magical powers ascribed to the blacksmith and the peril represented by his dangerous occupation (see Chapter 5).

14 *Tollund Man. He was an Iron Age bog-body, whose gut showed traces of ergot, a substance growing on infected barley, that causes hallucinations and burning sensations when ingested. The presence of ergot, and the man's position as if asleep, despite the strangulation noose around his throat, suggests he may have been a shaman.*

15 *Grauballe Man. Like Tollund Man, this individual was sacrificed during the Iron Age in Denmark. He was killed by having his throat savagely cut and he, too, had consumed ergot, causing him to hallucinate and dance about in agony, before coma and death set in. The manner of his death and the psychotropic drugs in his system may reflecct his status as a shaman, perhaps ritually killed for the well-being of his community.*

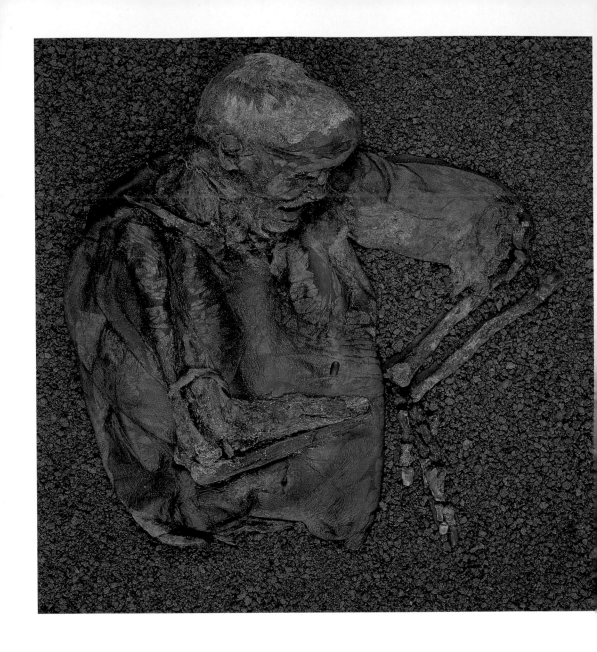

16 *Lindow Man, a British bog-sacrifice who died in the first century* AD. *He was subjected to a triple death: blows to the head, garotting and throat-cutting. He had traces of mistletoe in his gut. All this points to a ritual killing, and he may have been a special person, even a shaman.*

17 *New female grave at Wetwang, Yorkshire. This woman, who died in the Iron Age, perhaps in the third century* BC, *was special. Her grave, with its chariot and rich coral-decorated ornaments, proclaim her high rank. But a facial growth had disfigured her, marking her, perhaps, as touched by the gods.*

18 *Bronze 'cult-wagon' from Strettweg, Austria, of the seventh century* BC. *Depicted are a priestess or shaman, with a cauldron, and scenes of stag-sacrifice.*

19 *Nehalennia shrine reconstruction. The temples dedicated to Nehalennia were on the North Sea in Holland, in the Roman period. The picture shows a priest communing with the goddess.*

20 *Grave at Saint-Georges-les-Baillargeaux (Vienne), containing a knife and three razors. The tomb-furniture, with its ritual toolkit, may have been the possessions of a shaman.*

21 OPPOSITE *Great Langdale waterfall and rapids. This kind of turbulent water is exactly the kind of liminal place one would expect to be used by shamans.*

22 *Bronze image of hooved man from Bouray (Essonne), France.*

23 *Grave material from the Doctor's Grave, Stanway. The grave contained a board-game, in mid-play, a set of divining rods, a doctor's toolkit and a pot whose spout contained a hallucinogenic plant. So here, we may be seeing a shaman's grave.*

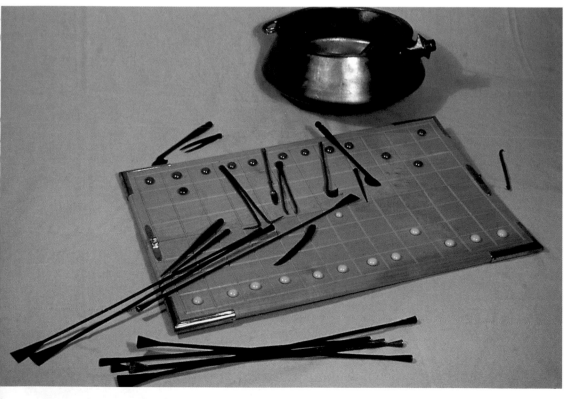

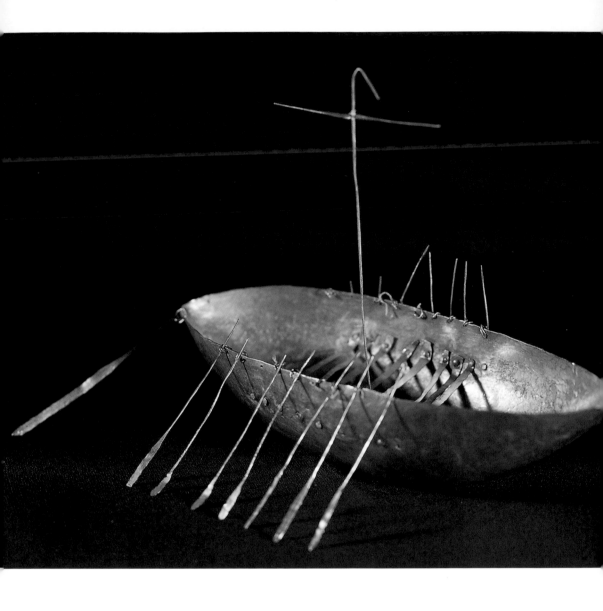

24 *Gold model of a boat from Broighter, Armagh, Ireland. The boat was deposited, with other precious metal objects, close to the shore, and may represent the sea-voyage of a shaman to the otherworld to consult the spirits.*

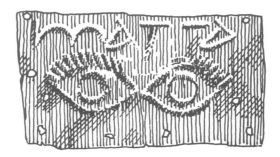

Healing the sick

'Shamans are at once doctors, priests, social workers and mystics.'[51] Scholars of traditional shamanism in circumpolar and other regions agree about the essential link between shamans and healing.[52] If we consider evidence from the western European Iron Age and Roman period, that same link can be discerned. Pliny recurrently associates the Druids with healing: the famous passage concerning mistletoe and golden sickles[53] speaks of the Druids as using the plant as a cure for infertility; elsewhere in the same work,[54] he alludes to the Druids' use of selago for healing eye disorders (see above) (Fig. 76). The contents of certain late Iron Age tombs lead us to suspect that they were the graves of priest-physicians: the Stanway burial (above), with its medical kit, 'divining rods' and narcotics, is highly suggestive of a shamanic healer; an earlier grave, dating to the third century BC at Tartigny (Oise) in northern France (see Chapter 5), contained 'sacramental' equipment, including a yew-wood vat, an iron knife and a combined scalpel and pincers, also made of iron.[55]

Medical personnel, as well as priests, were present at many of the thermal spring shrines in Roman Gaul and Britain; indeed, the two professions were almost certainly sometimes combined. The priest of Sulis at Bath, Calpurnius Receptus, who died (?still in office) at the age of seventy-five and whose tombstone was erected at the spa, could have been a physician.[56] We know from Ausonius that a Druid priest called Phoebicius officiated at the healing shrine of Belenus at Bordeaux during the later Roman empire.[57] Perhaps most significant of all is the inscribed mosaic, dating

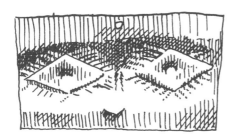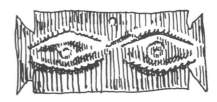

76 *Eye-plaques from Gallo-Roman healing sites. These small bronze anatomical votives were offered up in shrines by sick pilgrims seeking a cure for blindness and other eye-complaints.*

to the fourth century AD, presented to the temple to the healer-god Nodens at Lydney on the river Severn, which describes the pavement's dedicator as an 'Interpreter of Dreams'. This is a very shamanistic title and well known in the Greek world, as described by Artemidorus in his *Oneirocriticon*, written in about AD 150.[58] Even Senilis's name may carry significance, for it means 'Old Man' and was perhaps a title of respect: after all, we know from Caesar[59] that it took as long as twenty years to train a Druid.

GENDER-BENDING AND SHAMANISM

> For spirits when they please
> Can either sex assume, or both.
> John Milton, *Paradise Lost*[60]

A recurrent and widespread feature that characterizes and symbolizes the shaman's transgressive ability to cross boundaries between worlds and between states of being is the presentation of ambiguous, ambivalent and volatile gender-identity.[61] Gender lies at the very roots of personhood, of human identity; denial of one's biological birth-gender frees one from the constraints of 'normal' behaviour and any expression of gender-disturbance may signify the threshold situation of the ritualist divided between human and spirit dimensions, profane and sacred.[62] Gender-transference may equally serve to express the dangerous power of the shaman who, by access to all layers of the cosmos, was able to manipulate the supernatural forces for good or evil. Interestingly, some traditional systems maintain an ambivalence towards female ritualists: in early medieval Norse cult practice, it was considered effeminate for men to enter a trance state and thus communion with the spirit-world was reserved for female ritualists.[63] Among present-day traditions of the Khumbo people living in northeast Nepal, while some ritual practice is the preserve only of men, oracles undergoing trance-induced transgression to the otherworld in order to communicate with ancestral spirits are often women.[64] It seems as though for transference between the layers of the cosmos to take place, a female element in the ritualist's persona may frequently be deemed as necessary, even among communities where it was the norm for men to have control over religious activity.

Instability of gender may be expressed in several ways, including role-swapping and cross-dressing, for which there is substantial evidence in circumpolar shamanistic traditions, including those of Siberian and indigenous North American communities: male shamans belonging to the Chukchi of northeastern Siberia

77 OPPOSITE *The Kayhausen boy. This adolescent youth was killed, bound at the neck, hands and feet and placed in a peat bog in North Germany, perhaps as a human sacrifice, in the second–first century BC.*

adopt female attire while performing ritual actions.[65] Siberian shamans belong to a social gender separate from the biological male/female axis; among the Chukchi, women may only become shamans once they have reached the menopause: reproductive capacity is perceived as inimical to supernatural power.[66] In societies like these, then, only women of child-bearing age were perhaps regarded as sexually female. As in the case of women in early medieval European communities,[67] the end of their reproductive years brought opportunities for empowerment. Among many North American Indian groups,[68] the attainment of altered states of awareness is especially associated with both menopausal women and adolescent boys. In southern African San tradition, girls are perceived to be especially charged with supernatural force on reaching puberty.[69] This is interesting within the context of Iron Age European cult-practice, since a number of specially treated bog bodies[70] who were perhaps sacrificial victims, similarly belonged to 'liminal' age-groups: the woman from Haraldskaer was about fifty years old when she was garrotted and pinned down in a Jutland marsh; the bound woman from Great Houghton in Northamptonshire[71] was about forty when she died, and her lead torc, placed back-to-front, may signify her special status (lead is an unusual metal for ring-jewellery and, in the Classical world at least, was associated with cursing and underworld symbolism; the placement of the torc in a reversed position, its terminals at the back, is also highly idiosyncratic). The children from Kayhausen (Fig. 77), Yde and Windeby were all adolescents, on the edge of adulthood.

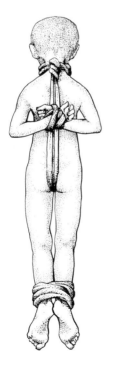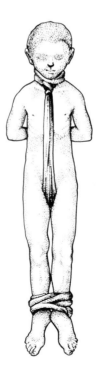

Indigenous American Navajo shamans are called 'two-spirits'[72] or 'changing ones';[73] in a similar manner to the Chukchi,[74] they deliberately assume oppositional identity by cross-dressing. Female saints in early medieval Europe engaged in transvestism,[75] partly in order to avoid sexual harassment but partly as an image of difference; early medieval Christian clergy, religious women in particular, were dislocated from normal gender-roles and this disjunction might be expressed both by physical seclusion and by ambiguous bodily presentation. In this way, both they and non-Christian shamans may be perceived as belonging to neither male nor female but to other genders which are not defined by biological sex. These 'other' genders served not only to express liminality but also the power of difference from norms. The Vestal Virgins of ancient Rome, keepers of the sacred hearth-flame of the goddess Vesta, once again were treated in accordance with neither gender but with being 'other': they dressed in distinctive white garments, had to swear an oath of chastity for their thirty years of office (the breach of which was punished hideously by burial alive) but were granted the 'male-only' privileges of being able to conduct business in their own right as independent agents rather than through husbands, fathers or brothers, as was normal.[76]

Transvestism among ancient European ritualists is recorded in a range of Classical literature. Plutarch[77] comments on cult-practice on the Greek island of Kos where, he says, a priest of Herakles donned female clothing as part of his preparation for sacrificial ritual. This is significant in two respects: firstly, Herakles was himself an ambiguous, transformative figure; like Prometheus, he was a demi-god, half-human, half-divine. Secondly, sacrifice is itself a transformatory ritual; by changing the victim's state from living to dead, the offering is transferred from the human to the spirit-world. Thus gender is used as a metaphor to express change and the ability of the religious functionary to oscillate between cosmic tiers or states of being. But, what is more, Herakles was himself associated with gender-swapping in Classical mythology: according to one legend, the hero's relationship with Omphale, queen of Lydia in Asia Minor, the two exchanged gender; he adopted female garments and he is often represented in ancient art as spinning with Omphale's slaves, clad in a woman's costume.[78] John Ferguson[79] draws attention to the frequency of transvestism as a dramatic device in Classical tradition, as a method of introducing irony, riddle, quandary and instability, much as occurs in Shakespearean and Restoration comedy and, indeed, in modern English pantomime. The symbolism of gender-change, particularly if the true sexuality of the transvestite is left obvious, could be seen as an agent for empowerment: the introduction of doubt serves to reinforce the control held by the being responsible for such uncertainty.

In his observations of ritual behaviour far away from the Aegean, in northern Europe, Tacitus described a priest who similarly cross-dressed for his encounter with the gods:

In the territory of the Naharvali one is shown a grove, hallowed from ancient times. The presiding priest dresses like a woman; the gods, translated into Latin, are Castor and Pollux. That expresses the character of the gods, but their name is Alci. There are no images, there is no trace of foreign cult, but they are certainly worshipped as young men and as brothers. [80]

Once more, as argued for Plutarch's Kos symbolism, the cult associated with Tacitus's transvestite clergy may give clues as to the context of such gender-swapping imagery. In Greek mythology, Castor and Polydeuces (Pollux) – the Dioskoroi (Dioscuri) – were the sons of Zeus; not only were they twins but they shared the gift of immortality between them, living alternately on Olympus and in the Underworld. The cult of the Dioscuri was introduced into Italy as early as 500 BC; the twin gods were particularly associated with horsemanship and attracted a large cult-following among the members of the equestrian class in Rome. In antiquity twins were regarded as special (and, indeed, in a world where infant mortality was rife, the survival of twins must have been regarded as all but miraculous). Identical twins might well have been perceived as charged with even greater mystery and, in some traditions, were perhaps seen as the embodiment of one split individual. So no wonder that Castor and Pollux, or their Germanic equivalents, were deities associated with 'two-spirit' shamans; twins would be a clear metaphor of paired worlds and the cross-dressing priest of the Naharvali may well have expressed the dualism of his gods by means of ambiguous gender. If the nuances of the Classical myth of life-death sharing were known in northern Europe, then such ambivalence is further explained. Certainly Tacitus himself would have been aware of the mythic origins of the divine twins and he may have invented or embellished tales about this obscure Germanic tribe living on the edge of the world.

Writing in the fifth century BC, the Greek historian Herodotus described transvestite prophets among the Scythians.[81] Like Tacitus, Herodotus was commenting on peoples on the edges of the known world, territories inhabited by strange beings, where weird, 'unGreek' things happened. The Amazons of Greek legend are a good example;[82] these terrifying beings were perceived as neither male nor female but assigned an alternative gender containing elements of male and female but at the same time apparently denying both.[83] The passage quoted below is significant not simply in terms of its presentation of cross-dressing ritualists but also in the way that the future was predicted by magical means:

There are many soothsayers in Scythia, and their method is to work with willow rods. They bring great bundles of them, which they put down on the ground; then they untie them, lay out each rod separately, and pronounce their prophecy. While they are speaking it, they collect the rods into a bundle again as before. This is the native mode of divination in Scythia; but the class of effeminate persons called 'Enarees' use a different method, which they say was taught them by Aphrodite: these people take a piece of the inner bark of the lime-tree and cut it into three pieces, which they keep twisting and untwisting round their fingers as they prophesy.[84]

The comment that these 'Enarees' were taught their divinatory craft by the Goddess of Love is perhaps significant: Aphrodite was born unnaturally, from sea-foam and thus might be considered as a symbol of sexual difference, like transvestites themselves. But it is also interesting that gender-bending seers occur elsewhere in ancient Greek tradition: the blind Tiresias of Athenian drama (see above) aptly illustrates the link between shaman and sexual ambivalence. Incidentally, Herodotus's description of divination-rods calls to mind the bronze and iron rods found in the late Iron Age burial at Stanway in Essex (Chapter 5).

It is sometimes possible to identify gender-instability in the material culture of antiquity; this ambiguity is sometimes apparently expressed in rituals associated with the disposal of the dead. Bryony Orme[85] draws attention to the Early Bronze Age cemetery at Brančin Slovakia where discrepant positioning of bodies according to gender (males laid on their right sides, females on their left) were flouted and a few biologically male corpses treated as though they belonged to women. The broadly coeval site of Golyamo Delchevo in northeast Bulgaria contains comparable evidence for special gender-categories: the grave goods from cemetery excavations exhibit three categories of gender-ascription – female, male and 'other'; the same pattern may be identified in the treatment of figurines (male, female and without sexual characteristics) which, although occurring only in the settlement areas inhabited by the living, betray similar tripartite gender-divisions.[86] Something essentially similar may have been expressed in the treatment of the dead buried in the Romano-British cemetery of Poundbury in Dorset, the bodies interred including six male skeletons each accompanied by bone hairpins, grave goods generally associated with females.[87] Such discrepant determinations may reflect biological sex, in which case deviants or the infertile might, perhaps, be treated as special but they may, instead, display other forms of social difference: it is even possible that those individuals rendered outside the male/female divide were liminal persons; one possible category of such people is the shaman, set apart from the community by virtue of specialist knowledge and access to other worlds.

The discrepant sexual treatment of the figurines from Golyamo Delchevo serves to illustrate the use of images in European antiquity as vehicles for exploring issues of difference or 'otherness' by means of gender. Certain anthropomorphic and zoomorphic figures may display sexual ambivalence, ambiguity or apparent 'asexuality' and it is possible to interpret such images as expressive of liminality, maybe even of ritualists' identity. The link between figurines and shamanism is well illustrated by shamanistic rites practised among certain Central and South American traditional communities, in whose cult images the spirits are said to reside for the duration of religious ceremonies while shamans negotiate with them, after which, when the spirits have departed, the figurines are smashed.[88] The Iron Age scholar Ian Stead suggests that this kind of interpretation might usefully be applied to the group of Iron Age chalk figurines from Garton Slack in northeast England (Fig. 78), some of which show signs of deliberate damage, including decapitation. Interestingly, these images are divided into two types: one is overtly male, with erect phalli, beards and swords, but the others depict apparently genderless beings. It could be argued that the two forms express adult maleness/warriorhood, on the one hand, and all other peoples in the community, on the other,[89] but an equally plausible explanation is that the most important categories of person were represented: warriors and ritualists. We should remember Caesar's comment about the Gauls whom he encountered in the mid-first century BC,[90] that the only individuals of any account in Gallic society were the noblemen and the Druids (Fig. 79). Other broadly coeval images likewise exhibit apparent genderlessness: the torc-wearing stone figures from Lanneunoc in Brittany and Alesia in Burgundy exemplify this minimalist artistic tradition. Whilst there may be other reasons for such lack of sexual detail on images like these, their seeming asexuality might be attributable to their liminal otherness, separate from male or female and thus special, close to the spirit-world. It is the very rarity of anthropomorphic imagery in the European Iron Age that leads to conclusions associated with specialness.

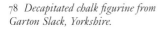

78 *Decapitated chalk figurine from Garton Slack, Yorkshire.*

79 *Apparently genderless chalk figure from a Romano-British pit-shrine at Deal, Kent. The deposition of a gleaming white figurine in a dark holy place may have endowed the image with particular power.*

As is so beautifully expressed in the passage from Milton quoted at the beginning of this section, there may be a close connection between ambivalent or ambiguous gender and the sacred. There is a rare but persistent tradition of dual-gendered imagery in European antiquity that may be charged with meaning associated with the societal *locus* of the being depicted in this manner. Ambivalence expresses instability, strangeness, boundary-transgression and the 'fluidity of meaning'[91] and it is tempting to interpret dual-gendered figures in relation to the 'two-spirit' shamans of circumpolar tradition. Sandra Hollimon[92] has drawn attention to the expression of gender-ambiguity among Siberian shamans by means of ceremonial masks, worn in ritual performance, 'that depicted their helping spirits as hermaphrodites'. Such dual-sexed images may be traced back into earlier European prehistory (see Chapter 5). To the east European Iron Age belongs a Transylvanian silver coin, the reverse of

80 *Gallo-Roman bronze figurine of an antlered woman, France.*

81 *Late Iron Age silver coin with horse-image, from Bratislava, Slovakia.*

82 *Gallo-Roman boar/sow from Cahors, France.*

which appears to depict a bearded and helmeted horseman with developed breasts.[93] A representation of a bi-sexual deity has been identified at the great healing sanctuary of Bolards in Burgundy;[94] the small and curious group of female figurines from Gaul wearing red-deer antlers (Fig. 80)[95] may also evoke gender-change as well as species transference (see below): female reindeer possess antlers but female red-deer do not, and so images of women thus adorned serve to transgress gender-boundaries and to project contradictory sexual messages. Animals could also be represented as sexually ambivalent or ambiguous: a late Iron Age silver coin from Bratislava displays a galloping horse (Fig. 81) with what may be interpreted either as three phalli or three teats (or both)[96] and a Gallo-Roman bronze figurine from Cahors depicts a wild boar, with tusks, stiff dorsal bristles but a row of sow's teats along its underbelly (Fig. 82).[97] It is tempting to interpret these beasts as spirit-animals, perhaps shamanic helpers who aided the shaman by enabling transgression between worlds, and who exhibited such ability by means of oscillating gender. In the same way, hermaphroditic human images may be intended to demonstrate shifting states of being.

Hermaphrodites are a well-known theme in Graeco-Roman art, particularly of the Hellenistic period.[98] A marble figure from Rome exhibits the paradox of 'chiastic torsion', wherein one view of the statue reveals one gender, the other the second gender.[99] Catherine Johns[100] refers to two bronze hermaphroditic figurines in the British Museum, one provenanced to the Thames in London (Fig. 83), the other probably from Italy: both date from the first-second century AD. Whilst in no way wishing to suggest that such images are themselves those of shamans, similar exploration of irony and contradiction are displayed, in a desire to contravene norms and to explore notions of tension, change, ambiguity and wholeness. Furthermore, boundary- transference may be illustrated in the images of certain Classical deities who are recurrently portrayed as androgynous beings, male but with soft, feminine treatment of face and body. The two gods most frequently depicted thus are Apollo and Dionysus, both of whom appear as effeminate-looking men in the western provinces of the Roman empire: the mosaic from the villa at Thruxton in Hampshire bears an image of Dionysus (Fig. 84) looking distinctly liminal in gender-

83 *Bronze figurine of hermaphrodite, found in the river Thames.*

terms;[101] likewise the marble group from Spoonley Wood in Gloucestershire shows a very female-looking representation of the god.[102] The bronze Apollos from the Thames at London, from Trier and from Mâlain in Burgundy,[103] equally exhibit androgynous characteristics. Such somatic treatment may be no more than convention, but it is striking that the cults of both divinities are associated with altered states and boundary-crossing. Apollo was responsible for prophecy, hunting, healing and music, all of which involve elements of transference: hunting and healing involve change (from death to life and from ill-health to health); prophecy and music are each linked with mind-alteration and attempts to reach the spirit-world. Dionysus was associated with the intoxication of wine and its use as a highway to other worlds. The ecstatic rites associated with his cults, involving maddened dancing Maenads, their minds bent by the god, are vividly displayed on the great silver platter from the late Roman Mildenhall treasure from Suffolk (Fig. 86).[104] An elaborate Corinthian capital from Cirencester (Fig. 85), probably once part of a Jupiter-column,[105] is carved with a Bacchic figure accompanied by bunches of grapes, whose bulging eyes appear to exhibit a wine-induced trance state.[106] Euripides's play *The Bacchae* shows very clearly how the wine-metaphor (see Chapter 5) is employed to project images of shifting values, oscillating realities and the capricious instability of the supernatural world. All of these issues are relevant to the shamanic experience.

84 *Mosaic with roundel depicting Dionysus, Thruxton Roman villa, Hampshire, England.*

85 *Bacchus on the capital of a Jupiter-column from Cirencester, England.*

86 *Maenads on the great dish from the Mildenhall treasure, Suffolk, England.*

SHAMANIC SHAPE-SHIFTERS

> Thus was Cairbre the cruel
> who seized Ireland south and north
> two cat's ears on his fair head
> a cat's fur through his ears
> *Cóir Anmann*[107]

This description of a medieval Welsh ruler illustrates a common phenomenon that runs through both archaeology and mythic literature, namely that of the shape-shifter, the being that belongs both to the world of humans and of beasts (Fig. 87). A great deal of current research concerned with shamanistic practice and identity dwells on the close links between shamans and their animal-helpers, spirit-creatures that facilitate the ritualist's encounters with the supernatural dimension; such dependence on animals may be evoked by the shaman's costume, that may include feathers, antler headdresses and pelts.[108] Trance is the medium through which the shaman's links with animals are expressed; during mind-altered states, ritualists experience the phenomenon of 'becoming' particular creatures,[109] while in a virtual world, a shamanic 'cyberspace' of spiritual force in which the dream becomes the world-paradigm.[110]

Both the material culture and imagery of Iron Age and Roman Europe contain resonances of a close and symbiotic linkage between human and animal that may be related to shamanistic practice. The animals selected as boundary-crossing metaphors tend to be those that, in themselves, contain intrinsic transgressive features: a good example in western European antiquity is the red deer which, by virtue of its seasonal growth and shedding of antlers, evokes metaphors of change; what is more, there was an ambiguity in the attitude of people towards deer: they were hunted and herded, killed and cared for and there is evidence, for instance in

87 LEFT *Cat-eared head on antefix from Caerleon.*

88 RIGHT *Pierced red-deer antlers from a Romano-British site at Hook's Cross, Hertfordshire, England.*

Neolithic and Iron Age Orkney, that red deer were tolerated near settlements, even though they would have competed with farming communities for agricultural resources, and that deer bones and antlers were carefully curated and deposited close to dwelling-places.[111]

A powerful and recurrent image in Gaul and Britain during the later Iron Age and Roman periods is that of a hybrid, monstrous creature, essentially human in form but with antlers or hooves. Arguably, such figures express liminality, cosmo-logical fluidity and movement between tiers of the cosmos, between earthly and sacred worlds. There is a case for identification of such creatures as shamans, for there is evidence that certain images depict people dressed up as beasts rather than the true monsters of Classical legend,[112] although the latter similarly evoke bound-ary motifs. Additionally, such half-beings may be read as transformative two-spirit persons in the midst of their soul-journeys between worlds. Transitional imagery like this may involve double-consciousness, the inward and outward vision of the shaman, as well as expressing difference from 'normal' people, marginality and empowerment, in so far as both human and animal are contained within one per-sona. The power to heal, to negotiate with spirits and to visit dead ancestors, all responsibilities associated with traditional shamanism, may be both expressed and enabled through hybrid imagery. The images themselves may be the result of trance-induced visions, shared with the community and forming part of the shaman's performance.[113]

The assumption of a beast's persona, by the donning of horns, antlers, animal-skins or feathers, may sometimes be detected in the archaeological record (see also Chapter 5). The modified antlers, drilled as if to be worn as headdresses, from sites such as the Iron Age temple at Digeon, Somme, where ten sets were discovered deposited in the sacred precinct,[114] and the pair from a Romano-British context at Hook's Cross, Hertfordshire (Fig. 88),[115] suggest that ritualists might have dressed up as beasts during ceremonies.[116] The late Iron Age silver coin from the Midlands, whose

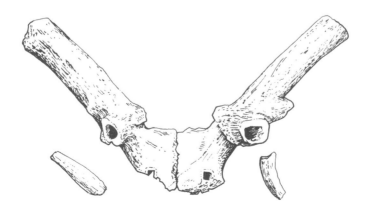

obverse bears the image of an antlered human face,[117] and the cross-legged antlered figure on the Danish Gundestrup cauldron (Fig. 59),[118] both appear to depict beings wearing masks, again as if to represent dressed-up people. The stag-men, probably dating to the early Iron Age, in the rock art of Camonica Valley in northern Italy may also represent ritualists in the guise of animals.[119] The antlered image at Gundestrup and many similar creatures depicted on stonework or metalwork from Roman-period Gaul and Britain are depicted seated cross-legged, an attitude that, at the same time, appears to represent sitting on the ground and, perhaps medita-tion or trance. Many such images wear torcs, a motif probably to be associated with special status, and some – for instance those from Autun and Sommerécourt – have detachable antlers, as if to signify seasonal change.[120] A unique bronze image dating to the second or first century BC, from Bouray, Essonne, France (Plate 22), depicts a human adorned with a great neck-ring, seated cross-legged; he is not antlered but his legs end in stag-hooves.[121]

Hybrid creatures are not merely confined to deer/humans in Iron Age and Roman Europe. Several pre-Roman Gallic coin issues, particularly in Brittany, depict a curious horse with a human face, driven or ridden by a horsewoman; a sim-ilar monster is represented on a flagon-lid from Reinheim in Germany, part of the grave-furniture of a high-ranking woman buried with great ceremony in the fourth century BC.[122] The bronze-bound wooden bucket interred in a rich late Iron Age tomb at Aylesford in Kent[123] bears the images of two 'pantomime' horses, clearly people wearing costumes. The late temple dedicated to the British hunter/healer god Nodens at Lydney on the river Severn[124] contained a number of votive objects in the form of dog images; one of them has a human face (Fig. 89).[125] Like deer, both horses and dogs might be regarded as boundary-crossing, transformative motifs: both are sensitive to precognition; each has a close and symbiotic relationship with humans and both were involved in warfare and hunting, transitional activities asso-ciated with abrupt transference between life and death. Inscriptions describe Nodens as a hunter and a healer, both related to altered states of being. Animals like these may well represent transformed shamans or spirit-animals, shamanic helpers paving the way for the soul-journey between worlds.

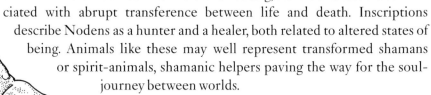

89 *Late Romano-British human-faced bronze dog-figurine from Lydney.*

One striking feature of traditional shamanistic art is the image of animals emerging from human figures. Patricia Sutherland[126] has alluded to this phenomenon in the context of Palaeo-Eskimo art, which appears to depict the theme of the shaman in a trance state experiencing the mind-altered perception that he or she is becoming a particular beast: similar themes occur in Bronze Age rock art (see Chapter 4). John Creighton[127] has drawn attention to some suggestive Iron Age coin imagery, notably that of a human head showing a horse disappearing into one ear and emerging from the other. Many coin issues depict boars standing on top of human heads, or wolves and boars riding horses,[128] perhaps reflective of similar trance experiences. The later Iron Age figure of a torc-wearing individual, with a great erect-crested boar striding along his torso from Euffigneix, Haute-Marne (see chapter 5, Fig. 62), may best be explained in this manner; indeed, most Iron Age boar images are depicted with prominent dorsal bristles, and this may represent danger or even death-trauma; in Namibian rock art, shamanic spirit-animals are represented thus, to indicate that they are dead or spirit-creatures.[129]

THE THREE-TIERED COSMOS: SEEING WITH THE INWARD EYE

> The meticulous naturalism of the details and the arbitrary combination of their relationship which surrealism copies from the dream, not only express the feeling that we live on two different levels, on two different spheres, but also that these regions of being penetrate one another so thoroughly that the one can neither be subordinated to nor set against the other as its antithesis.
>
> Arnold Hauser, *The Social History of Art*[130]

In the final section of this chapter, we wish to revisit the theme of surreality, introduced early on in the context of identifying shamanistic perception. The half-human, half-animal beings just discussed exemplify one aspect of surreality, in so far as each element in the blend is based upon nature; it is their mingling that creates disturbance, the idea of change and transformation so fundamental to the shamanic identity. But other forms of distortion may also be relevant to this enquiry; alongside the human/animal image, the repertoire of Iron Age and Roman European representation includes depictions that exhibit exaggeration, asymmetry and multiplication, all of which may be associated with trance imagery and perceptions of the spirit-world.[131] It is thus that we might venture to explain the exaggerated antlers on the stags depicted on the Iron Age rock art at Camonica Valley[132], the huge boar-crests on coins[133] and the enormously disporportionate heads on iconography such as the Bouray bronze figure[134] and the goddess from the Roman town of Caerwent.[135]

One of the most recurrent forms of surreal iconography is triplism, a schema that may be manifest in the presentation of whole figures, heads, horns or other

90 *Triple-head pot, Bavay (Nord), France.*

91 *Triple-horned bronze head from Hafenturm, Germany.*

body-parts. Whilst only conjecture, it could be that triplistic imagery relates to the shamanistic idea of the three-tiered cosmos – the lower world of the dead, the middle world of humans, beasts and materiality and the upper, spiritual domain. This notion of a triplistic universe, its layers – vertical or horizontal – permeable by shamans, is a widespread, recurrent cosmological concept. It is therefore quite possible that triadic iconography (Fig. 90) is associated with such a world-view. In terms of animal imagery, triple horns appear not only on Gallo-British bull-images of the Roman period but also on boars, horses and people (Fig. 91), the last two forms first occurring in the later Iron Age.[136] The linkage between triadic and hybrid human/ animal imagery is demonstrated by certain Gallo-Roman antlered human figures that are either themselves triple-headed or associated with three-faced beings: carvings from Autun and Bolards[137] exhibit this relationship.

One divine being popular in Gallo-British contexts is Mercury, a god who, in his persona as winged messenger and leader of dead souls, may well be grounded in shamanistic tradition. Mercury is not infrequently depicted in Gallo-Roman contexts as a triple-faced image,[138] and the votive assemblage from one of the most interesting Romano-British healing sanctuaries to have been investigated recently at Walsingham in Norfolk includes several representations of Mercury,[139] together with a curious bronze image of a person wearing a triple-horned cap (Fig. 92), rather similar to the schematic bust from a late Iron Age context at Hafenturm in Germany (Fig. 91)[140] and a stone carving from a Gallo-Roman healing shrine at Beire-le-Chatel in Burgundy.[141] The link between Mercury and shamanism is further supported by a little bronze image of the god found with a host of other figurines in a pot with late Roman coins at Southbroom in Wiltshire (Fig. 93).[142] The traditional Roman Mercury usually carries emblems that form part of a stock set of motifs, including a moneybag and a *caduceus* (herald's staff) or, sometimes, an offering-plate. But on the Wiltshire figure, the purse is inverted so that it resembles a rattle and in his other hand he holds a mirror; both these attributes would fit well within a shamanistic context: the rattle perhaps – like the shamanic drum – symbolic of the repetitive sound used to induce trance and summon the spirits, as testified by the rattle's significance in North American shamanism.[143] The rattle identified in the Romano-British religious context at Felmingham Hall, Norfolk (Fig. 54),[144] may have been used in this way. As we saw

92 *Bronze head wearing triple-horned cap, Walsingham, Norfolk.*

93 *Bronze figurine of Mercury with rattle, Southbroom, Wiltshire.*

earlier (Chapter 5), mirrors are found in a distinctive group of late Iron Age female graves in Britain, and may have been devices to show the double-consciousness of the ritualist who journeys between worlds and sees into both.

CONCLUSION

An exploration into the world of shamans and ritualists within the Classical world takes us into a peopled past; in other words, the presence of a rich literary tradition enables us to get closer to the object of our quest than is the case for earlier periods when, except for the end of the Iron Age, we are entirely reliant upon archaeological testimony. In this chapter, we have been able to use a combination of literature and material culture in order to build up a picture of ancient holy men and women, their ritual practice and the belief-systems that underpinned their activities. We have seen how Greek and Roman myth and religious texts abound with visionaries, soothsayers and 'two-spirit' persons, who meandered between the worlds of mortals and the spirits, and we have drawn attention to the importance placed on the religious interpretation of dreams and visions, themes not so far removed from the experience of the traditional shaman.

Two ideas dominate the discussion of both literature and iconography, both concerned with transition and each perhaps associated with the role of the shaman as a boundary-crosser: the depiction of ancient ritualists as trans-species and trans-gender persons. Shape-shifting between human and animal and between female and male results in the creation of new genders and new, monstrous types of being, both of which are associated with being different, being other and with belonging to earth-world and spirit-world. Furthermore, the archaeology provides us with evidence for toolkits, including medical equipment, associated with ritual burials and for the regalia that belonged to holy people in Roman and post-Roman Europe. Finally, we point to the prevalence of triplism in religious imagery, a phenomenon that can be explained, perhaps, in terms of a familiar shamanic idea, that of the three-tiered cosmos, a triple-layered universe inhabited by spirits, humans and dead ancestors or maleficent forces.

7 MYTHS AND MAGIC
Shape-Shifting and Shamanism in Early Celtic Literature

T he Warp-Spasm overtook him: it seemed each
hair was hammered into his head, so sharply they
shot upright. You would swear a fire-speck
tipped each hair. He squeezed one eye narrower
than the eye of a needle; he opened the other
wider than the mouth of a goblet. He bared
his jaws to the ear; he peeled back his lips
to the eye-teeth till his gullet showed. The
hero-halo rose up from the crown of his head.

The Táin[1]

It is thus that the Ulsterman Fergus describes the young Cú Chulainn when he was
about seven years old. The *Táin Bó Cúailnge* is part of a body of early medieval
mythic literature compiled in prose form by Irish and Welsh clerical redactors,
working in monastic establishments between the eleventh and fourteenth centuries. For us their interest lies in their accounts of legendary episodes and
characters clearly resonating with shamanic practice and identity. Many beings are
presented as liminal or boundary creatures, belonging both to the 'real' and supernatural worlds. Animals and people merge seamlessly one into the other; beasts
recurrently act as entrées to the otherworld. Individual heroes, like Cú Chulainn,
display idiosyncratic behaviour that mark them out as touched by the spirits: we
return to him later on in this chapter.

Several leitmotifs within the myths can be discerned that betray a possible
shamanistic origin. The most prominent of such *topoi* is transmogrification, the

ability of particular beings to shape-shift or skin-turn between human and animal form (especially wild animals, such as wolves, boars, deer and birds), and sometimes between genders; beasts and people may, in certain circumstances, understand each other's speech. The symbolism of colour is also important and, in particular, the imagery of piebald, speckled pelts, feathers and human hair, as evocative of double identities, 'two-spirits', creatures with a foot in the realms of both sacred and profane. In both Irish and Welsh medieval texts, animals emanating from the otherworld may be red and white. In Insular tradition, there are specific references to Druids, seers and diviners who predict the future while wearing speckled feather-cloaks or mantles of dappled animal-skins.

Clearly, the medieval vernacular myths need to be approached with care. We are never brought face-to-face with unequivocal shamans. Yet the resonances are strong (see Chapter 6) and, whether or not these mythic traditions had their genesis deep in the roots of pre-Christian paganism, there is close linkage between human and spirit-worlds throughout the myths, and accounts of particular beings who fulfilled many of the criteria associated with being a shaman: shape-changing, gender-bending, affinity with certain species of animal, possession, divinatory abilities and, above all, exhibition of being 'plugged-in' to the supernatural world. A good example is the Irish tradition of the *tarbhfhess* or 'bull-sleep', a divinatory ritual described in the mythic literature associated with what Piers Vitebsky has called a 'soul-journey', with the specific function, in the Insular context, of predicting the future ruler of Ireland: in this ceremony, a chosen individual is fed with sacrificial bull-flesh and broth, goes to sleep and experiences a vision of the next king, while Druids chant over him.[2]

SHAMANS AND BOUNDARY-CROSSERS IN WELSH MYTHOLOGY

Encounters with Otherworlds

> And he [Pwyll] could see a clearing in the wood as of a level field, and as his pack [of hounds] reached the edge of the clearing, he could see a stag in front of the other pack. And towards the middle of the clearing, lo, the pack that was pursuing it overtaking it and bringing it to the ground. And then he looked at the colour of the pack … and of all the hounds he had seen in the world, he had seen no dogs the same colour as these. The colour that was on them was a brilliant shining white, and their ears red; and as the exceeding whiteness of the dogs glittered, so glittered the exceeding redness of their ears …
>
> The First Branch of the *Mabinogi*[3]

The context for the above-quoted passage is the setting for an encounter between earth- and spirit-worlds. Pwyll is lord of Dyfed and, while out hunting with his hounds, he meets a foreign pack of dogs with a stag (Fig. 94) at bay, drives them off and steals their quarry, thus provoking the wrath of the strange hunter, who reveals himself to Pwyll as Arawn, lord of the otherworld, Annwfn. Arawn's identity is no surprise: the storyteller describes the weird appearance of his hounds, unlike any earthly beasts ever seen. This opening episode to the tale of Pwyll is important in so far as it sets off a series of encounters between the worlds of humans and supernatural beings. Arawn's dogs may be understood as dream-animals: their shimmering bi-coloured coats suggest as much. Pwyll atones for his hunting misconduct by taking Arawn's place in Annwfn for a year and by slaying Arawn's underworld enemy Hafgan. Significantly, on his return to Dyfed, Pwyll bears a new name, lord of Annwfn. The entire episode may be viewed as a visionary experience undergone by someone marked out as a soul-traveller, a shaman who visits the spirits and enjoys a special relationship with their domain.

The suggested identification of Pwyll as a shaman depends not simply upon his sojourn in Annwfn but also on his marriage to Rhiannon, the focus for the second half of the First Branch. The circumstances of his meeting with his future wife are highly charged and, from descriptions of her persona, we are led to infer that she comes from the otherworld.[4] Indeed, the place from which Pwyll first sets eyes on Rhiannon is demonstrably a liminal spot, a point of interaction between sacred and earthly domains, a mound named Gorsedd Arberth;[5] anyone who sits upon it is assured of a magical happening, either physical assault or a vision of something wondrous (depending, one assumes, upon whether the individual concerned is in tune or in conflict with spirit-forces). Pwyll announces that he is unafraid of what might befall him on the mound and rightly predicts that he will experience a wonder.

As he takes his seat there, he sees Rhiannon 'on a big pale white horse, with a garment of shining gold brocaded silk upon her, coming along the highway that led past the mound'. What occurs next betrays Rhiannon's supernatural

94 *Bronze stag from a ritual deposit made in the first century* BC *at Neuvy-en-Sullias, France.*

95 *The pre-Christian Gaulish horse-goddess Epona, from Kastel, Germany.*

96 OPPOSITE *Bronze boar-figurine from Gaer Fawr, Pembrokeshire, Wales.*

origins, for when Pwyll directs a courtier to intercept her, the horsewoman evades him with ease, even when the swiftest horse is ridden and when her own mount seems to be ambling. When Pwyll himself gallops after her, even he is powerless to apprehend her until he speaks to her; then she reins in her horse and replies that she has been searching for him. The upshot of the encounter is the marriage of Pwyll and Rhiannon.

This episode is a complex and multi-layered narrative, carrying with it a considerable body of imagery that may be applicable to shamanistic traditions. Pwyll himself has sojourned in the otherworld and is therefore already special, 'sensitized' to the supernatural dimension. He goes to an 'edgy' location which has a reputation for enabling visionary experience, and he sees what is clearly a supranormal being, a 'dream-woman'. Indeed, Rhiannon may be interpreted as a deity, perhaps a goddess of sovereignty, personification of the land and its prosperity.[6] She is essentially linked with horses, an association recurring in the persona of her son, Pryderi, and in various penances to which she is subjected, both in the First and Third Branches.[7] The symbolism of the horse as an otherworld creature[8] has been touched upon in previous chapters; the identification of Rhiannon with the pre-Christian Gaulish horse-goddess Epona (Fig. 95) is also significant, in terms of the former's divine origins. Pwyll is not divine himself but his close encounters with supernatural beings – first Arawn and then Rhiannon – suggest an ability to make contact with the spirit-world that has echoes in the role of the shaman. Indeed, Pwyll's half-hidden powers as a ritualist are, perhaps, hinted at in that words spoken by him are the only means of halting Rhiannon's mount; Piers Vitebsky[9] reminds us that 'the power of words lies not only in their meaning but in their musical effect', like chanting or drumming.

Some Welsh shape-shifters

The Fourth Branch of the *Mabinogi* has been interpreted[10] as a Creation or Origin myth. The story is set in Gwynedd, and the main *dramatis personae* are clearly supernatural entities, for they all demonstrate instability, transgression of boundaries and close affinities with the spirit-world. The central character is Math, lord of Gwynedd, a curious figure who possesses a magical wand and a strange quirk in so far as – except when at war or asleep – he must sit with his feet in the lap of a virgin. This peculiarity probably relates to Math's rulership as dependent upon a ritual union with the land itself, in a myth of sovereignty; if this were so, then the virginity of his footholder makes sense in terms of the symbolism of maiden purity and the potency of undissipated female sexuality. The catalyst for the unfolding story is the treachery of Math's two nephews, Gwydion and Gilfaethwy, who conspire to send their uncle off to war, thus leaving the virgin footholder, Goewin, at the mercy of Gilfaethwy's lust, a clear challenge to Math's rule. When he returns, Math punishes the brothers in a singular and significant manner: for three consecutive years, he transforms the youths into pairs of wild animals, hind and stag, boar and wild sow (Fig. 96) and wolf and she-wolf respectively, the genders changing over on each occasion. Math himself does not skin-turn but he is able to exact vengeance on his relatives by inducing their transmogrification.[11]

Later in the story, both Math and Gwydion exhibit their powers as magicians, in their conjurement of a supernatural wife for Gwydion's nephew Lleu, following the curse imposed on him by his mother Aranrhod, who has sworn that he will never marry a human woman.[12] One of us (MAG) has proposed elsewhere that the reason for Aranrhod's hatred of her son is probably best understood in terms of his probable conception as the result of incest between his mother and her brother Gwydion.[13] Math and Gwydion override the curse by producing for him Blodeuwedd, the 'flower-woman', made from the blooms of the oak, broom and meadowsweet. But because Blodeuwedd is not of the earth, she lacks human morals and she is both adulterous and murderous to her husband, plotting with her lover Gronw to kill him. Blodeuwedd's image is of a wild, anarchic creature born – significantly – of three wild plants that grow in different habitats, at different times

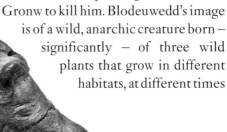

of the year perhaps, thus, encompassing space and time; the inclusion of the mead-owsweet ('medesweet') may have connections with mead and the uncontrolled behaviour induced by intoxication. Lleu himself deserves scrutiny as a marginal, boundary-crossing being, particularly in the paradoxical manner in which he can be killed:

'I cannot be slain within a house', said he, 'nor can I outside. I cannot be slain on horse-back, nor can I a-foot'. 'Why,' said she, 'in what manner then couldst thou be slain?' 'I will tell thee,' said he. 'By making a bath for me on a river bank, and making a vaulted frame over the tub, and thatching it well and snugly too thereafter, and bringing me a he-goat,' said he, 'and setting it beside the tub, and myself placing one foot on the back of the he-goat and the other on the edge of the tub. Whoever should smite me when so, he would bring about my death.'

The Fourth Branch of the *Mabinogi*[14]

The curious circumstances under which Lleu can die betray his origins as a being on the edge, halfway between human and spirit. This marginality is made even more distinctive in his fate after he is fatally injured by Gronw during his (somewhat naive) demonstration to his wife of his vulnerability for, mortally wounded by a poisoned spear-thrust, he gives a great howl and flies away in the shape of an eagle (Fig. 97).[15] The shape-changing theme is pursued in this final episode of the Fourth Branch: Gwydion comes upon Lleu, in his bird-form, perched in an oak tree and sings him down with magical poetry, changing him back to man-shape with a touch of his magic wand; he punishes Gronw with death but, since Blodeuwedd is not human, she cannot die and so Gwydion condemns her to live in perpetuity as an owl, a creature of the darkness, shunned and persecuted by all other birds.[16]

97 *Bronze figurine of an eagle from Woodeaton Romano-British temple-site, Oxfordshire.*

The shamanic cauldron: Brân and Ceridwen

I will give thee a cauldron, and the virtue of the cauldron is this: a man of thine slain to-day, cast him into the cauldron, and by tomorrow he will be as well as he was at the best, save that he will not have the power of speech

The Second Branch of the *Mabinogi* [17]

Brân, lord of Harlech, owner of this enchanted cauldron, is a larger-than-life figure, too massive for a house to contain him and able to wade across the sea from Wales to Ireland. The story tells of the cauldron's origins in Ireland, borne from a lake by a monstrous couple, and its sojourn in water brings to mind the watery deposition of Iron Age cauldrons, such as those from Carlingwark in Scotland and Llyn Fawr in South Wales. [18] Brân gives the vessel to Matholwch, king of Ireland, as reparation for a great insult done to him by Brân's half-brother Efnisien while a guest at Harlech, a visit designed to celebrate Matholwch's engagement to Brân's sister Branwen. Matholwch accepts the gift but later uses it as a weapon against the army of Harlech when war is declared over the Irish king's treatment of Branwen, restoring his warriors to life in the magical vessel. Finally, Efnisien atones for his role in starting the conflict between Wales and Ireland by jumping into the cauldron, stretching himself out inside it and bursting it to pieces. [19]

The story of Brân's cauldron is one of many medieval legends in which cauldrons are endowed with powers of death, rebirth and knowledge. [20] This particular vessel regenerates people slain in battle but since the reborn are no longer able to speak, they are marked out as still in thrall to the world of the dead; they are otherworld zombies, undead persons, lent back to earth-world but belonging to the spirits. As the vessel's owner, Brân is ultimately responsible for its transformatory powers and this, together with his supranormal physique suggest that this medieval mythic character contains remnants of a shamanic persona. What is more, at the end of the Second Branch, when both Ireland and Wales have been brought to their knees by the war, Brân meets a special death: mortally wounded in the foot by a poisoned spear, he commands that his head be cut off and carried by his followers for nearly a hundred years before being buried in London, its face towards France so as to repel any invaders from the east. Brân prophesies that the severed head would 'be as pleasant company to you as ever it was at best when it was on me' [21] and would remain uncorrupted all through its long journey to its final resting-place. The regeneration scene, described in this story, bears a strong resemblance to the Gundestrup cauldron 'army-plate' wherein a huge individual dips a warrior into a vat, while others line up behind (Fig. 64).

Another cauldron-keeper was Ceridwen, whose story is told in a myth preserved in a thirteenth-century text known as the Book of Taliesin, named after the famous sixth-century poet-prophet and thought to contain early elements. [22] Ceridwen is presented as a sorceress, keeper of the cauldron of knowledge in which she brews a magical stew of inspiration, designed as a gift for her ill-favoured son Afagddu as compensation for his ugliness. She appoints a young boy, Gwion, to watch over the vessel during the year the brew will take to cook but some drops of the boiling liquid splash onto his finger and, as he licks his sore hand, he unwittingly cheats Afagddu of his inheritance, imbibing the cauldron's wisdom instead. Like Brân's vessel, Ceridwen's cauldron explodes, leaving her son nothing and, in her rage, she chases Gwion, skin-turning both herself and the boy as she pursues him: she changes into various hunting animals and Gwion becomes her prey; finally she turns herself into a hen, Gwion into a wheat-grain and eats him. He is reborn to Ceridwen nine months later but her desire to murder him at birth cools when she sees how beautiful he is, so she leaves him afloat in a coracle to die or be rescued and he is recovered and brought up by a courtier of King Maelgwn of Gwynedd (a historically authentic ruler who died in AD 547), given the name of Taliesin and growing up to become the greatest satirist, poet and prophet in Wales.

Both Ceridwen and Gwion/Taliesin are clearly supernatural beings, endowed with the shamanic properties of shape-changing, prophecy and magic. Ceridwen can cast spells and has power over the gift of knowledge; Taliesin is utterly wise; his prophecies at Maelgwn's court are divinely inspired, as is his poetry. Taliesin and the Arthurian 'wizard' Merlin[23] were perceived as significant seers by early medieval thinkers: Taliesin, for instance, is presented as a historical figure, endowed with magical and prognosticatory (future-telling) powers.[24] Rachel Bromwich argues that in later Welsh poetic tradition Merlin was regarded as a genuine soothsayer;[25] he is depicted as a 'wild man' prophet associated with the deliverance of conquered lands from external oppressors,[26] just as the Gallo-British Druids were closely connected with freedom-fighters against Rome in the first centuries BC/AD.[27] The way that Taliesin received his wisdom from Ceridwen's cauldron of wisdom is significant, for it follows a pattern associated with other medieval seers, in both Irish and Norse myth,[28] in which prognosticatory, divinatory inspiration is heralded by placing the thumb or finger in the mouth. So Taliesin, the Irish seer Finn and Odin's pupil Sigurd all acquire wisdom by sucking a thumb or finger that has touched sacred food. Whilst it can be no more than pure speculation, it is worth noting that one of the Lindow bog bodies, decapitated and placed in a Cheshire peat marsh during the second century AD, had a vestigial extra thumb on his surviving right hand. It has been argued elsewhere[29] that physical abnormalities such as this might have led to the selection of sacrificial victims in pagan European antiquity, and that such persons might have enjoyed special status,

98 OPPOSITE   *Gilded silver cult cauldron from Gundestrup, Denmark. The vessel depicts mythological scenes on its thirteen decorated plates; it was dismantled and deliberately deposited on a small dry island within a bog at Raevemose, Jutland.*

perhaps as shamans, within their communities (we should remember that Anne Boleyn's extra finger was cited as evidence that she was a witch).[30]

Hilda Davidson[31] draws attention to an Irish divinatory ritual recorded in Cormac's ninth-century Glossary, known as the *imbas forosnai*, in which a seer in search of inspiration has to chew a piece of raw meat from a pig, a dog or a cat, then place it on a flagstone behind the door and chant an invocation to the spirits. In the context of a link between eating and divine knowledge, the cauldron attains particular significance, for it is the source of magical food.[32] In his study of traditional shamanistic practices, Piers Vitebsky reproduces a picture painted by a Peruvian Amazon shaman while under the influence of vision-inducing narcotics, wherein is depicted a group of other shamans seated cross-legged around a cauldron in which a hallucinogenic plant is being boiled.[33] In its broadest, most generic sense, the cauldron can be understood as the source of inspiration, knowledge, wisdom and entry to the otherworld dimension. Both the cauldron and the ritualist are the means by which earth-world and spirit-world meet. Ceridwen is both keeper of the cauldron and the cauldron (Fig. 98) itself: her cauldron contains the nourishment needed for the enlightenment of the human soul; her womb nourishes Taliesin, the Inspired One. The cauldron – perhaps in many traditions – can be seen in the context of a shamanic worldview, a symbol of the cosmos and the relationship between people and their universe.

SPIRITS, SEERS AND SOUL-JOURNEYS IN IRISH MYTHIC TRADITION

Between the seventh and twelfth centuries AD, Christian clerics working in Irish monasteries committed to writing a large and diverse body of mythical tradition, whose origins may have lain partly in court-storytelling (itself drawing upon ancestral memory), partly in monastic invention (for polemical, anti-pagan purposes) and partly in archaic resonances of pagan belief and ritual practice. In a study such as this, it is impossible to explore all medieval prose tales; rather we have chosen to examine one or two key texts and, in particular, the Ulster Cycle tale known as the *Táin Bó Cúailnge*, an epic myth that may have one of the earliest origins of all the Insular prose tales. James Mallory has described the *Táin* as presenting a picture of early medieval Ireland, fleshed out with detail from material culture from around the seventh century AD. But he and others[34] agree that these clerical 'redactors' of the myths used much earlier traditions as points of reference and that the *Táin* contains cosmogonic material associated with stories of creation. Of interest to us, in the search for ancient shamans, is the presence in these medieval Ulster tales of beings whose personae almost certainly owe much to shamanistic characteristics. The *Táin* and other coeval texts are full of references to heroic individuals or religious practitioners who are clearly in constant touch with the spirit-world and who exhibit the marginality or instability inherent in the traditional shaman; they are powerful, dangerous, and live on the edges of society: revered, feared and regarded with unease. In Classical tradition, figures like Orpheus, the musician,[35] who journeyed between the worlds of the living and the dead, may be cited as comparable beings.

Cú Chulainn: the 'warped man'

The main story-line of the *Táin Bó Cúailnge* is the bitter conflict between the two great Irish provinces of Ulster and Connacht, hostilities ostensibly sparked off by a contest over ownership of two huge, supernatural bulls. The Ulster champion is the young hero Cú Chulainn, a clearly liminal being with at least one foot in the spirit-world. Three aspects of his life, above all, mark him out as someone with a shamanic dimension: his journey to the otherworld, his affinity with shape-changing divinities and his own transformative, ambiguous nature. The expedition to the world of the dead has features in common with other hero-tales, notably that of Aeneas, legendary founder of Rome, whose visit to Hades to find his father Anchises is told in Book Six of the Augustan poet Virgil's *Aeneid*. Like Aeneas, Cú Chulainn is in danger from the spirit-lands because he is still alive and belongs to the realm of humans, and for both Aeneas and the Ulster champion, this element of risk is demonstrated by the hideous apparitions they encounter while in this alien world. Cú Chulainn is an unstable figure and his visit to the otherworld may be understood as a shamanic 'soul-journey', a voyage of the spirit,[36] perhaps while in an altered state of consciousness. The hero's affinity with the gods is shown time and again by his meetings with the battle-furies, the Morrigán and the Badbh: these are skin-turners, oscillating both between youth and old age and between woman and raven form, the former presumably relating to the ability of these beings to move between times as well as between species. The relationship between him and the goddesses is unstable: they help and protect him but, should he show his independence from them, they harm him. When he is on the point of death, the Badbh alights on his shoulder as a carrion bird, signalling the passage of his spirit from earth to underworld.

Cú Chulainn exhibits his 'boundary' symbolism or marginality in several ways. He is, on the one hand, very male, a warrior hero so strong that he breaks almost every weapon he touches; yet he is of almost feminine prettiness, with long braided stripy yellow hair and beardless. He spurns the Morrigán when she tries to seduce him and, when in a berserk state, he is shamed into his own mind again only by the approach of the naked Ulsterwomen. At one and the same time, he is made uneasy by raw female sexuality but his own androgynous persona upsets the older male heroes, such as Fergus and Conall.[37] There is a sense, too, in which Cú Chulainn exhibits species instability as well as gender-ambivalence: one episode, that serves to explain his change of name from Setanta (his birth-name), recounts how – as a young boy – he kills the watch dog of Culann the Smith while in a rage. In reparation for his violence, he elects to act as Culann's hound and guard the smith's forge, so he becomes Cú Chulainn – the Hound of Culann. His image as a transformative being is summed up in the *Táin* by Scáthach, a prophetess and the hero's weapons-trainer, when she describes his 'sweet shape-changing bright body'.[38]

It is the strange transformation that the young hero undergoes while in 'warp-spasm' – first occurring when he is a small child[39] – that excites the greatest interest in this complex mythic character. The quotation opening this chapter describes what happens to Cú Chulainn in brief, but there is a more detailed account worth quoting in full, for it presents a vivid image of liminality and boundary-transgression:

> The first warp-spasm seized Cú Chulainn, and made him into a monstrous thing, hideous and shapeless, unheard of. His shanks and his joints, every knuckle and organ from head to foot, shook like a tree in the flood or a reed in the stream. His body made a furious twist inside his skin, so that his feet and shins and knees switched to the rear and his heels and calves switched to the front ... On his head the temple-sinews stretched to the nape of his neck, each mighty, immense, measureless knob as big as the head of a month-old child. His face and features became a red bowl: he sucked one eye so deep into his head that a wild crane couldn't probe it onto his cheek out of the depths of his skull; the other eye fell out along his cheek. His mouth weirdly distorted: his cheek peeled back from his jaws until his gullet appeared, his lungs and liver

flapped in his mouth and throat, his lower jaw struck the upper a lion-killing blow, and fiery flakes large as a ram's fleece reached his mouth from his throat. His heart boomed loud in his breast like the baying of a watch-dog at its feed ... The hair of his head twisted like the tangle of a red thornbush stuck in a gap ...

The Táin[40]

This description, however exaggerated, appears to represent someone in the grip of an altered physical and mental state that could well derive, in origin at least, from observation of someone in the throes of a trance-induced visionary experience.[41] He exhibits classic signs of liminality, of belonging to two worlds, of being a two-spirit person; his body is turned inside-out, his internal organs are revealed, his entire physique is disarranged and normal symmetry disintegrates into lopsided asymmetry. Interestingly, the image presented here appears to display to an onlooker the signs of someone in an altered state of consciousness while, simultaneously, exhibiting imagery that might be seen by a ritualist during a trance experience: in other words, Cú Chulainn is presented as both visionary and vision.

The physical symptoms of the Ulster hero's warp-spasm or berserk state find resonance with iconographic representations that may be understood as divine or shamanic. The inversion of his body and the consonant visibility of his innards is highly reminiscent of the 'skeleton' figures depicted in the prehistoric rupestrine art of, for instance, Australia and Namibia[42] that are interpreted as evocative of shamanic vision-experience. Closer to home, in some of the Gallo-Roman healing sanctuaries, such as *Fontes Sequanae* in Burgundy and Chamalières in the Auvergne, anthropomorphic wooden images depict torsos with internal organs on display.[43] Likewise, Cú Chulainn's asymmetry – particularly that of his eyes – may be compared with somatic treatment found in both iconography and other mythic traditions (see Chapter 5). Apart from their very obvious sexuality, the odd female carved figures adorning so many medieval stone buildings (including churches), especially in Ireland, known as Sheela-Na-Gigs, frequently exhibit marked facial asymmetry: the image decorating Ballinacarriga Castle in Co. Cork is an example.[44] This kind of eye asymmetry, with one eye sunk and the other bulging, could relate to the shamanic ability to see both inwards to the 'thought-world' of the supernatural and outwards to the material world. It was with intense interest

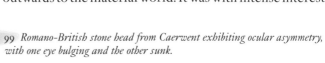

99 Romano-British stone head from Caerwent exhibiting ocular asymmetry, with one eye bulging and the other sunk.

that, during a recent scrutiny of a late Romano-British stone head studied many times (Fig. 99), one of us (MAG) realized that the head, found in a small shrine at the bottom of a town-house garden at Caerwent,[45] exhibits just this kind of ocular asymmetry. George Boon suggested that the head might have been the cult-property of people working in the household of a Christian who would have no truck with the pagan beliefs of his staff and relegated them to a place as far from his dwelling as possible. Incidentally, Cú Chulainn's physical peculiarities extend beyond his fits of warp-spasm and he is clearly presented as a 'special', suprahuman being:

> He had four dimples in each cheek – yellow, green, crimson and blue – and seven bright pupils, eye-jewels, in each kingly eye. Each foot had seven toes and each hand seven fingers.
>
> *The Táin*[46]

The additional digits on his feet and hands are interesting in the context of the apparent significance with which certain Iron Age people were regarded. Many bog bodies, understood by some scholars as sacrificial victims, show signs of physical abnormalities.[47] As we noted earlier, one of the Lindow bodies, interred in a Cheshire marsh in about AD 100, was that of a man with a vestigial extra thumb on his surviving right hand.

Prophecy and divination: some Irish seers

> 'I am Fedelma, and I am a woman poet of Connacht'
> 'Where do you come from?' Medb said.
> 'From learning verse and vision in Alba', the girl said.
> 'Have you the *imbas forosnai*, the Light of Foresight?' Medb said.
> 'Yes I have', the girl said.'
>
> *The Táin*[48]

Fedelma, the prophetess (Fig. 100), is a central figure in the *Táin*, whose main function is to prophesy Connacht's doom at the hand of Cú Chulainn. She is described as an otherworld being with long yellow hair, black eyelashes and eyebrows and three pupils in each eye. In her hand was a 'white-bronze' weaver's beam; she was dressed in a red-embroidered tunic and – significantly – a speckled cloak: in Irish mythical imagery, brindling (dappling) was a sign of belonging to the spirit-world, and – perhaps – signified liminality between earth and sacred realms. Fedelma's unusual colouring and strange eyes, so like those of Cú Chulainn, enhance her weirdness, and her presentation as an armed charioteer[49] upsets the 'normal' image of womanhood, as does the image of Medb herself. Indeed, in informing Medb that she hails from Alba, the prophetess is admitting to her otherworld status. Fedelma's prediction of Cú Chulainn's annihilation of Medb's army paints a chilling picture, which the Connacht queen is reluctant to accept. In answer to Medb's repeated question, 'Fedelma, prophetess, how seest thou the host?', the girl replies, 'I see it crimson, I see it red.' She describes the young hero thus:

> I see a battle: a fair man
> with much blood about his belt
> And a hero-halo around his head
> His brow is full of victories.

A very different kind of seer from Fedelma is the royal Ulster Druid Cathbadh, adviser to the court of King Conchobar. Cathbadh is a tutor to young heroes and he correctly predicts the fate of his pupil Cú Chulainn, pronouncing that 'He who arms for the first time today will achieve fame and greatness. But his life is short.' Conchobar's Druid makes other predictions about the future of Ulster, divining even before her birth that the beautiful Deirdre will bring about the ruin of the province.[50] Cathbadh interprets omens and proclaims the will of the gods and is held in greater awe than the king himself. In this way, he has a role almost identical to that of some Old Testament prophets, such as Samuel and Nathan, whose function was to mediate with God and curb the excesses of the king. When Samuel turned against Saul, the latter was doomed, for he had lost God's favour. The Biblical prophets were seers who knew things concealed from the rest of their community and possessed exceptional, suprahuman powers untrammelled by the constraints of space and time.[51] Like other Druids of Irish myth, Cathbadh's influence is expressed by his word-power; he is a satirist and can use speech to flay someone who crosses him or the gods.

In the same way as the Gaulish Druids of the first centuries BC and AD, Irish seers like Cathbadh were powerful political forces, at the forefront of matters concerning peace and war. They were crucial in determining future kings and used their connection with the gods to predict the correct person to succeed a deceased ruler. Their power is exemplified by the strange ritual of the *Tarbhfhess* or 'Bull Sleep', a mythical Druidic ceremony involving the sacrifice of a bull and the consumption of its meat by a chosen 'medium', who then fell asleep to the chanting of four Druids and dreamed of the next rightful king of Ireland. The implications of this curious ritual are firstly that the Druids invoked the spirit-forces in establishing the royal succession; secondly that the eating of bull-flesh in such a context induced a trance state and a very specific vision of the future, as if the meat itself acted as a psychotropic drug. The connection between bulls and supernatural power (Fig. 101)

100 *The Irish prophetess Fedelma, described in the early medieval prose tale* Táin Bó Cúailnge.

is understandable: cattle were the main measure-
ment of wealth in medieval Ireland, and the
numerous accounts of magical bulls and cows in the
mythic literature are testament to their almost
totemic symbolism. The *Táin* itself centres around
two supernatural bulls who were transmogrified swine-
herds, and possessed the ability to commune with the
spirits: in one episode, the Brown Bull of Ulster receives a
warning from the Badbh, one of the shape-shifting battle-
furies, who perches on his shoulder as a crow and whispers her advice to him.

Birdmen and soul-flights

> … if it is granted, say, that an animal can be turned into a piece of wood, bread into a
> stone, or a man into a bird, then none of these can remain firmly within the boundaries
> of its nature and we would be seen to assent to the ridiculous tales of *magi* who say that
> their ancestors were flying about in the substance of birds.
>
> Augustine, *de Mirabilis* [52]

So scorned a seventh-century Irish Christian cleric, mocking the notion of pagan
Druidic belief in the ability of their forebears to change into birds and fly to the
supernatural world. [53]

Birds play an important role in early Insular cosmologies; the medieval mythic
prose tales make repeated reference to the transmogrification of female war-spirits,
like the Badbh and the Morrigán, from human to carrion bird and it is frequently in
this theriomorphic state that they make contact with humans. The link between
birds and the spiritual domain is interesting and complex: the ability to fly has given
rise to the allegory of the human soul, freed from its body at death, to take flight and
join the ancestors in the otherworld. What is more, in many shamanistic systems,
flying may be associated with the shaman's soul-journey, undertaken while in
trance, when the seer can fly to the spirit-world: Siberian Tungus shamans were
depicted in the eighteenth century as having tails and wings. [54] In early Insular

101 ABOVE *Horned bronze head from Lezoux, France. This half-human, half-bull image is reminiscent of the
shape-shifters and supernatural bulls recorded in the* Táin.

102 OPPOSITE *Iron Age coin with two cranes, Maidstone.*

tradition, the image of birds as supernatural mediators was deeply entrenched in perceptions of the otherworld and in the imagery of ritualists in regular contact with that world. It may be that certain birds carried especially potent symbolism in this respect. Cranes (Fig. 102) figure in many of the myths: the Irish sea-god Manannán possessed a magical bag full of treasure made from the skin of a crane that had once been a woman, and Finn, mythic hero of the *Fenian Cycle* of tales, had a grandmother who saved him from falling over a cliff to his death as a lad, by turning herself into a crane and snatching him up in her beak while in flight. Adomnan's biography of the sixth-century Irish saint Columba, dated to *c.* AD 796, contains an account of his prophecy that an exhausted crane would arrive at Iona from the north coast of Ireland and that the monks must tend it and that when it had recovered they should send it on its way because 'it comes from the district of our fathers'.[55] The particular metaphoric value of cranes may be understood in terms of their observed behaviour in the natural environment, for not only are they wading-birds, thus combining association with flight and water, but they engage in social dancing;[56] they are also migrants and their disappearance for half the year might be perceived as reflective of their temporary sojourn in the otherworld and the shamanic soul-journey between human and sacred dimensions.

The Siege of Druim Damgaire is a medieval Irish mythic tale preserved in a fifteenth-century manuscript known as the Book of Lismore. It contains a fascinating account of a seer-shaman named Mog Ruith, a blind Druid whose magical powers were pitted against those of the Ulster king Cormac.[57] Mog Ruith's physical sightlessness marks him out as belonging to a widely recognized group of spirit-touched wise people whose inner vision is enhanced by their earthly blindness. Tiresias of Classical myth (see Chapter 6) is one of many ancient blind prophets; the Old Testament healer-seer Ahijah, consulted by the wife of the Israelite king Jeroboam,[58] was sightless, his powers dependent upon his ability to see into the supernatural world.[59] In preparation for contacting the spirits, Mog Ruith dons the hide of a brown bull, places a headdress of brindled feathers on his head and flies, chanting spells as he goes, to counteract the 'Druidic fire' conjured by King Cormac's own ritualists. His dappled feather headgear is significant in so far as piebald costumes, pelts or hair were coded messages to represent the shaman's liminal position between human and supernatural worlds (see above).

Mog Ruith (Fig. 103) was by no means the only bird-clad shaman recorded in the Insular literature. Cormac's ninth-century glossary[60] contains references to the wearing of bird-feather cloaks by Irish seer-poets:

> For it is of skins of birds white and many-coloured that the poet's toga is made from the girdle downwards, and of mallards' necks and crests from the girdle upwards to the neck.[61]

Once again, there is an allusion to speckled feathers but also to the iridescent plumage on the heads and necks of mallard ducks (Fig. 104), whose greeny-blue 'shot' feathers appear to change colour as the light catches them and thus provide an image of ambiguity and boundary-transference. The adoption of bird costumes symbolically transforms these Insular wise men and facilitates their soul-flight to divine the future from otherworld knowledge. Siberian shamans are recorded as being similarly attired,[62] and Joan Halifax[63] describes a female Finno-Ugrian shaman as performing rituals while clad in bird-dress.

The tale of *Da Derga's Hostel* (the *Togail Bruiden Da Derga*) is a medieval Irish text steeped in magic and the 'thought-world' of the shaman, that contains an account of King Conaire Mor, a mythical ruler closely associated with birds. Like many Insular kings and heroes, Conaire is bound by a series of divine prohibitions, known as *gessa* (sing. *geis*), pronounced at their rites of passage such as birth or assumption of sovereignty. Conaire's primary *geis* was an order not to kill birds. His father is described as a 'bird-man' who advised Conaire's mother of the injunction on the night of his conception.[64] This prohibition was attached to him throughout his lifetime and, on the occasion that he disobeyed the injunction and assailed a flock of birds, they immediately shed their feathers and mobbed him.[65] The text of the *Togail Bruiden* records the main series of *gessa* imposed upon Conaire Mor – when he is about to become king – by another bird-man, called Nemglan, a being about whom we are told little, although we can assume that, like Mog Ruith, he is a Druid-like prophet, a

103 OPPOSITE *Mog Ruith, the bird-man.*

104 RIGHT *Bronze image of a duck, Milber Down, Devon, England.*

shape-shifting shaman able to transfer between worlds as he can transform himself from human to animal shape. Tom Sjöblom[66] discusses the imposition of *gessa* on prominent Irish mythic figures – such as Conaire and Cú Chulainn – as being associated with their status as 'other': they were privileged, set apart, touched by the sacred and boundary-transgression and, as such, their powers required control by the seers, the shamanic mediators between people and the divine forces. Nemglan's role is 'that of a supersocietal controller of human society'.[67] Like Conaire, Cú Chulainn is proscribed by an animal-*geis*, that he must not eat dog-flesh, a prohibition presumably associated with his misdeed, while a young boy, when he kills Culann's hound and is subsequently renamed as the Hound of Culann, and with the connotations of cannibalism implied by breaking the injunction.

COMMUNING WITH ANIMALS

> Arthur said, 'Gwrhyr Interpreter of Tongues, it is right for thee to go on this quest. All tongues hast thou, and thou canst speak with some of the birds and the beasts.
>
> *Culhwch ac Olwen* [68]

The Tale of *Culhwch ac Olwen* belongs to the same group of medieval Welsh prose tales as the Four Branches of the *Mabinogi* and, indeed, may have origins as early as the tenth century. It is a quest tale in which the young hero Culhwch seeks to win the hand of Olwen by undergoing a set of Herculean tasks imposed on him by Olwen's father as a condition of his marriage, enlisting the help of his kinsman Arthur in so doing. The whole narrative is steeped in supernatural animal symbolism that involves shape-exchange, beasts with supernatural powers and cross-species communication. The very identity of Culhwch is essentially linked with animals, particularly pigs: the tale begins with an account of his mother who, when pregnant with him, went mad and ran dementedly around the countryside until she came to 'a place where a swineherd was keeping a herd of swine' and there gave birth, abandoning the baby to the pig-keeper. The child's guardian had him baptized and gave him the name Culhwch, meaning 'pig-run'. The association

197

between the boy and pigs (Fig. 105) continued: one of the most awesome tasks assigned to him by Olwen's father was to hunt the great boar Twrch Trwyth and extract the comb and shears lodged between the creature's ears. This animal is no ordinary beast but an erstwhile king shape-changed by God in punishment for his misdeeds. Needless to say, with Arthur's help, the great boar is overcome, after a chase covering Wales, Cornwall and Ireland.

In order to fulfil the 'impossible' conditions imposed on Culhwch by Olwen's father Ysbaddaden, the hero-band needs to find Mabon son of Modron, a Hound-Lord described as the youngest and oldest person in the world. In their search for him, Arthur and Culhwch turn for help to a range of supernatural animals, each more fabulous than the last. It is here that Gwrhyr, the tongue-master, comes into his own, for he is able to enlist aid from these creatures by speaking to them, Dr Doolittle-like, in their own language. Gwrhyr approaches the Ouzel of Cilgwri, the Stag of Rhedynfre, the Owl of Cwm Cawlwyd and the Eagle of Gwernabwy and they all agree to act as guides to the hunters. Finally, led by the Eagle, the band comes upon the wisest creature of all, the Salmon of Llyn Llyw who carries Gwrhyr and his companion Cei to the gates of the prison where Mabon is incarcerated.[69]

Culhwch ac Olwen is a dense, complex narrative that nonetheless contains one persistent thread, that of close linkage between animal, human and supernatural. We suspect that the genesis of the tale lies in resonances with an earlier, shamanic system in which animal-helpers aided liaison between upper and lower worlds. Elements in the story bear close resemblances to other episodes in Welsh myth relating to the involvement of beasts in enabling humans to access the spirit-world. Reference was made earlier in this chapter to Pwyll's encounter with the otherworld, a situation enabled by the hunted stag and Arawn's supernatural red-and-white hounds. In the Third Branch of the *Mabinogi*, Rhiannon's son Pryderi is enticed to the spirit-world by a magical boar – huge and shining white – which lures his hounds to pursue it, again acting as a go-between in order to bring about linkage between profane and sacred dimensions. It is clear in this context that animals were recognized as possessing special attributes not given to humans; they were in tune with the supernatural and through them gods could interact with people. Such a perspective is not too far removed from the notion of the shamanic animal-helper described in accounts of Siberian and other circumpolar religious traditions.

Medieval Irish mythology, too, has its share of animals that crossed the divide between earth and spirit domains, with far too many examples to examine here.[70] As in the Welsh narratives, the hunt is a prominent *topos* used in imaging encounters between humans and supernatural forces. Thus, in the twelfth-century Fenian Cycle, the eponymous hero Finn and his royal war-band the Fianna repeatedly come into contact with the otherworld while in pursuit of magical stags or boars,

---

105 *Bronze figurine of a dying boar, Muntham Court Roman temple, Sussex, England.*

their quarry acting as bait to entice earthly warriors to the world of the dead. In one tale, a ghost-woman from the *sídh* (an otherworld dwelling-place) of the god Donn mac Midir appears to Finn in the form of a fawn, acting as an intermediary to lure him to Donn's realm. Finn is an interesting mythic being in so far as his deer-imagery is persistent: his wife Sava is both doe and woman, and their son Oisín (Little Deer) retains an affinity with stags.[71] Finn is also intimately associated with wild boars: in one episode of the Fenian Cycle,[72] he is associated with a fierce wild boar known as the boar of Boann Ghulban, an animal with poison in his bristles. This creature is a shape-shifter: when the ageing Finn plots to rid himself of his young rival-in-love Diarmaid by persuading him to hunt the boar (and be killed by it), the animal turns out to be the young man's enchanted foster-brother.

Interestingly, the close affinity between humans and animals illustrated so graphically in the pagan myths of Wales and Ireland seeped into the early Christian tradition and several saints are recorded as having a close connection with 'animal-helpers'. One of these was Saint Ciarán of Saighir about whom a charming tale is told of his relationship with wild beasts, including a wild boar which, when tamed by the holy man, built a monastic cell using its teeth. It then joined other woodland creatures, a stag, a fox, badger and wolf as disciples of Ciarán and his fellow monks.[73] The Welsh female saint Dwynwen lived in the sixth century AD; she was a healer whose church and convent was established on the tiny island of Llanddwyn, off the Anglesey coast. Her holy well developed a reputation for curing all manner of diseases but was particularly effective in healing animals.[74] These early saints seem often to take on the mantle left by the pagan holy man or woman. Their affinity with wild creatures is just one way in which they resemble shamanistic beings; another is their marginality: their lives are frequently associated with belonging to the edges of society, as is the case with many seers, for instance in Japanese tradition.[75] They may be illegitimate, or of gentle and servile birth: Saint Brigit was the daughter of a nobleman and a slave; her mother gave birth to her on the threshold of her house and the Christian girl was brought up in a pagan Druid's household. The boundary-symbolism of Brigit is perhaps most evocatively displayed in her

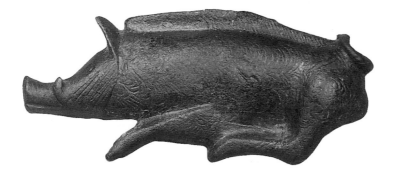

pagan/Christian persona: she was a goddess before she became a saint, and the seventh-century *Vita Brigitae* alludes to her nourishment with milk from an other-world cow.[76]

Liminal places and liminal times: living on the edge

> There is a distant isle,
> around which sea-horses glisten,
> a fair course on which the white wave
> surges,
> four pedestals uphold it....
>
> *Immram Brain* [77]

This chapter ends with consideration of shamanic perspectives associated with space and time. Richard Bradley[78] draws attention to the frequent use by traditional shamans of 'edgy' places, such as islands, caves, rivers, mountains or other marginal locations for sacrificial rituals. In terms of the early medieval Irish and Welsh mythic material, the same appears to be true. One of the most prominent images of access to the otherworld in the Insular literature is that of islands, powerful metaphors of liminality (Saint Dwynwen's island off an island is a good example of concentrated Insular symbolism). One important aspect of island-imagery concerns the need to make voyages over water to get to these remote places and, like the soul-flight of the shaman on its way to visit the spirit-world, the act of travelling is loaded with meaning, in terms of the search for enlightenment. This spiritual journey is well illustrated in early Christian Ireland by the motif of the *peregrinatio pro Dei amore*, the holy man's pilgrimage overseas to find God[79] undertaken by such early Christian clerics as the sixth-century Columbanus. The arduousness and peril of these voyages, the isolation and disjunction of the traveller from homeland and society, all contributed to the investment and gift of self-sacrifice and to the opportunity for contact with God.

It is interesting that this notion of sea journeys in search of the infinite is common both to early medieval Insular literature dealing with pagan myth and the lives of Christian saints. The clearest illustration of this commonality is in accounts of the voyages of Bran and St Brendan. The story of Bran is told in a seventh–eighth-century text known as the *Immram Brain* (the Voyage of Bran), the original (lost) manuscript of which was compiled at the monastic establishment of Druim Snechta.[80] Like Finn and Pwyll, Bran is a mortal hero lured by spirits to their world. He is enticed by sweet, enchanted music (Fig. 106) sung by a beautiful goddess and embarks on a voyage to the Happy Otherworld, a series of islands, the Land of Women, set in the western sea, a place where time stands still. In the early medieval Lives of Saint Brendan,[81] the eponymous cleric sets out in a coracle with fellow monks, in search of the Christian Isle of the Blessed which, once again, lies in the middle of the ocean. Brendan's first voyage-quest is a failure because, so his foster-mother tells him, he has 'attempted to reach so sacred a place in a vessel made of the (impure) skins of dead animals, instead of a boat made of wood'.[82] This detail in the story almost certainly contains echoes of an earlier, pre-Christian divinatory procedure, in which Druids or shamans, like Mog Ruith, used animal-skins in prophetic rituals presumably because of the perception of beasts as having especial affinity with the supernatural world.

If places could have spiritual meaning, in terms of access to the otherworld, so could time. The essential timelessness of Bran's Happy Otherworld has just been mentioned, and this suspension of the normal sequence of being is a common theme in the early Welsh and Irish mythic literature. The boundary-symbolism of medieval Insular socio-religious festivals is clear and well presented, for they occur at the edges of the seasons, when perceptible alterations of weather and daylight are particularly marked and important changes occurred in the farming year.[83] These festivals – Imbolc on 1 February, Beltane on 1 May, Lughnasadh in August and Samhain heralding winter at the end of October – were 'times of no being', when the normality of the everyday earthly world was frozen and the spirits were able to invade the human domain.

This encroachment of supernatural into natural worlds inverted order and produced a wild and forceful energy-field, where people lost control and weird events could take place. It is no coincidence that it was at these major seasonal festivals that significant, rite-of-passage events took place: the inauguration of kings, royal marriages, the forging of alliances and the declaration of war. Beltane welcomed in the summer, and was associated with transhumance and great Mayday bonfires through which, so the ninth-century commentator Cormac records, the Druids drove cattle, in a purificatory ritual that, at the same time, blessed the herds through contact with sacred fire, representative of the sun on earth. The first Druid to light a Beltane bonfire was named Mide; his fire spread all over the land of Ireland and, when the other Druids objected, Mide responded by cutting out their tongues, thereby rendering them powerless, for their ability to speak divinatory messages or satire was lost.

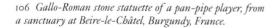

106 Gallo-Roman stone statuette of a pan-pipe player, from a sanctuary at Beire-le-Châtel, Burgundy, France.

Samhain was the context for a great assembly at the royal site of Tara in County Meath where, so the early medieval text tells us, both sacred and secular cere-monies were enacted, including the installation of the sacral king, the high king of Ireland who was believed to be as much a divinity as an earthly ruler. It was at Samhain that the superhuman heroes Cú Chulainn and Finn underwent their untimely and unnerving encounters with the world of the dead.[84]

These boundary-times were overseen by ritualists, by Druids, who alone could control both worlds and had the power to steer their communities through the minefield of lurking spirit-force and the undermining of frontiers between the sane, safe world of humans and the dangerous otherworld, so perilous to the living.

CONCLUSION

The rich assemblage of mythic literature from early medieval Wales and Ireland arguably contains a substantial body of pre-Christian material, and there is both overt and covert reference to religious specialists, including Druids, prophets, gender-switching and shape-changing characters of whom some, at least, would be familiar within a shamanic world-view. They are involved in healing, rebirth and divination; they have close affinities with animals and may have physical character-istics that mark them as special: Nemglan is a bird-man; so is Mog Ruith, who is also a blind seer; Fedelma has three pupils in each eye. The great Ulster Cú Chulainn is presented in the *Táin* as someone possessed by spirits; the description of his warp-spasm bears a strong resemblance to trance-induced behaviour.

In relating these Irish and Welsh texts to the quest for ancient shamans, perhaps the most significant issue is that of the way in which earth-world and the other-world encroach upon each other. Characters like Cú Chulainn and Pwyll regularly sojourned in the world of the dead and had powers to communicate with the spirits. Interestingly, the access-points from the land of humans to that of the supernatural recall those recognized within modern shamanic traditions: caves, islands, river-crossings, mountains, lakes and the sea. The important role played by cauldrons, in both the Welsh and Irish myths, may hark back to their symbolic prominence in prehistoric rituals associated, perhaps, with shared drug- or liquor-consumption (Chapter 5). One of the most tempting links between the material culture examined in Chapters 5 and 6 and the literature explored in this chapter concerns cauldrons of rebirth: the great Danish silver cauldron from Gundestrup, with its iconographic narrative, bears a scene in which warriors are placed upside down in a vat and, perhaps, reborn after death in battle. The First Branch of the *Mabinogi* relates just such an event, in the context of the war between Britain and Ireland. We should remember that dissolution and rebirth are, in many traditions, important elements in the initiation of a shaman.

8 EPILOGUE

This book has taken both its readers and its authors on a long journey that has ranged over a wide geographical area, and an enormous span of time: from the first humans to early medieval Ireland. The evidence upon which the study is based takes a range of forms: from cave art to Classical documents and from the earliest flutes to Celtic myths. The two authors come from widely divergent archaeological backgrounds. Stephen's specialism is human evolution and Stone Age material culture; Miranda's research interests lie in the evidence for ritual behaviour in the European Iron Age and the western Roman provinces. In writing *The Quest for the Shaman*, we encountered areas of paradox: in tapping into the evidence for ritualized activity in the earliest phases of human presence, there is a contradiction in terms of clarity and obscurity of message.

In dealing with such a remote period of the past, identifying the actions of persons who might have been shamans (in the broadest sense of the term) is problematic, simply because as we travel more deeply into the past, we find that less of the evidence survives and that we must be, accordingly, more tentative in its interpretation. Yet the evidence from these early periods may relate to behaviour that finds analogies in the traditional religious culture of certain present-day, or recent, social systems, particularly those of 'modern' hunter-gatherer communities. Inversely, testimonies from the late Iron Age, Roman and later periods are both clearer and, yet, more veiled by written sources. We are, of course, fortunate to possess such texts – which provide definite information concerning ritual practices, perceptions and belief – but the codification of religious action that occurs in developed political systems tends to marginalize or 'air-brush out' shamanism. Moreover, the texts give it scant overt attention and it is necessary to scrape away the layers of sophistication in order to get at the underlying animistic – and possibly shamanistic – traditions existing alongside or beneath *romanitas* as a sub-text that may, even then, have been branded as superstition. Similarly, when dealing with the earliest vernacular prose tales of Ireland and Wales, we need to circumnavigate the dangerous waters of Christendom and seek to probe beneath the manipulations of paganism that took place under the pen of Christian monastic redactors.

It is in the nature of epilogues that they seek to close the circle opened in the introductory text of Chapter i. Accordingly, it is necessary to revisit our opening remarks, where we sought both to discuss what we meant by the terms shaman and shamanism, on the one hand, and to present our approach, on the other. What has been exciting for us is the burgeoning realization that so many elements in 'traditional' shamanism are evidenced from ancient Europe and, furthermore, that – despite the wide differences in source-material between Stephen and Miranda's data-sets – it is possible to recognize threads of analogy in all the chapters. The archaeological evidence exhibits a degree of patterning which is manifested in repeated modes of expression, variously in art, the treatment of human bodies after death, and in perceptions about sacred places. But, over such a vast range of space and time, we postulate no more than a broad continuity of tradition. Detailed beliefs may have undergone profound changes without leaving a clear archaeological signature. We can see this for ourselves, for example, in the significant alterations in practice and belief that have taken place in the Christian Church over the last two millennia.

Of the many skeins of ritual behaviour presented in this book, it is useful to conclude by drawing out those threads that seem to us to be particularly significant in terms of shared and recurrent expression of activity. These may point to the presence of persons who were boundary-crossers between the worlds of humans and the divine powers, 'two-spirit' people, perhaps shamans. Some of these threads are summarized below.

We have exercised a degree of caution on whether entoptic images are reproduced in the range of art considered here. Even so, we have identified images potentially of this kind not only in discussion of the Palaeolithic evidence but also in respect of Iron Age coins and some 'abstract' motifs in the rock art of the western Alpine regions. We believe that some of the human/animal images known as 'therianthropes' can plausibly be construed as shamanic trance-images, although there remain other possible explanations. What is interesting is that these nightmare creatures, whilst rare, are present right from the earliest art known *c.* 32,000 years ago at Höhlenstein-Stadel in Bavaria and at Chauvet Cave in the Ardèche, and recur in the Italian Neolithic cult-caves. The latter seem to display two principal themes: secrecy and hunting. It is a commonplace that control of game is of vital importance to hunter-gatherer communities. In this context, the role of a shaman may sometimes have involved a soul-journey, through the veil of the cave wall, into the world of spirits. It may seem surprising, therefore, that hunting was important in

Neolithic Italy where the hunter-gatherer lifestyle had been superseded, for the most part, by a predominantly agricultural economic system. However, it would appear that hunting possessed high-status associations, in much the way that the playing of golf in western civilization is often perceived (and conducted) as an élite, and excluding, activity.

Relationships with animals are particularly important because shape-shifting into a range of animal forms is characteristic of the practice of shamanism. Moreover, it is normal for the subject to identify with a particular species of animal – such as the San with the eland. In this context, therefore, the occurrence of a range of, particularly megafaunal, remains in the Gravettian ceremonial graves, or with the interments in the later Mesolithic cemeteries of northwestern Europe, should be significant. However, it would be wrong to propound a simple monothetic explanation for an historical and social context in which *mythos* and *logos* existed side by side and supplied parallel and equally valid truths as the 'search engines' of the prehistoric societies involved. Several possibilities present themselves in the context of explaining aspects of grave furniture and burial practice. These include the protection of the body from disturbance by carnivores, the protection of the living from 'disturbance' by the undead, and the selection of the bones of particularly the larger herbivores reflecting the species with which the dead (when living) or their communities had had a close relationship, perhaps as shamanic helpers. Some of these issues are commented on further below.

Half-human, half-animal beings are endemic to the Bronze Age rupestrine art of Scandinavia, and to the coeval and later imagery carved on the rocks in the Camonica Valley and elsewhere in the western Alps. They are also recurrent in Iron Age and Roman-period images, whether as stone statues and reliefs or small bronze figurines. It is clearly unacceptable to try and impose any kind of unified cosmovisual structure on such an enormous range of space and time. But it may be possible to suggest that underlying the production of therianthropic representations may be the desire to exhibit boundary-crossing, or boundary-denial, by means of shape-shifting. The same may be true of the evidence for gender-crossing in the later periods covered by this book. The notion of shape-shifting or transmogrification may be associated with many different layers of meaning, but it fits well within a scenario of the 'two-spirit' ritualist or shaman, whose liminal state between earth-world and the domain of the spirits shows itself in terms of an unstable, unfixed individual who regularly 'travels' between the dimensions of the cosmos.

The issue of the seclusion of ritual sites, generally caves or rockshelters, is rarely addressed head-on in Palaeolithic studies. In part, this is because there may be doubt about both the level of the Palaeolithic floor and the location or form of the original Palaeolithic entrance. The latter may well have been altered by natural recession of the external rock face, a process heightened by the intensity of the Last Glacial Maximum *c.* 20,000 years ago. Nonetheless, we clearly need to look, as

Bacelar Alves has done in her study[1], entitled 'The architecture of the natural world', dealing with the schematic art of western Iberia, not just at individual depictions as combinations of pigment, technique and style, but at sites in their landscape. The fundamental question, which we are able to ask in western Iberia – and probably there to give the answer 'yes' because of the local survival of collective memories – is whether the sites, open air or cave, were selected as places for the depiction of rock art because they were already sacred. The content and range of the art at any one location may be controlled by the particular history of that site and by the mythologies or divine manifestations which informed its sanctity. Myths form part of the ancestral memory of any preliterate community and are handed down orally, changing over time in the process of re-telling. In this respect it is worth alluding to one of the statements displayed in the graphics of a wonderful exhibition put on to celebrate the 250th anniversary of the British Museum in 2003, the 'Museum of the Mind. Art and Memory in World Cultures': that people with strong powers of recall are always valued as special persons within their communities. One of the devices of such oral tradition, as an aid to memory, is the invention of monsters. We cannot know with confidence in any one case, therefore, whether therianthropes represent a shape-shifting shaman or a character from myth. One brilliant example of how the sanctity of a site may continue, but with the belief system which underpins it changing, is given by stories of the emergence of saints from fissures in cave walls in the western Iberian sites leading to the Christianization of the site. Once again, the issue of boundary-transgression is central to the argument about the possible identification of shamanistic activity. The sacred places used by 'two-spirit' persons may themselves express the liminality or threshold character of such sites. Caves are an important category, as are rivers, especially rapids, and deep pools. But we may look also at bogs where, during the Iron Age in northern Europe, they appear habitually to have been used as *terra inculta*, wild, uncultivated spaces, no-man's land, edgy places that led to the underworld and had to be propitiated by holy men and women. It may even be that some of these priests died and were deposited in these inhospitable but numinous places, whether as voluntary or unwilling sacrificial victims.

Chanting, drumming, dancing, sensory or sleep-deprivation, or control of breathing may all be involved in the inducement of trance. Psychotropic drugs are also regularly used by shamans in Amazonian communities in attempts to reach other worlds. This latter practice is by no means universal but it has been possible to identify hallucinogenic substances in later prehistoric and Roman-period contexts that are suggestive of their association with ritual activity. Thus, the presence of cannabis in the Hallstatt chieftain's tomb at Hochdorf in Germany in the sixth century BC, or the residue of artemisia trapped in the spout of a vessel deposited in the 'Doctor's Grave' at Stanway in Essex in the earlier first century AD, might be linked to the lives or deaths of these individuals. More suggestive still are the remains of ergot and other mind-altering materials in the gut-contents of several Iron Age bog bodies.

Two forms of treatment of the dead – which can be applied with equal validity to Gravettian ceremonial burials – have been noted in Scandinavian Mesolithic cemeteries.[2] Both can be encapsulated in the phrase 'holding the undead stone-still'. Thus, some of the Mesolithic burials are weighed down by, or symbolically covered with, a layer of stones. This practice seems to relate especially, but not exclusively, to burials of older people. The underlying concept seems to have been the restraint of spirits of the recently dead that were deemed to be subversive and whose continued participation in the affairs of the living may not have been welcome. Skeletons found in an extreme crouched position may be included here also. Some corpses in the cemetery of Skateholm 1 were trussed very tightly, including the binding of hands and feet. One thinks here also of the Gravettian burial, Kostenki 14 (Fig 10). One of the Mesolithic undead, from Bøgebakken grave 11, clearly was restive: the ultimate sanction of chthonic abortion was visited upon the occupant of that grave and the body was removed.[3]

If all this seems a little implausible, reference to discoveries from the Chukotka cemetery in Siberia may assist. Thirty years ago, Russian archaeologists excavated a tomb in a cemetery on the edge of the Bering Strait. This tomb is now known as 'Ekven Burial 154'. It was built of stone, wood and whalebone, and contained the skeleton of an elderly woman. The site is interpreted as the grave of a shaman who died 2,000 years ago. Some of the artifacts found with the body are interpreted as routine women's equipment but male items were present also. There were also objects used in dancing and curing, both activities typically involved in shamanic rituals. The people buried in the cemetery are believed to be direct ancestors of the Yup'ik who live in the region today, an Inuit people who live by hunting sea mammals. One of the most remarkable finds from the tomb was a burial mask (Fig. 107) with the holes for the eyes blocked by bone inserts. Such masks were probably designed to be placed on the shaman's face after death when the

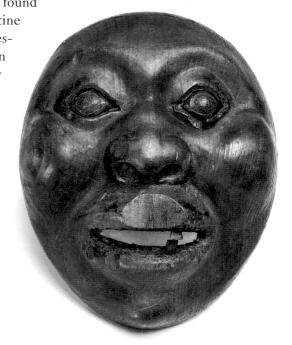

107 *Burial mask from the Ekven burial chamber.*

body was regarded as 'empty'. The purpose was to prevent the shaman's spirit from returning to her or his own body.

Actual or symbolic restraint, including binding, weighting or pinning down, has been identified as occasional practice, too, in later periods: the adult men crushed by great blocks of chalk and flint in the disused grain silos of Iron Age Danebury, southern England, and the hurdled men and women deposited in the remote and desolate marshes of Denmark, North Germany and the northern Netherlands, constitute just a few examples of persons perhaps deemed to be too charged with spirit-energy – even in death – for their bodies to be allowed to rest unrestrained. They may have been simply malcontents, foreign captives or criminals, but they could be interpreted as those whose lives belonged to the otherworld.

Evidence of ritual violence is present from the Palaeolithic onwards. We have quoted the possible evidence of hands that appear to have been mutilated, in particular those from the site of Gargas 'eternally crying out for help and mercy' (Fig 108), whilst noting that other interpretations are possible. Then, there is the case of depictions in parietal art of apparently speared humans, the so-called 'wounded men'. Such figures, at the sites of Pech Merle and Cougnac, have been re-interpreted by David Lewis-Williams[4] as spiritually, rather than physically, wounded. In this context, the spear-symbols may represent the pricking sensations of the shamanistic trance. One victim of Upper Palaeolithic violence, which still gives rise to a sense of alarm in many people, is the horse, defined in the soft clay of the cave wall, and then repeatedly 'stabbed', at Montespan in the Haute-Garonne. This is part of the 'fresque de la chasse' (the hunting fresco) which portrays a frieze of similarly stabbed horses. Neither horses nor bison experience shamanistic trances. Accordingly, it is harder to explain images of animals transfixed by spears or, bellies slashed, disgorging

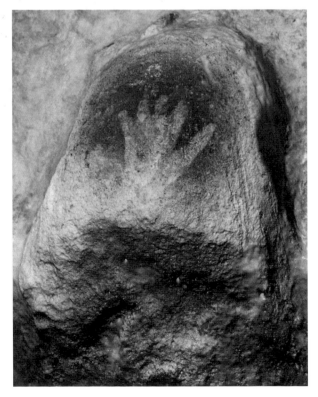

108 *Negative handprint with incomplete fingers, Gargas, Pyrénées.*

their entrails onto the ground. The explicatory route chosen by Lewis-Williams[5] was to view the latter event – which is part of a complex scene in the Lascaux shaft – as a metaphor of transformation post mortem into a shaman. Here, he makes the important point that such metaphors will have formed the fabric of local mythologies. Indeed, we will often not know whether some of the images we see are shamanistic or shamanistic with mythological roots *or* mythological or mythological with shamanistic roots.

Excessive and ritualized violence, both ante- and post-mortem, can be identified in the human remains of the European Iron Age and later. The multiple spear-attack on a body from one of the Garton Slack cemeteries in East Yorkshire bears a remarkable resemblance – in outward form at least – to the earlier images just mentioned. Several of the bog bodies were subjected to repeated and exaggerated violence both in life and as the causes of death: Lindow man was hit so hard on the head that his skull was fractured; he was garrotted and his throat cut. The Huldremose woman from Denmark had several injuries before death; and the young girl from Yde in Drenthe was stabbed in the neck before being strangled. Many of these bog victims were young, at the threshold of adulthood, a state that, in some traditional cultures, was so charged with energy that adolescent children were considered to have especially powerful shamanistic acuity. Another factor that may be significant about the Iron Age marsh bodies is that several suffered from physical disabilities: the Yde girl had such advanced scoliosis (curvature of the spine) that she must have lurched violently as she walked, and she was tiny. A number of the Gravettian burials were similarly affected: for example, the central 'female' from the Dolní Věstonice triple grave, the Barma Grande triple burial, and the adult male from the so-called shaman's grave at Brno.[6] It has been suggested also, in the case of the Ligurian burials, that above-average height may have been a factor in the selection of men for ceremonial cave burial.[7] It is possible that people may have been marked out as special, nurtured from babyhood and become seers because they were different; their handicap, or size, certainly seems to have been a factor in the selection of some as ritual murder victims.

We have said many times that shamanism involved public performance. We can offer Palaeolithic flutes, from the Aurignacian on, and even a drumstick found with the Gravettian burial at Brno. Like most firework parties, the exploding Gravettian figurines of Dolní Věstonice must have added some fun to life. Perhaps the Paviland ivory rods were used to divine the will of the spirit-world or were part of a 'medicine bundle' of sacred power. The Upper Palaeolithic caves offer not only some evidence, albeit not well dated, of initiation rites possibly accompanied by dancing, but also of the location of wall art in areas where there were particularly resonant calcite draperies. Perhaps these were 'played' to imitate animal noises, whilst the controlled movement of flickering oil lamps and brushwood torches made the beasts on the walls come to life: altogether a sort of Palaeolithic 'son et lumière'.

Likewise, Bronze Age rock-art figures, like the Swedish Järrestad Dancer, would have seemed to cavort in the guttering light of the fires lit at his feet. It may be worth remembering here that one of the best times to view engraved rock art in Sweden is by moonlight, when (we speak from experience) the drama is heightened by the noise of an elk crashing through nearby woodland. The little group of naked bronze dancers from Neuvy-en-Sullias, used as ritual tools at the very cusp between the end of the Iron Age and the Roman occupation of Gaul, must have been involved in ideas of performance. The Hallstatt chieftain, buried with pomp and ceremony at Hochdorf, was laid on a couch whose back was decorated with pairs of dancers opposed in sacred combat, perhaps to symbolize the fight for the dead man's soul. Flutes, pan-pipes and rattles all have a voice in the archaeological record for ritual activity during the later periods covered by this book.

Shamans may have worn regalia and would have used ritual equipment. The Palaeolithic and Mesolithic evidence is not strong in these areas. Pictorial representation of humans in cave art tends to be sketchy or schematic. Perhaps it is best to cite here the extensive 'regalia' of the Brno Gravettian burial and the Mesolithic antler headdress from Star Carr in northern England (Fig 1). Star Carr is a wetland site and such contexts, such 'edgy places' – caves, mountains, coasts, rivers and rapids – were recognized as locales where the tiers of the cosmos came together and shamans could cross boundaries. Here, it may be that the very location of sites – the passage graves of the Breton coast or the Boyne Valley – speak to us of a once shamanic world.

The evidence for regalia and ritual tools is more substantive for later periods. In the north European Bronze Age, we may point to the amazing gold cone-headdresses at Etzelsdorf and elsewhere, the Trundholm solar chariot and, most spectacular of recent discoveries, the Nebra sky-disc, perhaps used in divinatory practices. There is a range of sepulchral and shrine evidence for ritual regalia in the Iron Age and Roman periods: the sets of rods from the Stanway grave; the Coligny Calendar; the headdresses and sceptres from places like Felmingham Hall and Willingham Fen may all be cited. At the late Roman shrine to a British god, Nodens, at Lydney in Gloucestershire – a temple commanding fantastic views over the Severn Estuary and in sight of other temples in southwest England – a religious practitioner described himself, on an inscribed mosaic dedicated to the shrine, as an interpreter of dreams. He might have been a shaman in all but name, and at least one of the many images of dogs found here might have represented a shamanic animal-helper, for it is a double boundary-crosser: its canine body has a male human face but the row of teats along its underbelly proclaim it as a female animal.

Finally, we are sometimes confronted with images of people who may have been shamans in the midst of their soul-journeys. It is tempting so to interpret the winged human or animal figures depicted in Bronze Age Scandinavian rock art and on Iron Age coins, who could be perceived as flying between worlds. The bug-eyed faces staring out from the intricacies of Iron Age art on flagons, jewellery and weapons bear a marked resemblance to the faces of shamans undergoing the stress of trance and intervention with the spirits.

We are generally used to the origins of myth as rooted in the unreachable past. We will close with a myth created in 1961 by the Chilean poet, Pablo Neruda. It concerns a friend, killed abroad, who 'returns' home to Chile after his death. The poem is called 'El retrato en la roca', a 'portrait in stone'. It formed part of a collection entitled *The Stones of Chile* in which Neruda, exploring the mysteries of Nature, seeks to restore 'a sense of wonder, of the sacredness of the natural world'.[8]

a caballo …	out riding my horse …
miré y allí estaba mi amigo:	I looked and there was my friend:
de piedra era su rostro…	his face was formed in stone …
allí vino a parar el desterrado:	There the exile came to rest.
vive en su patria convertido en piedra	Transformed into stone, he lives in his own country

'El retrato en la roca' from *Las Piedras de Chile* by Pablo Neruda, translation by Ken Krabbenhoft.

109 *Reconstruction of a Scythian hemp vapour tent (see p. 122).*

CHAPTER 1 (pp. 9–18)
1 Vitebsky 1995, 96
2 Lorblanchet 1985, 74
3 2002
4 Jordan 2001, 87
5 Price 2001, 6
6 Hutton, 1993, 9
7 1995
8 Bradley 2000, 30
9 Such as Vitebsky, 1995
10 Walter 2001, 117
11 Watson 2001, 178
12 Bradley 2000, 126
13 Vitebsky 1995, 78–9
14 Hollimon 2001, 126
15 Gilchrist 1999, 59, 61
16 Dowson & Porr 2001, 173
17 Jordan 2001, 89
18 Vitebsky 1995, 12
19 Arsenault 2004
20 Jordan 2001, 91; Vitebsky 1995, 50–52
21 Gilchrist 1999, 95
22 Loring 1997, 200, 202

CHAPTER 2 (pp. 19–64)
1 Borges 1975, 38–39
2 Davies 2001, 204
3 Smith et al. 1999
4 These are uncalibrated radiocarbon dates
5 Mellars 2000
6 The dating of the Châtelperronian layers in the Grotte du Renne is highly problematic but the result quoted here probably provides the best estimate of the age of the Neanderthal child from that site (Hublin et al. 1996)
7 Note that the difference in the two St Césaire determinations is more apparent than real: a radiocarbon age of 33,000 is probably equivalent

to the calendar age of 36,000 years ago provided by the TL determination (Bowen 2000)
8 For references to sites and dates see Smith et al. 1999
9 Street and Terberger 2001
10 http://www.pnas.org/cgi/content/abstract/2035108100v1
11 Richter et al. 2000; Clottes 1996, 122
12 Pettitt and Bahn 2003
13 For three reasons: first, nearly fifty charcoal samples have now been dated and fall into two clusters of c. 31,500 and 26,000 years ago, with the early cluster including all the drawings directly dated. Second, the art both overlies and underlies bear scratches in different sections of the cave wall. The presence of bears and humans clearly, therefore, interdigitated. (Perhaps the human visits to the cave were made in summer when hibernating bears would have been absent.) Radiocarbon dates on bear bones have yielded seven results which fall between 30,700 and 29,000 years ago, a range consistent with the dating of the art. Third, study of the blocked entrance to the cave shows this was effected by cliff collapse around 20,000 years ago. Therefore, the art of Chauvet cannot belong to the Magdalenian – the classic period of florescence of cave art in western Europe – because there was no possibility of human access to the cave at the time. I am indebted to Jean Clottes for valuable discussion on Chauvet.
14 1981

15 Zvelebil and Jordan 1997, 120
16 S. Green 1989, 73
17 S. Aldhouse-Green 2000a
18 1999
19 2002: 189–92
20 Vitebsky 1995
21 2002, 89, 192
22 Lewis-Williams 2002, 196
23 D'Errico et al. 1998; Zilhão 2001
24 2001, 40
25 S. Aldhouse-Green 2000; Mussi 1990; Mussi 1995
26 Gamble 1991; Mussi et al. 2000
27 Armstrong 2000, 14
28 Pagel, M. and Mace, R. 2004. The cultural wealth of nations. Nature 428: 275–78
29 1992, 26
30 Marjorie Irene Green (1917–1975), née Stinchcombe, is Stephen Aldhouse-Green's mother
31 Duarte et al. 1999
32 Zilhão 2000
33 Ward and Stringer 1997
34 Palmer 2000, 210
35 Barham and Robson-Brown 2000
36 S. Aldhouse-Green 2001
37 The Krapina strata are as follows, from top to base:
8–9 Cave Bear zone – mostly temperate fauna, some indication of warming
5–7 Merck's Rhinoceros zone – faunal remains indicate cold to temperate climate
2–4 'Homo sapiens' zone' – faunal remains indicate warm to temperate climate; this 'hominid zone' yielded 800 human bones, representing the remains of up to forty-three Neanderthals; an interglacial fauna including a range of herbivores and a

number of carnivores (bear, hyaena, leopard and wild cat)

1 Rolled fluvial sediments

38 Most Neanderthal remains came from layers 3 and 4, Gorjanović's 'Homo sapiens zone', with the exception of a small collection of bones from layer 8. All layers yielded stone tools

39 Trinkaus & Shipman 1993, 167–71, 364

40 1987

41 Taylor 2002, 208

42 2002, 208

43 Reported in Culotta 1999, 19; Palmer 2000, 93–95

44 Taylor 2002, 209

45 After M. Aldhouse-Green 2001a, 56–61; Taylor 2002

46 Currant et al. 1989

47 Richards et al. 2000

48 Barham et al. 1999: 78–79. Another broadly contempoary site with comparable treatment of human remains is Maszycka Cave in southern Poland (Kozlowski 1993)

49 2002, 210–12

50 Soffer 2000

51 Rhys Jones, pers. comm.

52 Berger and Trinkaus 1995

53 Trinkaus 1995

54 Bronowski 1973, 64

55 I am tempted to wonder whether the legs might not have been removed (post mortem) for consumption. Certainly, however, the cranium seems to have been removed only after the decay of the atlanto-occipital ligaments and, by then, its soft parts would have so far decayed to make it unappealing even to a Neanderthal used only to 'basse cuisine' (Paul Pettitt in litt.). I wonder, however, whether it can really have been worse than the rotten meat I once consumed when taking part in fieldwork in the Sudan (SAG)

56 S. Aldhouse-Green 2001, 116

57 'Ouranic' is an adjective from the Greek word 'ouranos' (heaven), just as 'chthonic' refers to the underworld

58 The term 'cosmovision' is taken from the title of an article by one of the authors (M. Aldhouse-Green 2001c). It was used there to describe perceptions about the universe and the worlds of the supernatural

59 Mussi et al. 2000, 120

60 Lewis-Williams and Dowson 1988

61 Lewis-Williams 1997, 326

62 1995, 29

63 Helvenston and Bahn 2002

64 'Neuropsychology and Upper Palaeolithic art: observations on the progress of altered states of consciousness', Cambridge Arch. Journal 14 (April 2004), pp. 107–111

65 2002, 212

66 Wilbert 1997, 318

67 2002, 212

68 Saunders 2002, 212

69 D'Errico et al. 2001

70 Richter et al. 2000, 86

71 After McBrearty and Brooks 2000, fig 13, p 530

72 Grün et al. 1990; Sillen and Morris 1996

73 Knight et al. 1995

74 1969

75 Douglas 1967

76 Jones and MacGregor 2002b, 11

77 Scarre 2002c, 231

78 Jones and MacGregor 2000b, 8

79 Chapman 2000, 54–67; Scarre 2002, 231

80 Bahn and Vertut 1997, 115

81 Albert Camus 1995, 62

82 Camus 1994, 79

83 Saunders 2002, 217

84 Bradley 2002, 112

85 Dr Martin Howley, Humanities Librarian, QE II Library, Memorial University of Newfoundland

86 See S. Aldhouse-Green 2000b for fuller descriptions and referencing – except Arene Candide (Pettitt et al. 2003)

87 2002, 11

88 Trinkaus et al. 2000, 1130

89 Oliva 1996

90 Trinkaus 2000, 147, 191

91 Underhill 1965, 110–11; S. Aldhouse-Green 2000a, 116–17

92 Barma Grande 2–4. Mussi (1995)

93 The quote comes from Shakespeare's Coriolanus

94 Dolní Věstonice skeletons, left to right, are DV XIII, XV and XIV (Klíma 1995, Abb. 76)

95 Trinkaus et al. 2001

96 Klíma 1987b

97 Jones and MacGregor 2000b, 8

98 Trinkaus et al. 2001

99 Klein 1999, 499

100 Parker Pearson, 2002

101 I am indebted to Paul Pettitt for valuable discussion on this point

102 Zilhão and Trinkaus 2002; Duarte 2002

103 Bradley 2000, 5–13

104 Vitebsky 1995, 60–61

105 Zachrisson and Iregren 1974, 11–14

106 Ingold 1986, 257–58

107 Trinkaus et al. 2000

108 In litt. Alf Webb; see S. Aldhouse-Green 2000b, 234

109 Stiner 1999

110 Mussi 1990, 135

111 Mussi 1990, 135

112 2000

113 2000

114 White 2003, fig. 48, p. 84

115 Soffer et al. 1993

116 2003

117 Guenther 1997

118 Hughes 1997, 3

119 Including Ucko and Rosenfeld 1967; Lorblanchet 1995; Bahn and Vertut 1997; Lewis-Williams 2002

120 Clottes 1999, 171–72

121 1962, 100

122 Bahn and Vertut 1997, 105

123 Clottes 1997b

124 Davis 1984

125 1988

126 Clottes 1997a, 43

127 Pfeiffer 1982

128 Mithen 1988, 322

129 Turk 1997

130 Lewis-Williams 1981

131 Gillieson 1996, 5–6

132 Davis 1984

133 D'Errico and Villa 1997; D'Errico et al. 1998

134 Richter et al. 2000, 73

135 Bosinski 1990, 69–70

136 Buisson 1990, 421–22

137 Brade 1975; 1982; Buisson 1990, 429

138 Clottes 1995, 76–80

139 Lorblanchet 1995, 175–78

140 Otte 1994; Bahn 1998, 201–05

141 A good example is that from La Roche Lalinde in the Dordogne (Bahn and Vertut 1988, 69–70). The artifact is covered with an engraved geometric design and is stained with red ochre.

142 Paul Pettitt in a paper given to a conference on Creswell Art in European Context, Creswell, 15–17 April 2004

143 Geneste 2003, 46

144 Geneste 2003

145 Philippe and Fosse 2003, 56

146 Garcia 2003, 39–41

147 Bégouen and Clottes 1984, 412

148 González-Echegaray and Freeman 1981

149 Borges 1975, 36–37

150 Lewis-Williams 2002, 207

151 The Höhle Fels finds also include carvings of a horse head and water bird. See Conard 2003

152 Saladin D'Anglure 1994

153 Bégouen and Clottes 1984

154 Bednarik 2003

155 White 2003, 121–22

156 Hutton 2001, 131–33

157 Clottes and Lewis-Williams 2001, 149–231

CHAPTER 3 (pp. 65–88)

1 Mary Douglas 1970, 36

2 Mithen 2003

3 1992

4 1992, 72

5 O'Hare 1990, 137

6 Cunnington 1929 (113, pl. 22, 1)

7 The date is in tree-ring (dendrochronological) years

8 1991

9 1992, 91

10 1992, 133–34, 140–41
11 Leach 1976, 72
12 1992, 142–43,168
13 Tilley 1996, 68
14 1996
15 English Heritage 2004. The calibrated age is 8500 to 8250 BC
16 Davies 1925
17 Mithen 1994, 120–32
18 Clark 1975, 198
19 Tilley 1996, 43
20 Zvelebil 2003, 10
21 Zvelebil 2003, 11–12
22 Zvelebil 1992
23 Chaix *et al.* 1997
24 Mithen 1994, 120–32; Jacobs 1995
25 Jacobs 1995
26 Mithen 1994, 126; Jacobs 1995, 367
27 Zvelebil and Jordan 1997, 117–19
28 Zvelebil 2003, 13
29 Larsson 1984; 1989
30 1996, 33–69
31 Zvelebil 2003, 11
32 Lubbock 1865, xxx
33 *Odyssey* 17, 291–327
34 2002
35 Larsson 2002, 181–82
36 2002, 180
37 Albrethsen and Petersen 1975; 1976
38 Tilley 1996, 44–48
39 Gvozdover 1995, 44
40 White and Bisson 1998
41 Scarre 2002b, 100
42 2002b
43 Scarre 2002b, 85
44 Thomas 2003, 69–70
45 Scarre 2002a, 177
46 Cummings 2002, 109–10
47 Scarre 2002b, 94
48 Tomb IIIC
49 2002b, 100
50 1995; 1996a–b
51 1995, 261
52 1996b
53 Pentikäinen 1984, 125, 148
54 2002
55 2001
56 1991
57 Stringer and McKie 1996, 134–36
58 1999, 173
59 Flood 1990
60 Whitley *et al.* 1999
61 Atkinson 1956, 183–85
62 Campbell 1988, 241
63 Miles and Palmer 1995; Gosden and Lock 1998, 2
64 Hawkes 1951, 83
65 Rumsey 1994, 127–28
66 1982
67 Ong 1982, 5–8
68 Lord 1960, 68–98
69 Ong 1982, 20–23
70 Ong 1982, 23–24
71 Lord 1960; Ong 1982, 59–60
72 1982, 44
73 1992, 27–33, 49
74 1992, 33

75 Ong 1982, 69–70
76 Connerton 1989
77 Sherratt 1991. The term 'narcotic' is used very loosely here, as it was by Sherratt
78 In his 'Introduction' to *The Quiet American* (London: William Heinemann), pp. xxi–xxii
79 'Snow' is cocaine. Song written by Bert Jansch in 1965 (Logo Songs Ltd.)
80 Near Kabushiya in 1968/69.
81 For example, Fly Agaric is common in birch woodlands and *could* have been a Palaeolithic narcotic
82 Russell and McGowan 2003
83 Dronfield 1996b

CHAPTER 4 (pp. 89–110).
1 i.e. art carved on living rock-faces
2 Layton 1992; Bradley 1997; Chaloupka 1993; Lewis-Williams 2001a; Blackmore 1996
3 1997, 8, 10
4 Bradley 2000, 28
5 Bradley 1997, 10
6 2001b
7 Lewis-Williams 2001a; Clottes & Lewis-Williams 1998; Dowson & Porr 2001; Lewis-Williams & Dowson 1988
8 Chaloupka undated, 22; 1993, 77–98; Bradley 1995, 55; Lewis-Williams & Dowson 1990, 5–16
9 2001a, 23
10 Coles 1994; 2001
11 Anati 1965; Priuli 1988; 1996
12 Coles 1999, 171–72
13 Coles 1999, 167–187
14 *op. cit.*, 179
15 *op. cit.*, 1999, 180, fig. 13
16 e.g. *op. cit.*, fig. 7
17 Coles 1999, 176, 184
18 Coles 1999, 179, 185
19 *op. cit.* 179
20 Coles 1990
21 Coles 2000, 83–4
22 To point to a 'modern' analogy, the symbolism of fire and water is clearly reflected, for instance, in Act 2 of Mozart's opera *The Magic Flute* where the principal characters, Tamino and Pamina, pass through the two elements in their achievement of enlightenment, in what is clearly an 18th-century Masonic ritual
23 Coles 1999, 185
24 Seen and 'brass-rubbed' by the authors in May 1988
25 Coles 1990, 42, figs. 11g, 25
26 Coles 2000, 51, pl. 63; Bertilsson 1987, fig. 52:10
27 Coles 1990, fig. 84b
28 Briard 1987, 128–29
29 2001, 50
30 Coles 1990, 33, fig. 19c

31 Bertilsson 1987, fig. 52:8
32 Coles 1990, 67, fig. 61
33 Coles 1990, 23–27
34 Coles 2000, 48
35 *op. cit.* 53, pls. 67–8
36 Coles 2000, 54, pl. 69
37 Vitebsky 1995, 18
38 Coles 1990, fig. 11b; Green, M. 1991, 81–2, figs. 62–4
39 Coles 2000, 40
40 Devlet 2001, 47, 49
41 Walter 2001, 105–119
42 Scott Schnell 1999; Nicola Cook pers. comm
43 Rozwadowski 2001, 70–71
44 Coles 1990, 41
45 Coles 1994, 44
46 Bradley 1997, 43, after Layton 1992
47 Coles 2000, pl. 70
48 Coles 1990, fig. 10e
49 Larsson 1997, 84, fig. 29
50 Coles 2000, 47, pl. 57; Larsson 1997, 83, fig. 28
51 Coles 2000, 47
52 Coles 2000, 46, pl. 55
53 2001, 18
54 Aldhouse-Green, M. 2001a, 126
55 Bertilsson 1987, 73, 76
56 Coles 1994, 29
57 Coles 2000, 60–61, pls. 81–83
58 Coles 1999, 176
59 Book VI
60 Coles 2000, 38, pl. 45
61 Coles 2000, 35, pl. 40
62 Coles 2000, 34, fig. 67
63 Bradley 1995, 55
64 Rozwadowski 2001, 75
65 Creighton 2000, 47. Paul Pettit suggests an alternative to the view that the cupmarks represent entoptic phenomena, namely that they represent clusters or lines of barrows and thus cemeteries.
66 Bertilsson 1987, 73, 113
67 *op. cit.*, 76
68 Vitebsky 1995, 15
69 1994, 44
70 2000, 98–99
71 Coles 1994, 17–19
72 Coles 2000, 123
73 For a discussion on the significance of emphasis in Scandinavian rock art see Coles 2003, 567–571
74 Coles 1990, 14; 1994, 17
75 Bertilsson 1987, 185
76 Anati 1965, 34–35
77 1998, 145–57
78 Vitebsky 1995, 17
79 Scarre 1998, 145–157
80 1987, 13–14
81 Priuli 1988, 4; 1996, 109, fig. 186
82 Priuli 1996, 107, fig. 184
83 Anati 1965, 36–37, 152, 186, 211
84 Aldhouse-Green, M. 2001a, 30
85 Blackmore 1996; Aldhouse-Green, M. 2001c
86 1965, 236

87 Priuli 1988, 78; Aldhouse-Green, M. 2001b, fig. 7.2
88 Priuli 1996, 29, fig. 51
89 Aldhouse-Green, M. 2001b, fig. 7.2
90 Such images are recorded in Gallo-British iconography of the Roman period: Aldhouse-Green, M. 2001b, figs. 7.5–7.7
91 Priuli 1988, 77, 80; Anati 1965, 171; Aldhouse-Green, M. 2001b, fig. 7.4
92 Anati 1965, 215
93 Priuli 1988, 81–83
94 de Lumley 1995; Briard 1987, 96–7; Priuli 1996, 47, no. 82; 55, no. 92
95 Priuli 1996, 126, fig. 211; 1988, 55
96 Priuli 1996, fig. 211
97 Anati 1965, 216–17
98 Vitebsky 1995, 18
99 Anati 1965, 92
100 op. cit. 213, 220, 225
101 Priuli 1996, 121, Fig. 201
102 Deyts 1999, 83
103 Priuli 1996, 41, no. 75; 114, fig. 193
104 Clottes & Lewis-Williams 1998, 46, pl. 44; Bahn & Vertut 1988, 104
105 Priuli 1988, 55
106 Priuli 1996, 81, fig. 143
107 Priuli 1988, 32
108 Priuli 1996, 122, fig. 204
109 Scarre 1998, 145–57; Priuli 1996, 61, no. 100
110 Anati 1965, 106–7
111 Priuli 1996, 102
112 Coles 2000, 99–101
113 Green, M. 1998b; Mikalson 1975
114 Springer 1999
115 Eluère 1987, 50–60; Menghin 1999, 172–175
116 Hesiod Works and Days lines 381–383; trans. Wender 1973, 71
117 Schulz 2002; Pernicka 2003
118 Glob 1974, pl. 39; Green, M. 1991, fig. 23
119 Glob 1974, 99–125; Jensen 1978, 36; Ashbee 1989, 539–546; Piggott 1983, 114–116
120 Green, M. 1991, 112–119
121 Green, M. 1991, 67–68; Champion et al. 1984, 285; Jensen 1982, 163–65; Pare 1989, 80–100

CHAPTER 5 (pp. 111–142)
1 Library of History V, 31, 2–3
2 Aldhouse-Green, M. 2001a
3 Hillman 1986, 103
4 1999, 68
5 1986, 99–115
6 Green, M. 1997b, 59; Aldhouse-Green, M. 2000, 8
7 Stead, Bourke & Brothwell 1986; Turner 1995, 10–18
8 Natural History XVI, 95
9 Hillman 1986, 99–115; Holden Holden 1995, 76–82; Scaife 1995, 83–85
10 Aldhouse-Green, M. 2001a, 169
11 Jones & Jones 1976, 76; Green, M. 1995, 60

12 Fischer undated, 6
13 Gebuhr 2001; Van der Sanden 1995, 146–165; 1996, 131
14 Glob 1969, 112–115
15 Thompson 2003, 217–244
16 Tacitus Germania 19; trans. Mattingly 1948, 116
17 Van der Sanden 1996, 129
18 Fagles 1982, 38
19 Fagles 1982, 174
20 1995, 146
21 Gilchrist 1999, 88, 107, 116–117; Foxhall 1994
22 1995, 57
23 Tacitus The Histories IV, 61; trans. Wellesley 1964, 247
24 Histories IV, 65; trans. Wellesley 1964, 250
25 1999
26 Green, M. 1995, 62; Jones & Jones 1976, 55
27 Van der Sanden & Capelle 2001
28 Coles 1990; 1998
29 Aldhouse-Green, M. 2000
30 Green, M. 1997a, 898–911
31 1998, 165
32 Coles 1990, 320–322
33 Coles 1998, 165
34 Green, M. 1999a, 57
35 Deyts 1983
36 Van der Sanden & Capelle 2001, 14, fig. 6
37 Vitebsky 1995, 11
38 Anisimov 1963, 85
39 Hayen 1971, 88–123; 1987, 117–36; Aldhouse-Green, M. 2000, 17–18; Van der Sanden & Capelle 2001, 75–76
40 Raftery 1996, 260, 285–87, pl. 44, figs. 382–84
41 Van der Sanden & Capelle 2001, 80, fig. 77
42 Pitts 2001, 327–329
43 Herodotus Histories IV, 73–74; trans. de Sélincourt 1965, 265–266
44 Although Paul Pettitt has commented that the vapour would have to be quite strong in order to induce a hallucinogenic trips, and that Herodotus' Scythians may simply have been 'stoned and enjoying themselves' (pers. comm.)
45 Sherratt 1991, 52; Creighton 1995, 295
46 Holl 2002, 9
47 Crummy 1997a; 1997b; Carr 2002
48 Tacitus Germania 10; trans. Mattingly 1948, 108–109
49 2000, 52
50 Perrin 2000a
51 Paddy Coker, pers. comm.
52 Poux et al, 2002, 57–110
53 2001, 19
54 Galliou 1984, 24–36; Vencl 1994, 299–326
55 Arnold 2001, 14–19
56 Bibracte 2000, nos. 39, 348; Fitzpatrick 2000a
57 Arnold 2001, 14–19

58 Paul Pettitt, pers. comm.
59 2003
60 1987, 182–204
61 op. cit., 191
62 op. cit., 195
63 Rozwadowski 2001, 72
64 Green, M. 1996, 114
65 Green 1998c
66 Aldhouse-Green, M. 2001a, 190, fig. 76
67 Raftery 1994, 184
68 Green, M. 1997b, 63
69 Gilbert 1978, 159–87
70 Green, M. 1998a
71 Dronfield 1993, 181
72 2000, 47–49
73 Fulford & Creighton 1998, 331–342
74 Green, M. 1996, 117
75 op. cit. 126
76 Hill 2001, 2–3
77 Duval 1987, 53–64
78 e.g. Aldhouse-Green, M. 2001b, figs. 7.5–7.7
79 Vitebsky 1995, 64
80 Green, M. 1996, fig. 32
81 op. cit. fig. 34
82 op. cit. fig. 43
83 Green, M. 1996, 59, 69
84 Aldhouse-Green, M. 2001b, figs 7.2, 7.4; see also Chapter 4
85 op. cit., figs. 7.3, 7.8
86 Green, M. 1996, fig. 87; Megaw & Megaw 1989, 101
87 Green 1997a, fig. 6
88 2000, 40–54
89 op. cit., 44–45, fig. 2.6
90 Green, M. 1998a, 219–240; Aldhouse-Green, M.2001b, 201–230
91 Duval 1987, 31.
92 2000, 45–47
93 Creighton 2000; Aldhouse-Green, M. 2003
94 2001, 165–77
95 MacInnes 1989, 10–24
96 Green, M. 1998a; Aldhouse-Green, M. 2001c
97 Vitebsky 1995; Aldhouse-Green, M. 2001b
98 Green, M. 1989, fig. 46
99 1996
100 Green, M. 1992, figs. 3.4, 5.9
101 op. cit. fig. 3.4
102 Priuli 1996, 100, fig. 176; Bradley 1997, 197
103 1995; 2000, 52–53
104 1995, 84
105 Aldhouse-Green, M. 2002
106 Firelight-induced visions may have been equally responsible for some of the Palaeolithic cave art (see Chapter 2)
107 Keller & Keller 1996, 23
108 2000, 41–42
109 Scott 1990, 186; Ó Cathasaigh 1977
110 Creighton 2000, 40
111 Grinsell 1953, 175
112 Vitebsky 1995, 11, 60–61

113 Aldhouse-Green, M. 2001a, 114, fig. 48
114 Jones & Jones 1976, 29
115 Taplin 1988, 44–71
116 Vitebsky 1995, 101
117 *Germania* 40
118 Bradley 1990; Bridgford 1997
119 Fox 1946
120 Stead 1985, 11
121 Savory 1976, pl. VI
122 Aldhouse-Green, M. 2002
123 Savory 1976, fig. 28; Fox 1946, pl. x
124 Bibracte 2000 & pers. comm.
125 Aldhouse-Green, M. 2001a, 148–49
126 *Germania* 39
127 Green, M. 1978, pls. 54–56
128 Bibracte 2000, no. 5; Fellmann 1999, 133–175
129 Vitebsky 1995, 104
130 Perrin 2000a
131 V, 31, 3
132 *Histories* 4.54
133 1995, 116–117
134 Green, M. 1997b, 97
135 1995, 78
136 Vitebsky 1995, 18; Bradley 2000, 12
137 Tomlin 1988, 98, 130
138 Chapman 2001
139 *Commemoratio Professorum Burdigalensium*; Chadwick 1966, 82; Green, M. 1997b, 15
140 Perrin 2000b
141 e.g. I. 35
142 Bibracte 2000, no. 7; Aldhouse-Green, M. 2001a, 181
143 *de Divinatione* I. 90
144 Duval & Pinault 1986
145 Green, M. 1998b, 198–99
146 Pritchett 1963, 345; Mikalson 1975, ix
147 1996
148 Aldhouse-Green, M. 2001a, 170, fig. 61
149 Bradley 2000, 12
150 *op. cit.*, 28–32
151 Drinkwater 1983, 111
152 Aldhouse-Green, M. 2001a, 194; Parker Pearson 1999, 70–71
153 Vitesbky 1995, 50–52
154 1999, 95
155 *Geography* IV, 4,6; Green, M. 1997b, 105
156 Stead 1991, 593
157 Stead 1991, 591–595
158 Fitzpatrick 2000b, 15–29
159 Lambot 1998; Aldhouse-Green, M. 2001a, 130–131
160 Bibracte 2000, no. 12
161 Bibracte 2000, no. 25
162 Fitzpatrick 2000a
163 Green, M. 1986, fig. 61; Dent 1985, 85–92
164 Knüsel 2002, and *see* chapter 6
165 Bibracte 2000, no. 26

CHAPTER 6 (pp. 143–178)
1 Aeschylus *Prometheus Bound*, trans. Vellacott 1961, 35
2 Aldhouse-Green, M. 2001c
3 Hansen 2000, 57–65
4 Dowden 2000, 246
5 *Nemean Odes* I, 60–61
6 the 'Pseudo-Hesiodic' *Melampodia*, probably pre-dating Hesiod and thus at least as early as the eighth century BC: Schwartz 1960, 128–29, 211–215; Lamberton 1988, 134
7 Fagles trans. 1982, 111
8 Fagles trans. 1982, 174
9 *op. cit.* 175
10 Vellacott trans. 1973, 197
11 Schwartz 1960, 211–215
12 Coles 1998, 168
13 Rasmussen 2000, 11
14 Wheeler & Wheeler 1932, 102–103
15 van Driel-Murray 1999, 134
16 *Geography* VII, 2, 3
17 1999, 131
18 Lewis-Williams 2001b, 22–23
19 Aldhouse-Green, M. 2001a, 190, fig. 76
20 Dio Cassius *Roman History* LXII, 6, 1–2; trans. Cary 1925, 91–93
21 Vitebsky 1995, 116, 128, 135–136
22 1999, 1–20
23 Meaney 1989, 9–40.
24 Corder & Richmond 1938, 68ff; Green, M. 1978, 47
25 Green, M. 1976, 210
26 *op. cit.*, 220, pl. XXVf
27 *op. cit.*, 219
28 Green, M. 1991, 102–103; Williams *et al.* 1996, 155–158, fig. 91
29 1996, 81–89
30 Aldhouse-Green, M. 2001b, fig. 7.8
31 2001, 119
32 2001, 58
33 Künzl 1983, 57, 59, 79
34 2002
35 Hoppál 1992, 117–131
36 *Saga* 4, 81–8
37 *Histories* IX.6, 485
38 Meaney 1981
39 2001a, 22
40 Green, M. 1989, fig. 45; Aldhouse-Green, M. 2000, 13
41 Green, M. 1989, fig. 43
42 Fitzpatrick 2000a, 49; Lejars & Perrin 2000, 40
43 Arnold 1990, 163–76
44 Knüsel 2002
45 Painter 1997, 99–102
46 De la Bedoyère 1999, 102
47 Shepherd 1998
48 Fulford 2001, 199–218
49 2001, 89
50 *Natural History* XXIV, 62; *Germania* 40
51 Vitebsky 1995, 10
52 Alekseev 1997, 153–64
53 *Natural History* XVI, 95
54 XXIV
55 Bibracte 2000, no. 41; Aldhouse-Green, M. 2001a, 185–186, figs. 71, 72
56 Green, M. 1997b, 114–119
57 *op. cit.*, 90
58 Hansen 2000, 57–65
59 VI, 14
60 John Milton *Paradise Lost* I
61 Vitebsky 1995, 93; St Pierre & Soldier 1995, 56; Green, M. 1997b; Aldhouse-Green, M. 2001c; 2001e
62 Aldhouse-Green, M. 2001c
63 Siikala 1992, 81, after Knüsel 2002
64 Diemberger 1993, 101
65 Vitebsky 1995, 93; Green, M. 1997b; Aldhouse-Green, M. 2001c; 2001e
66 Hollimon 2001, 124, 126
67 Gilchrist 1999, 107–108
68 Underhill 1965, 83
69 Lewis-Williams 2001b, 31
70 Aldhouse-Green, M. 2001a, 152–7
71 Chapman 2001
72 Jacobs *et al.* 1997
73 Roscoe 1998
74 Underhill 1965, 93; St Pierre & Soldier 1995, 56
75 Gilchrist 1997, 43, 56
76 Plutarch *Life of Numa* 9–10; Ferguson 1980, 57–8
77 *Quaestiones Graecae* 58
78 Kampen 1996, 233–46, figs. 98, 99
79 1972, 19
80 Tacitus *Germania* 43; trans. Mattingly 1948, 136
81 Taylor 1996, 210–211
82 Herodotus IV, 118–119; King 1995, 138–167
83 DuBois 1982, 34–36. Myths like these may have their origins in the reality of Iron Age warrior-women whose graves have been found in Central Asian contexts: Parker Pearson 1999, 61–63
84 Herodotus *The Histories* IV, 63–69; trans. de Sélincourt 1964, 263
85 1981, 239
86 Bailey 1994, 321–331
87 Carr 2001, 112–113
88 Stead 1988, 9–29; Stahl 1986, 134–50
89 Green, M. 1997a, 898–911
90 VI, 13
91 Sørensen 1991, 121
92 2001, 126
93 Megaw 1970, pl. IV
94 Deyts 1999, 90, no. 49
95 Green, M. 1995, 168; Boucher 1976, nos. 317–18; Deyts 1992, 40; Aldhouse-Green, M. 2001b, fig. 7.10
96 Zachar 1987, pl. 201; Green, M. 1997a, fig. 2
97 Green, M. 1997a, fig. 5; Dayet 1954, 34–335
98 Smith 1991, 130–134
99 Pardo 1993, 62–64; Bober & Rubinstein 1986, 130
100 1982, figs. 12, 86
101 Henig 1995, pl. XIV
102 Henig 1993, fig. 1
103 Green, M. 1976, 223; 1989, figs. 17, 24
104 Henig 1995, fig. 86
105 Jupiter-columns are mainly found

in eastern Gaul and the Rhineland. They are composite monuments erected in the Roman period in honour of the sky-god Jupiter, and consist of a basal plinth carved with divine images, a high pillar, sometimes decorated to represent a tree, surmounted by a sculptured group (resembling St George and the Dragon) comprising Jupiter on horseback, thunderbolt in hand, riding down a monster, with a human body and snakes for legs. The iconography is generally interpreted as depicting the triumph of light over darkness, life over death and order over chaos

106 Green, M. 1984, fig. 68
107 Howell 1988, 23; Stokes 1897, 384
108 Vitebsky 1995; Devlet 2001, 50; Sutherland 2001, 135–145
109 Creighton 2000, 43
110 Chipp 1968, 397–455; Read 1982, 125–127
111 Loring 1997, 185–220; Aronsson 1991, 5; Sharples 2000; Jones 1998, 301–24; Parker Pearson & Sharples 1999, 21; Parker Pearson et al. 1999, 149–52
112 King 1995, 138–167
113 Aldhouse-Green, M. 2001c
114 Meniel 1987, 89–100
115 Green, M. 1997b, 58; Tony Rook pers. comm.
116 The pierced antlers from the Mesolithic site of Star Carr in Yorkshire indicate that this kind of headgear was being worn on ritual occasions long before the Iron Age or Roman periods: Champion et al. 1984, 89–110.
117 Boon 1982
118 Olmsted 1979, pl. 2A; Taylor 1992, 66–71; Kaul et al. 1991, fig. 221
119 Priuli 1988, 77–78, 84; 1996, 29
120 Aldhouse-Green, M. 2001b
121 op. cit.
122 Aldhouse-Green, M. 2001c
123 Fitzpatrick 2000a, 49
124 Wheeler & Wheeler 1932
125 Green, M. 1997a, fig. 7
126 2001, 138
127 2000, 43
128 Green, M. 1992, 158–160, fig. 6.23
129 Green 2001c
130 Hauser 1962, 224
131 Green, M. 1998a, 219–40
132 Priuli 1996, 100, fig. 176
133 Green 1992, fig. 6.23
134 Green, M. 1989, fig. 37
135 Green, M. 1996, fig. 83
136 Green, M. 1998a, 219–240
137 Aldhouse-Green, M. 2001b; Devauges 1974, 434; Planson & Pommeret 1986, fig. 44
138 Green, M. 1989, 174
139 Bagnall Smith 1999, nos. 1–3, 18
140 Green, M. 1998a, 219–240

141 Deyts 1976, no. 21
142 Green, M. 1976, pl. IIIh
143 Vitebsky 1995, 49
144 Gilbert 1987 and see chapter 5

CHAPTER 7 (pp. 179–202)
1 from The Táin, trans. Kinsella 1969, 77
2 Mac Cana 1983, 117; Aldhouse-Green, M. 2001d, 102–117
3 from the First Branch of the Mabinogi, trans. Jones & Jones 1976, 3
4 Aldhouse-Green, M. 2001d
5 Jones & Jones 1976, 9
6 Green, M. 1995, 51; Aldhouse-Green, M. 2001d
7 Green, M. 1995, 52–53
8 Green, M. 1997c; Wood 1997
9 1995, 78
10 Carey 1991, 24–38
11 Jones & Jones 1976, 61–63
12 op. cit., 68
13 Green, M. 1995, 58
14 Jones & Jones 1976, 70
15 op. cit., 71
16 op. cit., 74
17 from the Second Branch of the Mabinogi; trans. Jones & Jones 1976, 29
18 Green 1998c
19 op. cit. 37
20 Green, M. 1998c
21 Jones & Jones 1976, 38
22 Jones & Jones 1976, xxiii; Wood 1989, 52–65
23 as described in the twelfth-century Black Book of Carmarthen
24 Wood 1989, 52–65
25 1966–68, 30–37
26 Wood 1989
27 Webster 1999, 1–20
28 Davidson 1989, 66–78
29 Aldhouse-Green, M. 2001a, 160
30 We are grateful to Paul Pettitt for this observation
31 1989, 66–78
32 Green, M. 1998c
33 Vitebsky 1995, 8–9
34 Mallory 1992, 103–159; O hUiginn 1992, 62
35 See Henig 1995, fig. 91
36 Alver 1989, 125–6
37 Lowe 2000, 119–129
38 Kinsella 1969, 36
39 Mallory (ed.) 1992, 12
40 from the Táin, trans. Kinsella 1969, 153
41 Paul Pettitt has observed that the 'warp spasm' sounds very like the effects of ergot poisoning.
42 Vitebsky 1995; Blackmore 1996; Clottes & Lewis-Williams 1998
43 Green, M. 1999a; Romeuf 1986; Deyts 1993
44 McMahon & Roberts 2001, 88
45 Boon 1976
46 Kinsella 1969, 158
47 Aldhouse-Green, M. 2001a, 157–160

48 Kinsella 1969, 60–63
49 Kelly 1992, 90–91
50 Green, M. 1997b, 129
51 Porter 1989
52 Augustine de Mirabilius I, 17, in Smyth 1995, 23–44
53 Smyth op. cit.
54 Halifax 1982
55 MacQueen 1989, 37
56 For a discussion on the symbolism of cranes at Neolithic Çatalhöyük see Russell & McGowan 2003, 445–455.
57 Sjoestedt 1926, 1–123; Smyth 1995, 23–44
58 I Kings 14, vv 1–18
59 Porter 1989, 100–115
60 Best & O'Brien 1954–1983, 780
61 Stokes 1905, 13, note 4
62 Eliade 1968, 136–137
63 1982
64 Sjöblom 1996, 233–251
65 Smyth 1995, 23–44
66 1996, 233–51
67 Sjöblom op. cit.
68 from Culhwch ac Olwen, trans. Jones & Jones 1976, 123–124
69 Jones & Jones 1976, 124–126
70 Green, M. 1992, 190–195
71 Green, M. 1992, 166–67; Mac Cana 1983, 104; O'Fáolain 1954
72 Green, M. 1992, 171; Campbell 1870–72, 193–202
73 Mac Cana 1983, 41–42
74 Henken 1987, 227–32
75 Blacker 1986, 116–123
76 Green 1995, 198–202; Bray 1987, 209–215; McCone 1990, 185–86.
77 from Immram Brain, after Mac Cana 1970, 124
78 2000
79 Green, M. 1999b, 60; Lehane 1994, 147; Wooding 2000
80 Mac Cana 1972, 102–142; 1976, 95–115
81 Nagy 1997, 284–86
82 op. cit., 285
83 Green, M. 1997b, 35–36
84 Green, M. 1997b, 35; O'Rahilly 1946; Mac Cana 1970, 126–28; Binchy 1958, 113–138; de Vries 1963; O'Hogáin 1990; Macalister 1931

CHAPTER 8 (pp. 203–211)
1 Bacelar Alves 2002
2 Strassburg 2000, 179–82
3 Strassburg 2000, 183
4 2002, 277–84
5 2002, 262–66
6 Pettitt 2002, 12–13.
7 Mussi 1995, 835.
8 Franco 1975

BIBLIOGRAPHY

Key works for further reading are marked with an asterisk

Albrethsen, S.E. and Petersen, E.B. 1975. *Gràvene på Bøgebakken Vedbaek.* Poul Kristensen: Herning.
—— 1976. Excavation of a Mesolithic cemetery at Vedbaek, Denmark. *Acta Archaeologica* 47, 1-28.
Aldhouse-Green, M.J. 2000. *Seeing the wood for the trees: the symbolism of trees and wood in ancient Gaul and Britain.* Aberystwyth: Centre for Advanced Welsh and Celtic Studies, University of Wales Aberystwyth.
* —— 2001a. *Dying for the Gods. Human Sacrifice in Iron Age and Roman Europe.* Stroud: Tempus.
—— 2001b. Animal Iconographies: Metaphor, Meaning and Identity (or why Chinese dragons don't have wings), in G. Davies, A. Gardner & K. Lockyear (eds) *TRAC 2000. Proceedings of the Tenth Annual Theoretical Roman Archaeology Conference London 2000.* Oxford: Oxbow, 80-93.
—— 2001c. Cosmovision and Metaphor: Monsters and Shamans in Gallo-British Cult-Expression, *European Journal of Archaeology* 4 (2), 201-230.
—— 2001d. Pagan Celtic Iconography and the Concept of Sacral Kingship, *Zeitschrift für Celtische Philologie* 52, 102-117.
—— 2001e. Gender-bending images: permeating boundaries in ancient European iconography, in R.J. Wallis & K. Lymer (eds), *A Permeability of Boundaries? New Approaches to the Archaeology of Art, Religion and Folklore.* Oxford: British Archaeological Reports (IS), No. 936, 19-29.
—— 2002. Any Old Iron! Symbolism & Ironworking in Iron Age Europe, in M. Aldhouse Green & P.V. Webster (eds) *Artefacts and Archaeology. Aspects of the Celtic and Roman World.* Cardiff: University of Wales Press, 8-19.

—— 2003. Metaphors, meaning and money: contextualising some symbols on Iron Age coins (Lecture delivered at *Celtic Coinage 2001*, a conference at the Ashmolean Museum, Oxford 6th-7th December 2001, in press.
* Aldhouse-Green, S.H.R. (ed.) 2000a. *Paviland Cave and the 'Red Lady': a Definitive Report.* Bristol: Western Academic & Specialist Press.
—— 2000b. Climate, ceremony, pilgrimage and Paviland: the 'Red Lady' in his palaeoecological and technoetic context. In Aldhouse-Green (ed.) 2000a: 227-46.
—— 2000c. Palaeolithic and Mesolithic Wales. In Lynch, F., Aldhouse-Green, S.H.R. and Davies, J.L. *Prehistoric Wales.* Stroud: Alan Sutton, 1-41.
—— 2001. 'Ex Africa aliquid semper novi': the view from Pontnewydd. In Milliken, S. and Cook, J. (eds) 2001. *A Very Remote Period Indeed. Papers on the Palaeolithic presented to Derek Roe.* Oxford: Oxbow Books, 114-19.
Alekseev, A. 1997. Healing techniques among Evén Shamans, in M.M. Balzer (ed.) *Shamanic Worlds. Rituals and Lore of Siberia and Central Asia.* Armonk, NY: North Castle/Sharpe, 153-64.
Alver, B.G. 1989. Concepts of the soul in Norwegian Tradition, in R. Kvideland & H.K. Sehmsdorf (eds) *Nordic Folklore.* Bloomington & Indianapolis: Indiana University Press, 110-127.
Alves, L. 2001. Rock art and enchanted moors: the significance of rock carvings in the folklore of north-west Iberia. In Wallis, R.J. (eds) 2001. *A Permeability of Boundaries? New Approaches to the Archaeology of Art, Religion and Folklore.* Oxford: British Archaeological Reports (IS), 936, 71-78.

Anisimov, A.F. 1963. The Shaman's Tent of the Evenks and the Origin of the Shamanistic Rite, in H.N. Michael (ed.) *Studies in Siberian Shamanism*. Toronto: University of Toronto Press/Arctic Institute of North America, 84-123.

Armstrong, K. 2000. *The Battle for God. Fundamentalism in Judaism, Christianity and Islam*. London: HarperCollins.

Arnold, B. 2001. Power Drinking in Iron Age Europe, *British Archaeology* 57, February 2001, 14-19.

Arnold, C.J. 1990. The Anglo-Saxon Cemeteries on the Isle of Wight: An Appraisal of Nineteenth-century Excavation Data, in S. Southworth (ed.), *Anglo-Saxon Cemeteries. A Reappraisal*. Stroud: Alan Sutton, 163-176.

Arsenault, D. 2004. From natural settings to spiritual places in the Algonkian sacred landscape: an archaeological, ethnohistorical and ethnographic analysis of Canadian Shield rock art sites. In Chippindale, C. and Nash, G. (eds) *Pictures in Place: the Figured Landscapes of Rock-Art*. Cambridge: Cambridge University Press, 289-317.

Ashbee, P. 1989. The Trundholm Horse's Trappings: a Chamfrein?, *Antiquity* 63, no. 240, 539-46.

Ashton, N. and Lewis, S. 2002. Deserted Britain: declining populations in the British Late Middle Pleistocene. *Antiquity* 76: 388-96.

Atkinson, R.J.C. 1956. *Stonehenge*. London: Hamish Hamilton.

Bacelar Alves, L. 2002. The architecture of the natural world: rock art in western Iberia. In Scarre (ed.) 2002a: 51-69.

Bagnall Smith, J. 1999. Votive Objects and Objects of Votive Significance from Great Walsingham, Norfolk, *Britannia* 30, 21-56.

Bahn, P.G. 1998. *The Cambridge Illustrated History of Prehistoric Art*. Cambridge: Cambridge University Press.

—— 2003. Human figures in portable art of the European Upper Palaeolithic. *Antiquity* 77: 410-12.

* Bahn, P.G. and Vertut, J. 1997. *Journey through the Ice Age*. London: Weidenfeld and Nicolson.

Bailey, D. 1994. Reading figurines as individuals, *World Archaeology* 25, 321-331.

Baker, P.A. 2001. Medicine, Culture and Military Identity, in Davies *et al.* (eds), 48-68.

Barham, L., Priestly. P. and Targett, A. 1999. *In Search of Cheddar Man*. Stroud: Tempus.

Barham, L. and Robson-Brown, K. (eds) 2001. *Human Roots. Africa and Asia in the Middle Pleistocene*. Bristol: Western Academic and Specialist Press Ltd.

Bar-Yosef, O. 2000. The Middle and Early Upper Palaeolithic in Southwest Asia and neighboring regions. In Bar-Yosef, O. and Pilbeam, D. (eds) *The Geography of Neandertals and Modern Humans in Europe and the Greater Mediterranean*, pp. 107-56. Harvard: Peabody Museum of Archaeology and Ethnology.

Baudry, M-T. (ed.) 1984. *L'Art des Cavernes: Atlas des Grottes ornées paléolithiques françaises*. Paris: Ministère de la Culture.

Beck, J.W., Richards, D.A, *et al.* 2001. Extremely large variations of atmospheric 14C concentration during the last glacial period. *Science* 292, 2453-58.

Bednarik, R.G. 2003. Seafaring in the Pleistocene. *Cambridge Archaeological Journal* 13(1): 41-66.

Bedoyère, G. de la 1999. *The Golden Age of Roman Britain*. Stroud: Tempus.

Bégouen, Comte H. and Vallois, H.V. 1927. Etudes des empreintes de pieds humains du Tuc d'Audoubert, de Cabrerets et Ganties. *Congrès international d'Anthropologie et d'Archéologie préhistorique*, pp 323-37 and plates 7-9. Amsterdam.

—— 1928. Les Empreintes préhistoriques: grottes du Tuc d'Audoubert (Ariège), de Cabrerets (Lot) et de Ganties-Montespan (Hte-Garonne). *Revue anthropologique* 33, 16.

Bégouen, R. and Clottes, J. 1984. Grotte du Tuc d'Audoubert. In Baudry (ed.) 1984, 410-15.

Bémont, C. 1983-84. *L'Art Celtique en Gaule 1983-1984*. Paris: Direction des Musées de France.

Benoit, F. 1969. *L'Art primitif Méditerranéen de la Vallée du Rhône*. Aix-en-Provence: Annales de la Faculté des Lettres.

Berger, T.D. and Trinkaus, E. 1995. Patterns of trauma among the Neanderthals. *Journal of Archaeological Science* 22, 841-52.

Berlin, B., & Kay, P., 1969. *Basic Color Terms: their Universality and Evolution*. Berkeley (CA): University of California Press.

Bertilsson, U. 1987. *The Rock Carvings of Northern Bohuslän. Spatial Structures and Social Symbols*. Stockholm: Stockholm Studies in Archaeology 7: Institutionen för Arkeologi: Stockholms Universitet.

Best, R.I. & O'Brien, M.A. (eds) 1954-1983. *The Book of Leinster*. Dublin: Institute for Advanced Studies IV.

Bibracte, Musée de la Civilisation Celtique 2000. *Les Druides Gaulois. Exposition Temporaire 29 Avril – 5 Novembre 2000. Catalogue des Objets Exposées*. Glux-en-Glenne: Centre Archéologique Européen du Mont Beuvray.

Binchy, D.A. 1958. The Fair of Tailtu and the Feast of Tara, *Eriu* 18, 113-138.

Bird, J. 1996. A Romano-British priestly head-dress from Farley Heath, *Surrey Archaeological Collections* 83, 81-89.

Bischoff, J.L., Shamp, D.D., *et al.* 2003. The Sima de los Huesos hominids date to beyond U/Th equilibrium (>350 kyr) and perhaps to 400 – 500 kyr: new radiometric dates. *Journal of Archaeological Science* 30, 275-80.

Blacker, C. 1989. The Seer as a Healer in Japan, in Davidson (ed.), 116-123.

Blackmore, J. 1996. Outlining a 'new' region: the rock art of the Omburo Ost, Namibia. Lecture delivered at the

Theoretical Archaeology Group Conference, University of Liverpool (16-18 December, 1996).

Bober, P.B. & Rubinstein, R. 1986. *Renaissance Artists and Antique Sculptures: a handbook of sources.* London: Harvey Miller.

Boon, G.C. 1976. The Shrine of the Head, Caerwent, in G.C. Boon & J.M. Lewis (eds) *Welsh Antiquity.* Cardiff: National Museum of Wales, 163-175.

Borges, J.L. 1975. *In Praise of Darkness.* London: Allen Lane.

Bosinski, G. 1990. *Homo sapiens: l'histoire des chasseurs du paléolithique supérieur.* Paris: Editions Errance.

Bott, E. 1987. The Kava Ceremonial as a dream structure, in M. Douglas (ed.) *Constructive Drinking. Perspectives on Drink from Anthropology.* Cambridge: Cambridge University Press, 182-204.

Boucher, S. 1976. *Recherches sur les bronzes figures de Gaule préromaine et romaine.* Paris/Rome: Bibliothèque des Ecoles Françaises à Athènes et de Rome, Palais Farnèse.

Bowen, D.Q. 2000. Calibration and correlation with the GRIP and GISP2 Greenland ice cores of radiocarbon ages from Paviland (Goat's Hole), Gower. In Aldhouse-Green (ed.) 2000a, 61-63.

Brade, C. 1975. *Die Mittelalterlichen Kernspaltflöten Mittel- und Nordeuropas.* Neumünster: Karl Wachholtz Verlag.

—— 1982. The prehistoric flute - did it exist? *The Galpin Society Journal* 35, 138-50.

Bradley, R. 1990. *The Passage of Arms.* Cambridge: Cambridge University Press.

—— 1997. *Rock Art and the Prehistory of Atlantic Europe.* London: Routledge.

*—— 2000. *An Archaeology of Natural Places.* London: Routledge.

—— 2002. *The Past in Prehistoric Societies.* London: Routledge.

Bray, D.A. 1987. 'The image of Saint Brigit in the early Irish Church', *Etudes Celtiques* 24, 209-215.

Brewer, R.J. 1986. *Corpus Signorum Imperii Romani. Corpus of Sculpture of the Roman World. Wales.* London/Oxford: British Academy/Oxford University Press.

Briard, J. 1987. *Mythes et Symboles de l'Europe Pré-Celtique: les Religions de l'âge du bronze 2500-800 av. JC.* Paris: Errance.

Bridgeford, S. 1997. Mightier than the pen? An edgewise look at Irish Bronze Age swords, in J. Carman (ed.) *Material harm. Archaeological Studies of War and Violence.* Glasgow: Cruithne Press, 95-115.

Bromwich, R. 1966-68. Y Cyneirdd a'r Traddodiad Cymraeg, *Bulletin of the Board of Celtic Studies* 22, 30-37.

Bronowski, J. 1973. *The Ascent of Man.* London: BBC Books; Boston: Little, Brown and Company.

Buisson, D. 1990. Les flûtes paléolithiques d'Isturitz (Pyrénées-Atlantiques). *Bulletin de la Société Préhistorique Française* 87, 420-33.

Buleli, N'Sanda 1993. Iron-making techniques in the Kivu region of Zaïre: some of the differences between the South Maniema region and North Ivu, in Thurston Shaw *et al.* (eds) *The Archaeology of Africa.* London: Routledge, 468-477.

Bulloch, A.W. 1985. *Callimachus. The Fifth Hymn.* Cambridge: Cambridge University Press.

Callow, P. & Cornford, J.M. (eds) 1986. *La Cotte de St. Brelade 1961—1978: excavations by C B M McBurney.* Norwich: Geo Books.

Campbell, J.F. 1870-72. Fionn's Echantment, *Revue Celtique* 1, 193-202.

Campbell, J. (ed.) 1982. *The Anglo-Saxons.* Harmondsworth: Penguin.

Camus, A. 1994. *Le Premier Homme.* Paris: Gallimard.

—— 1995. *The First Man.* London: Hamish Hamilton.

Cardillo, M. and Lister, A. 2002. Death in the slow lane. *Nature* 419 (3 October 2002), 440-41.

Carr, G. 2001. Romanisation and the Body, in Davies *et al.* (eds) 112-124.

—— 2002. A Time to Live, a Time to Heal and a Time to Die: Healing and divination in later Iron Age and Early Roman Britain, in G. Carr & P. Baker (eds) *New Approaches in Medical Archaeology.* Oxford: Oxbow, 58-73.

Carey, J. 1991. A British Myth of Origins?, *History of Religions* (University of Chicago), 24-38.

Cervera, J., Arsuaga, J-L., Bermúdez de Castro, J. M. and Carbonell, E. 1999. *Atapuerca: un Millón de Años de Historia.* 3rd edition. Madrid: Plot Ediciones S.A. and Editorial Complutense.

* Chadwick, N. 1966. *The Druids.* Cardiff: University of Wales Press.

Chaix, L., Bridault, A. and Picavet, R. 1997. A tamed brown bear (*Ursus arctos* L.) of the Late Mesolithic from La Grande-Rivoire (Isère, France). *Journal of Archaeological Science* 24, 1067-1074.

Chaloupka, G. undated *Burrunguy. Nourlangie Rock.* Sydney: Northart, National Library of Australia/ Australian Museum.

Chaloupka, G. 1993. 'you gotta have style', in Lorblanchet & Bahn (eds), 77-98.

Chapman, J. 1981. *The Vinča Culture of South-East Europe.* Oxford: British Archaeological Reports. International Series 117.

—— 2002. Colourful prehistories: the problem with the Berlin and Kay colour paradigm. In Jones and MacGregor (eds) 2002a: 45-72.

Champion, T., Gamble, C., Shennan, S. & Whittle, A. 1984. *Prehistoric Europe.* London: Academic Press.

Chipp, H.B. 1968. *Theories of Modern Art.* Berkeley/Los Angeles: University of California Press.

Clark, G. 1975. *The Earlier Stone Age Settlement of Scandinavia.* Cambridge: Cambridge University Press.

Clottes, J. 1995. *Les Cavernes de Niaux.* Paris: Seuil.

* —— 1996. Epilogue: Chauvet Cave today. In Chauvet, J-M., Deschamps, E. B. and Hillaire, C. 1996. *Chauvet Cave: the Discovery of the World's Oldest Paintings.* London: Thames & Hudson, 89—128.

—— 1997a. New laboratory techniques and their impact on palaeolithic cave art. In Conkey, M.W., Soffer, O., Stratmann, D. & Jablonski, N.G. (eds). 1997. *Beyond Art: Pleistocene Image and Symbol*, San Francisco: Memoirs of the California Academy of Sciences 23, pp 37-52.

—— 1997b. Art of the light and art of the depths. In Conkey, M.W., Soffer, O., Stratmann, D. & Jablonski, N.G. (eds). 1997. *Beyond Art: Pleistocene Image and Symbol*. San Francisco: Memoirs of the California Academy of Sciences 23, pp 203-16.

—— 1999. Twenty thousand years of palaeolithic cave art in southern France. In Coles, J., Bewley, R. and Mellars, P. (eds) *World Prehistory: Studies in Honour of Grahame Clark*, published as *Proceedings of the British Academy* 99, 161-75.

* Clottes, J. (ed.) 2003. *Return to Chauvet Cave. Excavating the Birthplace of Art: the First Full Report*. London: Thames & Hudson.

* Clottes, J. and Lewis-Williams, D. 1998. *The Shamans of Prehistory. Trance and Magic in the Painted Caves*. New York: Harry N. Abrams.

—— 2001 *Les Chamanes de la Préhistoire. Texte Intégral, Polémique et Réponses*. Paris: La Maison des Roches.

Clottes, J., Rouzaud, F. and Wahl, L. 1984. Grotte de Fontanet. In Baudry (ed.) 1984, 433-37.

Clottes, J. and Simonnet, R. 1972. Le réseau René Clastres de la caverne de Niaux. *Bulletin de la Société Préhistorique Française* 69, 293-323.

—— 1972. Le Réseau René Clastres. In Baudry (ed.) 1984, 424-27.

Coles, B. 1990. Anthropomorphic Wooden Figures from Britain and Ireland, *Proceedings of the Prehistoric Society* 56, 315-333.

—— 1998. Wood species for Wooden Figures: a glimpse of a pattern, in A. Gibson & D.D.A. Simpson (eds) *Prehistoric Religion & Ritual*. Stroud: Sutton Publishing, 163-169.

Coles, J. 1990. *Images of the Past. A Guide to the rock carvings and other ancient monuments of Northern Bohuslän*. Uddevalle: Hällristningsmuseet, Vitlycke.

—— 1994. *Rock Carvings of Uppland*. Uppsala: Societas Archaeologica Uppsaliensis.

—— 1999. The Dancer on the Rock: record and analysis at Järrestad, Sweden, *Proceedings of the Prehistoric Society* 65, 167-187.

* —— 2000. *Patterns in a rocky land: Rock Carvings in South-West Uppland, Sweden*. Uppsala: Department of Archaeology & Ancient History, University of Uppsala.

—— 2003. A measure of conviction: recording emphasis in Scandinavian rock carvings, *Antiquity* 77, no. 297, 555-571.

Collis, J. 2000. Survey and settlement in Central France: Celts, Arverni and Julius Caesar. Newport: University of Wales College, Newport, SCARAB Seminar 3.5.00.

Conard, N.J. 2003. Palaeolithic ivory sculptures from southwestern Germany and the origins of figurative art. *Nature* 426: 830-32.

* Conkey, M.W., Soffer, O., Stratmann, D. & Jablonski, N.G. (eds). 1997. *Beyond Art: Pleistocene image and symbol*. San Francisco: Memoirs of the California Academy of Sciences 23.

Connerton, P. 1989. *How Societies Remember*. Cambridge: Cambridge University Press.

Corder, P. & Richmond, I.A. 1938. A Romano-British Interment with Buckets and Sceptres from Brough, East Yorkshire, *Antiquaries Journal* 18, 68ff.

Creighton, J. 1995. Visions of power: imagery & symbols in late Iron Age Britain, *Britannia* 26, 285-301.

* —— 2000. *Coins and Power in Late Iron Age Britain*. Cambridge: Cambridge University Press.

Crummy, P. 1997a. Britain's earliest doctor?, *Rescue News* 73, 7.

—— 1997b. Colchester. The Stanway Burials, *Current Archaeology* 153, 2, no. 9, 337-341.

Culotta, E. 1999. Neanderthals were cannibals, bones show. *Science* 286, 18-19.

Cummings, V. 2002. All cultural things: actual and conceptual monuments in the Neolithic of western Britain. In Scarre (ed.) 2002a, 107-21.

Cunnington, M.E. 1929. *Woodhenge*. Devizes: Simpson.

Currant, A. P., Jacobi, R.M. and Stringer, C.B. 1989. Excavations at Gough's Cave, Somerset, 1986-7. *Antiquity* 63, 131-36.

Davidson, H.E. 1989. 'The Seer's Thumb', in H.E. Davidson ed., 66-78.

* Davidson, H.E. 1989 (ed.). *The Seer in Celtic and Other Traditions*. Edinburgh: John Donald.

Davies, G., Gardner, A. & Lockyear K. (eds) 2001. *TRAC 2000. Proceedings of the Tenth Theoretical Archaeology Conference, London 2000*. Oxford: Oxbow.

Davies, J. 1996. *The Making of Wales*. Stroud: Alan Sutton.

Davies, J.A. 1925. Fourth Report on Aveline's Hole. *Proceedings of the University of Bristol Spelaeological Society* 2: 104-14.

Davies, W. 2001. A very model of a modern human industry: new perspectives on the origin and spread of the Aurignacian in Europe. *Proceedings of the Prehistoric Society* 67, 195-217.

Davis, W. 1984. Representation and knowledge in the prehistoric rock art of Africa. *African Archaeological Journal* 2, 7-35.

Dayet, M. 1954. 'Le sanglier à trois cornes de Cabinet des Medailles', *Revue Archéologique de l'est et du centre-est* 5, 334-335.

D'Errico, F. 1991. La signification des galets engravés aziliens et le mythe des calendriers lunaires préhistoriques. *Annales de la Fondation Thyssen*.

D'Errico, F., Henshilwood, C. and Nilssen, P. 2001. An engraved bone fragment from *c.* 70,000-year-old

Middle Stone Age levels at Bloombos Cave, South Africa: implications for the origins of symbolism and language. *Antiquity* 75 (288), 309-18.

D'Errico, F. and Villa, P. 1997. Holes and grooves: the contribution of microscopy and taphonomy to the problem of art origins. *Journal of Human Evolution* 33, 1-31.

D'Errico, F., Villa, P., Pinto Llona, A.C. and Ruiz Idarraga, R. 1997. A Middle Palaeolithic origin of music ? Using cave-bear bone accumulations to assess the Divje Babe I bone 'flute'. *Antiquity* 72, 65-79.

D'Errico, F., Zilhao, J., Julien, M., Baffier, D. & J. Pelegrin. 1998. Neanderthal acculturation in Western Europe? A critical review of the evidence and its interpretation. *Current Anthropology* 39, supplement, pp.1-44.

De Lumley, H. 1995. *Le grandiose et le sacré. Gravures protohistoriques et historiques de la région du Mont Bégo.* Paris: Epona.

De Sélincourt, A. 1964. *Herodotus. The Histories.* Penguin: Harmondsworth.

* Demakopoulou, K., Eluère,C., Jensen, J., Jockenhövel, A. & Mohen, J.-P. 1999. *Gods and Heroes of the European Bronze Age.* London: Thames & Hudson.

Dent, J. 1985. Three Cart Burials from Wetwang, Yorkshire, *Antiquity* 59, 185-192.

Devauges, J.-B. 1974. Circonscription de Bourgogne, *Gallia* 32, 434.

Devlet, E. 2001. Rock art and the material culture of Siberian and Central Asian shamanism, in Price (ed.), 43-55.

Deyts, S. 1976. *Sculptures Gallo-Romaine Mythologiques et Religieuses.* Paris: Editions de Musées Nationaux.

—— 1983. *Les bois sculptés des Sources de la Seine.* Paris: CNRS/ XLIIe supplément à *Gallia.*

—— 1992. *Images des Dieux de la Gaule.* Paris: Errance.

—— 1999. *A la rencontre des Dieux gaulois un défi à César.* Paris: Musée des Antiquités Nationales.

Diamond, J. 2002. Evolution, consequences and future of plant and animal domestication. *Nature* 418 (8 August 2002), 700-707.

Dickinson, T.M. 1992. An Anglo-Saxon 'cunning woman' from Bidford-on-Avon, in M.O.H. Carver (ed.), *In Search of Cult: Archaeological Investigations in Honour of Philip Rahtz.* Woodbridge: Boydell Press, 45-54.

Diemberger, H. 1993. Blood, sperm, soul and the mountain: Gender relations, kinship and cosmovision among the Khumbo (N.E. Nepal), in T. del Valle (ed.) 1993. *Gendered Anthropology.* London: Routledge.

Dillehay, T.D. 2003. Tracking the first Americans. *Nature* 425: 23-25.

Douglas, M. 1970. *Natural Symbols.* London: Cresset Press.

* Dowden, K. 2000. *European Paganism: The Realities of Cult from Antiquity to the Middle Ages.* London: Routledge.

Dowson, T. & Porr, M. 2001. Special objects - special creatures: shamanistic imagery and the Aurignacian art of South-West Germany, in Price (ed.), 165-177.

Drinkwater, J. 1983. *Roman Gaul.* London: Croom Helm.

* Dronfield, J. 1993. Ways of seeing, ways of telling: Irish passage tomb art, style and the universality of vision, in M. Lorblanchet & P.G. Bahn (eds) *Rock Art Studies: The Post-Stylistic Era or Where do we go from here?.* Oxford: Oxbow Monograph 35, 179-93.

* —— 1995. Migraine, light and hallucinogens: the neurocognitive basis of Irish megalithic art. *Oxford Journal of Archaeology* 14, 261-75.

* —— 1996a. The vision thing: diagnosis of endogenous derivation in abstract arts. *Current Anthropology* 37, 373-91.

* —— 1996b. Entering alternative realities: cognition, art and architecture in Irish passage-tombs. *Cambridge Archaeological Journal* 6, 37-74.

Duarte, C. 2002. The burial taphonomy and ritual. In Zilhão and Trinkaus (eds) 2002: 187-201.

Duarte, C., Maurício, J., *et al.* 1999. The early Upper Palaeolithic human skeleton from the Abrigo do Lagar Velho (Portugal) and modern human emergence in Iberia. *Proceedings of the National Academy of Sciences USA* 96, 7604-7609.

DuBois, P. 1982. *Centaurs and Amazons: women and the Prehistory of the Great Chain of Being.* Ann Arbor (MI): University of Michigan Press.

Duval, P.-M. 1987. *Monnaies Gauloises et Mythes Celtiques.* Paris: Hermann.

Duval, P.-M. & Pinault, G. 1986. *Recueil des Inscriptions Gauloises (RIG).* Vol. III. *Les Calendriers (Coligny, Villards d'Héria).* Paris: CNRS. XLVe Supplément à *Gallia.*

* Eliade, M. 1968. *Le Chamanisme et les techniques archaiques de l'exstase.* Paris: Payot.

Eluère, C. 1987. *L'Or des Celtes.* Fribourg: Bibliothèque des Arts.

Enard, W., Przeworski, M., Fisher, S.E., Lai, C.S.L., Wiebe, V., Kitano, T., Monaco, A.P. and Pääbo, S. 2002. Molecular evolution of *FOXP2*, a gene involved in speech and language. *Nature* 418, 869-72.

English Heritage 2004. Britain's earliest cemetery revealed. http://accessibility.englishheritage.org.uk/Default.asp? WCI=NewsItem&WCE=343 (accessed 18/01/2004)

Espérandieu, E. 1915. *Recueil Général des Bas-Reliefs de la Gaule Romaine et pré-Romaine* vol. 6. Paris: Imprimerie Nationale.

Fagles, R. 1982 trans. *Sophocles. The Three Theban Plays.* Harmondsworth: Penguin.

Farizy, C. 1990. The transition from Middle to Upper Palaeolithic at Arcy-sur-Cure (Yonne, France): technological, economic and social aspects. In Mellars, P.A. (ed.) *The Emergence of Modern Humans: an Archaeological Perspective.* Edinburgh: Edinburgh University Press, 303-26.

Fellmann, R. 1999. Das Zink-Täfelschen vom Thormebodewald auf der Engehalbinsel bei Bern und seine keltische Inschrift, *Archaeologie im Kanton Bern* 4, 133-175.

Ferguson, J. 1972. *A Companion to Greek Tragedy.* Austin (Texas): University of Texas Press.

—— 1980. *Greek and Roman Religion. A Source Book.* Park Ridge (NJ): Noyes Press.

Finlayson, B. 1998. *Wild Harvesters. The First People in Scotland.* Edinburgh: Canongate Books.

Fischer, B. 2003. Coinage and wine in Gaul, in P. de Jersey (ed.) *Celtic Coinage 2001 (Proceedings of a Conference held at the Ashmolean Museum, Oxford, December 2001).* Oxford: British Archaeological Reports.

Fischer, Christian undated. *The Tollund Man and the Elling Woman.* Silkeborg: Silkeborg Museum.

Fitzhugh, W.W. and Prusinski, J. 2003. Crossroads of continents – Ekven burial chamber. http://.www.mnh.si.edu/arctic/features/croads/ekven.html. Consulted 7.9.03.

* Fitzpatrick, A.P. 1996. Night and day: the symbolism of astral signs on later Iron Age anthropomorphic short swords, *Proceedings of the Prehistoric Society* 62, 273-298.

—— 2000a. Les Druides en Grande-Bretagne, in Guichard & Perrin (eds), 47-49.

—— 2000b. Ritual, Sequence and Structure in Late Iron Age mortuary practices in north-west Europe, in J. Pearce, M. Millett & M. Struck (eds) *Burial, Society and Context in the Roman World.* Oxford: Oxbow, 15-29.

Flannery, T. 2001. *The Eternal Frontier: an Ecological History of North America and its Peoples.* London: William Heinemann.

* Flood, J. 1990. *Archaeology of the Dreamtime. The Story of Prehistoric Australia and its People.* London: Yale University Press.

Forcey, C., Hawthorne, J. & Witcher, R. (eds) *TRAC 97. Proceedings of the Seventh Annual Theoretical Archaeology Conference Nottingham 1997.* Oxford: Oxbow.

Fox, C. 1946. *A Find of the Early Iron Age from Llyn Cerrig Bach, Anglesey.* Cardiff: National Museum of Wales.

Foxhall, L. 1994. Pandora unbound: a feminist critique of Foucault's *History of Sexuality,* in A. Cornwall & N. Lindisfarne (eds) *Dislocating Masculinity.* London: Routledge, 133-146.

Franco, J. 1975. Introduction. In Neruda, P. *Selected Poems.* London: Penguin Books, 13-23.

Fulford, M. 2001. Links with the Past: Pervasive 'Ritual' Behaviour in Roman Britain, *Britannia* 32, 199-218.

Fulford, M. & Creighton, J. 1998. A Late Iron Age Mirror Burial from Latchmere Green, near Silchester, Hampshire, *Proceedings of the Prehistoric Society* 64, 331-342.

Galliou, P. 1984. Days of Wine and Roses? Early Armorica and the Atlantic Wine Trade, in S. Macready & F.H. Thompson (eds) *Cross-Channel Trade between Gaul and Britain in the Pre-Roman Iron Age.* London: Society of Antiquaries of London, 24-36.

Gamble, C. 1986. *The Palaeolithic Settlement of Europe.* Cambridge: Cambridge University Press.

* —— 1991. The social context for European Palaeolithic art. *Proceedings of the Prehistoric Society* 57, 3-15.

—— 1995. The earliest occupation of Europe: the environmental background. In Roebroeks and Kolfschoten (eds) 1995, 279-95.

—— 1999. *The Palaeolithic Societies of Europe.* Cambridge: Cambridge University Press.

Garcia, M.A. 2003. The prints and traces of humans and animals. In Clottes (ed.) 2003, 34-43.

Garland, R. 1995. *The Eye of the Beholder: Deformity and Disability in the Graeco-Roman World.* Ithaca, New York: Cornell University Press.

Gazin-Schwartz, A. and Holtorf, C. 1999. 'As long as ever I've known it ...': on folklore and archaeology. In Gazin-Schwartz, A. and Holtorf, C. (eds) 1999. *Archaeology and Folklore,* pp 3-25. London: Routledge.

Gebühr, M. 2002. *Moorleichen in Schleswig-Holstein.* Schleswig: Archäologisches Landesmuseum Schloß Gottorf.

Geneste, J-M. 2003. Visiting the cave and human activities. In Clottes (ed.) 2003, 44-50.

Giedion, S. 1962. *The Eternal Present. The Beginnings of Art.* London.

Gilbert, H. 1978. The Felmingham Hall Hoard, *Bulletin of the Board of Celtic Studies* 28, part 1, 159-187.

Gilchrist, R. 1997. Ambivalent Bodies: gender and medieval archaeology, in J. Moore & E. Scott (eds) *Invisible People and Processes: writing gender and childhood into European Archaeology.* Leicester: Leicester University Press, 42-58.

—— 1999. *Gender and Archaeology.* London: Routledge.

Gillies, W. 1981. The Craftsman in Early Celtic Literature, *Scottish Archaeological Forum* 11 (*Early Technology in North Britain*), 70-85.

Gillieson, D. 1996. *Caves: Processes, Development and Management.* Oxford: Blackwell.

Glob, P.V. 1969. *The Bog People.* London: Faber & Faber.

—— 1974. *The Mound People.* London: Faber & Faber.

Gore, R. 2000. People Like Us. *National Geographic* 198 (1), 90-117.

Gosden, C. and Lock, G. 1998. Prehistoric histories. *World Archaeology* 30, 2-12.

Green, H.S. 1989. The stone age cave archaeology of south Wales. In Ford, T.D. (ed.) *Limestones and Caves of Wales.* Cambridge: Cambridge University Press, pp. 70-78.

Green, M.J. 1976. *The Religions of Civilian Roman Britain.* Oxford: British Archaeological Reports (BS), No. 24.

—— 1978. *A Corpus of Small Cult Objects from the Military Areas of Roman Britain.* Oxford: British Archaeological Reports (BS) no. 52.

—— 1984. *The Wheel as a Cult-Symbol in the Romano-Celtic World.* Brussels: Latomus.

—— 1989. *Symbol and Image in Celtic Religious Art.* London: Routledge.

—— 1991. *The Sun-Gods of Ancient Europe.* London: Batsford.

—— 1992. *Animals in Celtic Life and Myth*. London: Routledge.

—— 1995. *Celtic Goddesses. Warriors, Virgins and Mothers*. London: British Museum Press.

—— 1996. *Celtic Art. Reading the Messages*. London: Weidenfeld & Nicolson.

—— 1997a. Images in opposition: polarity, ambivalence and liminality in cult representation, *Antiquity* 71, 898-911.

* —— 1997b. *Exploring the World of the Druids*. London and New York: Thames & Hudson.

—— 1997c. The Symbolic Horse in Pagan Celtic Europe: An Archaeological Perspective, in S. Davies & N.A. Jones (eds) *The Horse in Celtic Culture*. Cardiff: University of Wales Press, 1-22.

—— 1998a. Crossing the Boundaries: Triple Horns and Emblematic Transference, *European Journal of Archaeology* 1 (2), 219-240.

—— 1998b. The Time Lords: Ritual Calendars, Druids and the Sacred Year, in A. Gibson & D. Simpson (eds) *Prehistoric Ritual and Religion*. Stroud: Alan Sutton, 190-202.

—— 1998c. Vessels of Death: Sacred Cauldrons in Archaeology & Myth, *Antiquaries Journal* 78, 63-84.

—— 1999a. *Pilgrims in Stone. Stone Images from the Gallo-Roman Sanctuary of Fontes Sequanae*. Oxford: Archaeopress/British Archaeological Reports (IS), No. 754.

—— 1999b. Back to the Future. Resonances of the past in myth and material culture, in A. Gazin-Schwartz & C. Holtorf (eds) *Archaeology and Folklore*. London: Routledge, 48-66.

Grinsell, L.V. 1953. *The Ancient Burial-Mounds of England*. London: Methuen.

Grün, R., Beaumont, P.B. and Stringer, C.B. 1990. ESR dating evidence for early modern humans at Border Cave in South Africa. *Nature* 344, 537-40.

Guenther, M, 1991. Animals in bushman thought, myth and art. In Ingold, T, Riches, D, & Woodburn, J, (eds). *Hunters and Gatherers. Volume 2: property, power and ideology*, pp 192-202. Oxford: Berg.

Guenther, M.G. 1997. African Foragers. In Vogel, J.O., (ed.). 1997. *Encyclopedia of Precolonial Africa*, pp 179-84. London: Altamira Press.

* Guichard, V. & Perrin, F. (eds). *Les Druides*. Paris: Errance (L'Archéologue Hors Série No. 2).

Guthrie, R.D. 1990. *Frozen Fauna of the Mammoth Steppe*. Chicago: Chicago University Press.

Gvozdover, M. 1995. *Art of the Mammoth Hunters: the finds from Avdeevo*. Oxford: Oxbow Monograph 49.

Hahn, J., Müller-Beck, H. and Taute, W. 1973. *Eiszeithöhlen im Lonetal*. Stuttgart: Müller & Gräff.

Halifax, J. 1982. *Shaman. The Wounded Healer*. New York: Crossroads.

Hansen, H.L. 2000. The truth without nonsense: Remarks on Artemidorus' *Interpretation of Dreams*, in R.L.

Wildfang & J. Isager (eds) *Divination and Portents in the Roman World*. Odense: Odense University Press, 57-65.

Hauser, A. 1962. *The Social History of Art 4: Naturalism, Impressionism, The Film Age*. London: Routledge.

Havelock, EA 1963. *Preface to Plato*. Cambridge, Mass: Harvard University Press.

Hawkes, J. 1951. *A Guide to the Prehistoric and Roman Monuments in England and Wales*. London: Chatto and Windus.

Hayden, B., Chisholm, B. and Schwarcz, H. P. 1987. Fishing and foraging: marine resources in the Upper Palaeolithic of France. In Soffer, O. (ed.) *The Pleistocene Old World: Regional Perspectives*. Plenum Press: New York, 279-291.

Hayen, H. 1971. 'Hölzerne Kultfiguren am Bohlenweg XLII (Ip) im Wittemoor (Gemeinde Berne, Landkreis Wesermarsch), *Die Kunde* 22, 88-123.

—— 1987. Peatbog Archaeology in Lower Saxony, West Germany, in J. Coles & A. Lawson (eds) *European Wetlands in Prehistory*. Oxford: 117-136.

Haynes, G. 2002. *The Early Settlement of North America: the Clovis Era*. Cambridge: Cambridge University Press.

* Helvenston, P.A. and Bahn, P.G. 2002. *Desperately Seeking Trance Plants: Testing the 'Three Stages of Trance' Model*. New York: RJ Communications LLC.

—— 2002. Testing the 'Three Stages of Trance' model. *Cambridge Archaeological Journal* 13 (2): 213-24.

Henig, M. 1993. *A Handbook of Roman Art. A Survey of the Visual Arts of the Roman World*. Oxford: Phaidon.

—— 1995. *The Art of Roman Britain*. London: Batsford.

Henken, E.R. 1987. *Traditions of the Welsh Saints*. Cambridge: Boydell & Brewer.

Herbert, E.W. 1993. *Iron, Gender and Power: rituals of transformation in African Societies*. Bloomington: Indiana University Press.

Hill, J.D. 1995. *Ritual and Rubbish in the Iron Age of Wessex*. Oxford: British Archaeological Reports (BS), No. 242.

—— 2001. A New Cart/Chariot Burial from Wetwang, East Yorkshire, *PAST* 38, August 2001, 2-3.

Hillman, Gordon 1986. Plant Foods in Ancient Diet: The Archaeological Role of Palaeofaeces in General and Lindow Man's Gut Contents in Particular, in I.M. Stead, J.B. Bourke & Don Brothwell, *Lindow Man. The Body in the Bog*. London: British Museum Publications, 99-115.

Hingley, R. 1997. Iron, ironworking and regeneration: a study of the symbolic meaning of metalworking in Iron Age Britain, in A. Gwilt & C. Haselgrove (eds) *Reconstructing Iron Age Societies*. Oxford: Oxbow Monograph 71, 9-18.

Hoggart, R. 1992. *The Uses of Literacy*. London: Penguin Books.

Holden, T.G. 1995. The Last Meals of the Lindow Bog Men, in Turner & Scaife (eds), 76-82.

* Holl, J. 2002. *An Investigation into Three Romano-British Religious Sites in Surrey.* Bristol: University of Bristol, unpub. dissertation.

* Hollimon, S. 2001. The gendered peopling of North America: Addressing the antiquity of systems of multiple genders, in Price (ed.), 123-134.

Hoppál, M. 1992. Shamanism: an archaic and/or recent system of beliefs, in Siikala & Hoppál (eds), 117-131.

* Housley, R.A. 1998. The return of the natives: AMS radiocarbon dating of Magdalenian artefacts and recolonisation of northern Europe after the last ice age. In Bayley, J. (ed.) *Science in Archaeology: an Agenda for the Future.* London: English Heritage, 9-20.

* Howell, R. 1988. *A History of Gwent.* Llandysul: Gomer Press.

* Hublin, J-J., Spoor, F., Braun, M., Zonneveld, S. and Condemi, S. 1996. A late Neanderthal associated with Upper Palaeolithic artefacts. *Nature* 381, 224-26.

* Hughes, T. 1997. *Tales from Ovid. Twenty-four passages from the Metamorphoses.* London: Faber and Faber.

* Hutton, R. 1993. *The Shamans of Siberia.* Glastonbury: the Isle of Avalon Press.

Hutton, R. 2001. *Shamans: Siberian Spirituality and the Western Imagination.* London: Hambledon and London.

Ingold, T. 1992. Comment on 'Beyond the original affluent society' by N. Bird-David. *Current Anthropology* 33, 34-47.

* —— 1986. *The appropriation of Nature.* Manchester: Manchester University Press.

* Jacobs, D., Thomas, W. & Lang S. (eds), 1997. *Two-Spirit People: Native American Gender, Sexuality & Spirituality.* Illinois: University of Illinois Press.

Jacobs, K.W. 1995. Returning to Oleni'ostrov: social, economic and skeletal dimensions of a boreal forest Mesolithic cemetery. *Journal of Anthropological Archaeology* 14: 359-403.

Jensen, J. 1978. *The Prehistory of Denmark.* Copenhagen: Nationalmuseet.

Jensen, J. 1982. *The Prehistory of Denmark.* London: Methuen.

Johns, C. 1982. *Sex or symbol: erotic images of Greece and Rome.* London: British Museum Publications.

Jones, A. 1998. 'Where Eagles Dare. Landscapes, animals and the Neolithic of Orkney', *Journal of Material Culture* 3 (3), 301-324.

Jones, A. and MacGregor, G. 2002. Introduction: wonderful things – colour studies in archaeology from Munsell to materiality. In Jones and MacGregor (eds) 2002: 1-21.

* Jones, A. and MacGregor, G. (eds) 2002. *Colouring the Past: the Significance of Colour in Archaeological Research.* Oxford: Berg.

Jones, G. & Jones, T. Trans. 1976. *The Mabinogion.* London: Dent.

Jones, R.L. 1986. The flora and vegetation of La Cotte de St Brelade and its environs. In Callow, P. & Cornford, J.M.

1986. *La Cotte de St. Brelade 1961–1978: excavations by C B M McBurney.* Norwich: Geo Books, 99-106.

Jordan, P. 2001. The materiality of shamanism as a 'worldview: Praxis, artefacts and landscape, in Price (ed.), 87-104.

Jundi, S. & Hill, J.D. 1998. Brooches & Identities in first century AD Britain: more than meets the eye?, in Forcey *et al.* (eds), 125-137.

Kampen, N.B. 1996. Omphale and the instability of gender, in N.B. Kampen (ed.) *Sexuality in ancient art. Near East, Egypt, Greece and Italy.* Cambridge: Cambridge University Press, 233-246.

Kaul, F., Marazov, I., Best, J. & de Vries, N. 1991. *Thracian Tales on the Gundestrup Cauldron.* Amsterdam: Najade Press.

Keller, C.M. & Keller, J.D. 1996. *Cognition and Tool Use. The Blacksmith at Work.* Cambridge: Cambridge University Press.

Kelly, P. 1992. The Táin as Literature, in Mallory (ed.), 69-102.

King, H. 1995. Half-Human Creatures, in J. Cherry (ed.) *Mythical Beasts.* London: British Museum Press, 138-167.

Kinsella, T. 1969. *The Táin.* Oxford: Oxford University Press.

Klein. R.G. 1995. Anatomy, behavior and modern human origins. *Journal of World Prehistory* 9, 167-198.

* —— 1999. *The Human Career.* 2nd edition. Chicago: University of Chicago Press.

Klíma, B. 1995. *Dolní Věstonice II.* Liège: ERAUL 73.

Knight, C., Power, C. and Watts, I. 1995. The human symbolic revolution: a Darwinian account. *Cambridge Archaeological Journal* 5, 75-114.

Knüsel, C. 2002. Of Crystal Balls, Political Power and Changing Contexts: What the Clever Women of Salerno Inherited, in P. Baker & G. Carr (eds), *New Approaches in Medical Archaeology.* Oxford: Oxbow, 172-194.

Kolen, J. 1999. Hominids without homes: on the nature of Middle Palaeolithic settlement in Europe. In Roebroeks, W. & Gamble, C. (eds) 1999. *The Middle Palaeolithic Occupation of Europe.* Leiden: University of Leiden, 139-75.

Kozlowski, S. K. (1993) Maszycka Cave: a Magdalenian site in Southern Poland. *Jahrbuch der Romisch-Germanischen Zentralmuseum Mainz* 40 Teil 1. 115.

Krings, M., Stone, A., *et al.* 1997. Neanderthal DNA sequences and the origin of modern humans. *Cell* 90, 19-30.

—— 1999. DNA sequence of the DNA hypervariable region II from the Neanderthal type specimen. *Proceedings of the National Academy of Sciences (USA)* 96, 5581-5.

Krings, M., Capelli, C., *et al.* S. 2000. A view of Neanderthal genetic diversity. *Nature Genetics* 26, 144-6.

Künzl, E. 1983. *Medizinische Instrumente aus Sepulkralfunden der römischen Kaiserzeit.* Köln: Rheinland Verlag.

Lamberton, R. 1988. *Hesiod.* Newhaven & London: Yale University Press.

Lambot, B. 1998. Les Morts d'Acy Romance (Ardennes) à La Tène Finale. Pratiques funéraires, aspects religieuses et hiérarchie sociale, *Etudes et Documents Fouillés* 4. *Les Celtes. Rites Funéraires en Gaule du Nord entre le Vie et le Ier siècle avant Jésus-Christ.* Namur: Ministère de la Région Walionne, 75-87.

Langbroek, M. 2001. Debating Neanderthals and Modern Humans in late Pleistocene Europe. *Archaeological Dialogues* 8 (2), 123-51.

Larsson, L. 1984. The Skateholm project. A late Mesolithic settlement and cemetery complex at a southern Swedish bay. *Meddelanden från Lunds Universitets Historiska Museum* (NS) 5, 5-38.

—— 1989. Late Mesolithic settlements and cemeteries at Skateholm, southern Sweden. In Bonsall, C. (ed.) *The Mesolithic in Europe*, pp. 367-78. Edinburgh: John Donald.

—— 1997. *Materiell Kultur och Religiosa Symboler.* Umeå: Institutionen för Arkeologi Umeå Universitet/Arkeologicka Studier Vid Umeå Universitet 4.

—— 2002. Food for the living, food for the dead. *Before Farming*, 177-87. Bristol: Western Academic & Specialist Press

* Layton, R 1992. *Australian Rock Art: a new synthesis.* London: Routledge.

Le Guillou, Y. 2003. Depictions of humans. In Clottes (ed.) 2003: 167-71.

Leach, E. 1976. *Culture and Communication.* Cambridge: Cambridge University Press.

Lejars, T. & Perrin, F. 2000. 'Des Tombes de Druides', in Guichard & Perrin (eds), 37-40.

Lehane, B. 1994. *Early Celtic Christianity.* Cardiff: Constable.

Leroi-Gourhan, A. 1961. Les fouilles d'Arcy-sur-Cure. *Gallia Préhistoire* 4, 3-16.

Lévêque, F., Backer, A.M and Guilbaud, M. 1993. *Context of a Late Neanderthal. Implications of Multidisciplinary Research for the Transition to Upper Palaeolithic Adaptations at Saint-Césaire, Charente-Maritime, France.* Madison, Wisconsin: Prehistory Press.

* Lewis-Williams, J.D. 1981. *Believing and Seeing: symbolic meanings in southern San rock paintings.* London: Academic Press.

—— 1991. Wrestling with analogy: a methodological dilemma in palaeolithic art research. *Proceedings of the Prehistoric Society* 57 (1), 149-62.

* —— 1997. Harnessing the brain: vision and shamanism in palaeolithic western Europe. In Conkey *et al.* (eds) 1997, 321-42.

* —— 2001a. 'Southern African shamanistic rock art in its social and cognitive contexts', in Price (ed.), 17-39.

—— 2001b. 'Shamanism in Upper Palaeolithic Rock-Art', Lecture delivered in the Dept of Drama, University of Bristol 23ʳᵈ October 2001.

* —— 2002. *The Mind in the Cave: Consciousness and the Origins of Art.* London and New York: Thames & Hudson.

* Lewis-Williams, J.D. & Dowson, T.A. 1988. The signs of all times: entoptic phenomena in Upper Palaeolithic Art, *Current Anthropology* 29 (2), 201-245.

* —— 1990a. Through the Veil: San rock paintings and the rock face, *South African Archaeological Bulletin* 45, 5-16.

* —— 1990b. On palaeolithic art and the neuropsychological model. *Current Anthropology* 31: 407-8.

Lorblanchet, M. 1984. Grotte de Pech-Merle. In Baudry (ed.) 1984: 467-74.

—— 1984. Symbolisme des empreintes en Australie. *Histoire et Archéologie* 90: 63-76.

—— 1995. *Les Grottes Ornées de la Préhistoire: Nouveaux Regards.* Paris: Editions Errance.

* Lorblanchet, M. & Sieveking, A. 1997. The Monsters of Pergouset, *Cambridge Journal of Archaeology* 7 (1), 37-56.

Lord, A.B. 1960. *The Singer of Tales.* Harvard Studies in Comparative Literature, 24. Cambridge, Mass: Harvard University Press.

Loring, S. 1997. On the trail of the Caribou House: Some reflections on Innu caribou hunters in northern Ntessinan (Labrador), in L.J. Jackson & P.T. Thacker (eds), *Caribou and Reindeer Hunters of the Northern Hemisphere.* Avebury: Aldershot, 185-220.

Lowe, J. 2000. Kicking over the Traces: The Instability of Cú Chulainn, *Studia Celtica* 34, 119-129.

Lubbock, J. [Lord Avebury] 1865. *Pre-historic Times, as Illustrated by Ancient Remains, and the Manners and Customs of Modern Savages.* London: Williams and Norgate.

Macalister, R.A.S. 1931. *Tara. A Pagan Sanctuary of Ancient Ireland.* London: Methuen.

Mac Cana, P. 1970. *Celtic Mythology.* London: Newnes.

—— 1972. Mongán mac Fiachna and "Immram Brain", *Eriu* 23, 102-142.

—— 1976. The sinless otherworld of Immram Brain, *Eriu* 27, 95-115.

—— 1983 *Celtic Mythology.* London: Newnes.

MacInnes, J. 1989. The Seer in Gaelic Tradition, in Davidson (ed.), 10-24.

MacQueen, J. 1989. The Saint as Seer. Adomnan's Account of Columba, in Davidson (ed.), 37-51.

Malinowski, B. 1923. The problem of meaning in primitive languages. In Ogden, C.K. and Richards, I.A. (eds) *The Meaning of Meaning: a Study of the Influence of Language upon Thought and of the Science of Symbolism.* Kegan Paul: London, 451-510.

Mayle, P. 1989. *A Year in Provence.* London: Hamish Hamilton.

McBrearty S. and Brooks A.S. 2000. The revolution that

wasn't: a new interpretation of the origin of modern human behavior. *Journal of Human Evolution* 39 (5), 453-563.

McCone, K. 1982. Brigit in the seventh century – a saint with three lives, *Perítia* I, 107-145.

—— 1990. *Pagan Past and Christian Present in Early Irish Literature.* Maynooth: An Sagart.

McMahon, J. & Roberts, J. 2001. *The Sheela-Na-Gigs of Ireland and Britain.* Cork: Mercier Press.

Mallory, J.P. 1992. The World of Cú Chulainn. The Archaeology of the Táin Bó Cúailnge, in Mallory (ed.), 103-159.

Mallory, J.P. 1992 (ed.) *Aspects of the Táin.* Belfast: December Publications.

Mattingly, H. 1948. (trans.) *Tacitus on Britain and Germany.* West Drayton: Penguin.

May, J. 2003. Eogan of Knowth. *Current Archaeology* 188: 328-34.

Meaney, A.-L. 1981. *Anglo-Saxon Amulets and Curing Stones.* Oxford: British Archaeological Reports (BS), No. 96.

* —— 1989. Women, witchcraft and magic in Anglo-Saxon England, in D.G. Scragg (ed.). *Superstition and Popular Medicine in Anglo-Saxon England.* Manchester: Manchester Centre for Anglo-Saxon Studies, 9-40.

Megaw, J.V.S. 1970. *Art of the European Iron Age.* New York: Harper & Row.

Megaw, R. & V. 1989. *Celtic Art. From its Beginnings to the Book of Kells.* London and New York: Thames & Hudson.

Mellars, P.A. 1994. The Upper Palaeolithic Revolution. In Cunliffe, B. (ed.) 1994. *The Oxford Illustrated Prehistory of Europe.* Oxford: Oxford University Press, 42-78.

—— 1999. The Neanderthal problem continued. *Current Anthropology* 40(1): 341-64.

—— 2000. Châtelperronian chronology and the case for Neanderthal/Modern Human 'acculturation' in western Europe. In Stringer, Barton and Finlayson (eds) 2000: 33-39.

Menghin, W. 1999. The Berlin Gold Hat: A Ceremonial Head-dress of the Late Bronze Age, in Demakopoulou *et al.*, 172-175.

Menghin, W. & Schauer, P. 1983. *Der Goldhegel von Etzelsdorf: Kultgerät der Späten Bronzezeit.* Nürnberg: Nürnberg Germanisches National Museum.

Meniel, P. 1987. *Chasse et élevage chez les Gaulois (450-52 J.C.).* Paris: Errance.

Mikalson, J.D. 1975. *The Sacred and Civil Calendar of the Athenian Year.* Princeton: Princeton University Press.

Miles, D. and Palmer, S. 1995. White Horse Hill. *Current Archaeology* 142, XII, 10, 372-78.

Mithen, S.J. 1988. Looking and learning: Upper Palaeolithic art and information gathering. *World Archaeology* 19, 297-327.

—— 1994. The Mesolithic age. In Cunliffe, B. (ed.) 1994. *The Oxford Illustrated Prehistory of Europe.* Oxford: Oxford University Press, 79-135.

* —— 1996. *The Prehistory of the Mind.* London and New York: Thames & Hudson.

* —— 2003. *After the Ice: a Global Human History, 20,000-5,000 BP.* London: Weidenfeld and Nicolson.

Mohen, J-P. 1990. *The World of Megaliths.* New York: Facts on File.

Mussi, M. 1990. Continuity and change in Italy at the Last Glacial Maximum. In Soffer, O. and Gamble, C. (eds) *The World at 18 000 BP. Volume One: High Latitudes.* London: Unwin Hyman, 126-47.

—— 1995. Rituels funéraires dans les sépultures gravettiennes des grottes de Grimaldi et de la grotte delle Arène Candide: une mise au point. In Otte M. (ed.) *Nature et Culture.* Liège: ERAUL 68, 831-44

Mussi, M., Cinq-Mars, J. and Bolduc, P. 2000. Echoes from the mammoth steppe: the case of the Balzi Rossi. In Roebroeks *et al.* 2000, 105-24.

Nagy, J.F. 1997. *Conversing with Angels and Ancients.* Dublin: Four Courts Press.

Naipaul, V.S. 1981. *The Return of Eva Peron.* Harmondsworth: Penguin Books.

Newall, V. 1989. The Role of the Seer within the Punjabi Asian Minority of Britain, in Davidson (ed.), 133-46.

Neruda, P. 1995. *Love Poems.* London: Harvill Press.

Neruda, P. 1975. *The Stones of Chile (La Piedras de Chile)* transl. K. Krabbenhoft. Harmondsworth: Penguin Books.

Ó Cathasaigh, T. 1977. *The Heroic Biography of Cormac Ma Airt.* Dublin: University College Dublin Institute for Advanced Studies.

O'Fáolain, E. 1954. *Irish Sagas and Folk-Tales.* Oxford: Oxford University Press.

O'Hare, G.B. 1990. A preliminary study of polished stone artefacts in prehistoric southern Italy. *Proceedings of the Prehistoric Society* 56, 123-52.

Ó'hÓgáin, D. 1990. *The Encyclopaedia of Irish Folklore, Legend and Romance.* London:

—— 1999. *The Sacred Isle. Belief and Religion In pre-Christian Ireland.* Cambridge: Boydell Press.

Ó hUiginn, R. 1992. The background and development of the Táin Bó Cúailnge, in Mallory (ed.), 29-67.

Oliva, M, 1996. Mladopalaeoliticky hrob Brono II jako príspevek k pocátkum samanismu, *Archeologické rozhledy* 48: 353-84, 537-42.

* Olmsted, G.S. 1979. *The Gundestrup Cauldron.* Brussels: Latomus.

Ong, W.J. 1982. *Orality and Literacy. The Technologizing of the Word.* London: Methuen.

O'Rahilly, T.F. 1946. *Early Irish History and Mythology.* Dublin: Institute for Advanced Studies.

Orme, B. 1981. *Anthropology for Archaeologists.* London: Duckworth.

Otte, M. (ed.) 1994. *Sons Originels: Préhistoire de la Musique.* (Actes du Colloque de Musicologie, 1992: Etudes et Recherches Archéologiques de l'Université de Liège 61). Liège: Université de Liège.

Painter, K. 1993. Silver Hoards from Britain in their Late-Roman Context, *L'Antiquité Tardive* 5, 93-110.

Pales, L. 1976. *Les Empreintes de pieds humains dans les cavernes. Les empreintes du réseau Clastres et de la caverne de Niaux.* Paris: Editions Masson, Archives de l'Institut de paléontologie humaine, Mém. 36.

Pales, L. and Vialou, D. 1984. Grotte de l'Aldène. In Baudry (ed.) 1984: 340-42.

Palmer, D. 2000. *Neanderthal.* London: Channel 4 Books.

Pardo, M. 1993. Artifice as seduction in Titian, in J.G. Turner (ed.) *Sexuality and gender in early modern Europe: institutions, texts, images.* Cambridge: Cambridge University Press.

* Parker Pearson, M. 1999. *The Archaeology of Death and Burial.* Stroud: Alan Sutton Publishing.

—— 2002. The dead beneath their feet: housewarming *c.* 1000BC – roundhouse rituals at Cladh Hallan. *Past* 40, 1-2.

Parker Pearson, M. & Sharples, N. 1999. *Between Land and Sea. Excavations at Dun Vulan, South Uist.* Sheffield: Sheffield Academic Press.

Parker Pearson, M., Sharples, N. & Mulville, J. 1999. Excavations at Dun Vulan: a correction, *Antiquity* 73, 149-152.

* Pentikäinen, J. 1984. The Sámi shaman – mediator between man and universe. In Hoppál, M. (ed.) 1984. *Shamanism in Eurasia.* Göttingen: Edition Herodot, 125-48.

Pernicka, E. 2003. 'The Sky Disk of Nebra', Lecture delivered at the University of Bristol Archaeological Society 25.3.03.

Perrin, F. 2000a. Le Gui, in Guichard & Perrin (eds), 21-22.

—— 2000b. Diviciacus, un druide, in Guichard & Perrin (eds), 42-43.

Pettitt, P.B. 1997. High resolution Neanderthals? Interpreting Middle Palaeolithic intrasite spatial data. *World Archaeology* 29(2): 208-24.

* —— 2002a. When burial begins. *British Archaeology* 66 (August 2002): 8-13.

—— 2002b. The Neanderthal dead: exploring mortuary variability in Middle Palaeolithic Eurasia. *Before Farming, the Archaeology and Anthropology of hunter-gatherers* 2002/1 (4). www.waspress.co.uk/

Pettitt, P.B. and Bader, O.N. 2000. Direct AMS radiocarbon dates for the Sungir mid Upper Palaeolithic burials. *Antiquity* 74, 269-70.

Pettitt, P. and Bahn, P. 2003. Current problems in dating palaeolithic cave art: Candamo and Chauvet. *Antiquity* 77, 134-41.

Pettitt, P.B., Richards, M., Maggi, R. and Formicola, V. 2003. The Gravettian burial known as the Prince ('Il Principe'): new evidence for his age and diet. *Antiquity* 77, 15-19.

Pfeiffer, J. 1982. *The Creative Explosion.* New York: Harper and Row.

Philippe, M. and Fosse, P. 2003. The animal bones on the cave floor. In Clottes (ed.) 2003: 51-56.

Piggott, S. 1983. *The Earliest Wheeled Transport: From the Atlantic Coast to the Caspian Sea.* London: Thames & Hudson.

Pitts, M. 2001. Fiskerton, *Current Archaeology* 176, 327-329.

Planson, E. & Pommeret, C. 1986. *Les Bolards.* Paris: Ministère de la Culture/Imprimérie Nationale.

Porter, J.R. 1989. The Seer in Ancient Israel, in Davidson (ed.), 100-115.

* Price, N. 2001. An Archaeology of Altered States: Shamanism and Material Culture Studies, in N. Price (ed.) *The Archaeology of Shamanism.* London: Routledge, 3-16.

* Price, N. (ed.). 2001. *The Archaeology of Shamanism.* London: Routledge.

Pritchett, W.K. 1963. *Ancient Athenian Calendars on Stone.* Berkeley/Los Angeles: University of California Press.

Priuli, A. 1988. *Incisioni Rupestri della Val Camonica.* Collana, Torino: Quaderni di Cultura Alpina.

—— 1996. *Le Piu Antiche Manifestazioni Spirituali Arte Rupestre Paleoiconografia Camuna e delle genti Alpine.* Torino: Collana. I Grandi Libri.

Raftery, B. 1994. *Pagan Celtic Ireland. The Enigma of the Irish Iron Age.* London and New York: Thames & Hudson.

—— 1996. *Trackway Excavations in the Mountdillon Bogs, Co. Longford, 1985-1991.* Dublin: Irish Archaeological Wetland Unit Transactions, 3).

Ramirez, B.R. and Behrmann, R. de B. 1991. Southern Europe: post palaeolithic art in Spain. State of the issue. In Bahn, P.G. and Fossati, A. (eds) *Rock Art Studies: News of the World I,* pp. 35-40. Oxford: Oxbow monograph 72.

Rasmussen, S.W. 2000. Cicero's Stand on Prodigies: A Non-existent Dilemma, in Wildfang & Isager (eds), 9-24.

Read, H. 1982. What is Revolutionary Art?, in F. Frascina & C. Harrison (eds) *Modern Art and Modernism.* London: Harper & Row, 123-127.

Richards, M.P., Jacobi, R., Currant, A., Stringer, C., and Hedges, R.E.M. 2000. Gough's Cave and Sun Hole Cave human stable isotope values indicate a high animal protein diet in the British Upper Palaeolithic. *Journal of Archaeological Science* 27, 1-3.

Richards, M.P., Pettitt, P.B., Stiner, M. and Trinkaus, E. 2001. Stable isotope evidence for increasing dietary breadth in the European mid-Upper Palaeolithic. *Proceedings of the National Academy of Science* (USA) 98 (11), 6528-32.

Richter, D., Waiblinger, F., Rink, W.J. and Wagner, G.A. 2000. Thermoluminescence, Electron Spin Resonance and 14C dating of the Late Middle and Early Upper Palaeolithic palaeolithic site of Geissenklösterle Cave in southern Germany. *Journal of Archaeological Science* 27(1), 71-89.

persistence in the Pavlovian. *Journal of Archaeological Science* 28, 1291-1308.

* Turk, I. (ed.) 1997. *Mousterian Bone Flute and Other Finds from Divje Babe I Cave Site in Slovenia.* Ljubljana: Institut za Archaeolgijo.

* Turner, R.C. 1995. The Lindow Bog Bodies, in R.C. Turner & R.G. Scaife (eds) *Bog Bodies. New Discoveries & New Perspectives.* London: British Museum Press, 10-18.

* Turner, R.C. & Scaife, R.G. 1995 (eds) *Bog Bodies. New Discoveries and New Perspectives.* London: British Museum Press.

* Ucko, P.J. & Rosenfeld. A. 1967. *Palaeolithic Cave Art.* London: Weidenfeld & Nicolson.

Underhill, R.M. 1965. *Red Man's Religion.* Chicago, IL: University of Chicago Press.

Van der Sanden, W. 1995. Bog Bodies on the Continent: Developments since 1965, with special reference to the Netherlands, in Turner & Scaife (eds), 146-165.

* —— 1996. *Through Nature to Eternity. The bog bodies of northwest Europe.* Amsterdam: Batavian Lion International.

Van der Sanden, W. & Capelle, T. 2001. *Mosens Guder. Antropomorfe traefigurer fra Nord- og Nordvesteuropas fortid.* Silkeborg: Silkeborg Museum.

Vandermeersch, B. 1993. Was the Saint-Césaire discovery a burial? In Lévêque *et al.* 1993, 129-31.

Van Driel-Murray, C. 1999. And did those Feet in Ancient Time – Feet and Shoes as a material projection of the self, in P. Baker, C. Forcey, S. Jundi & R. Eitcher (eds) *TRAC 98. Proceedings of the Eighth Annual Theoretical Archaeology Conference.* Oxford: Oxbow, 131-140.

Vellacott, P. 1961. (trans.) *Aeschylus Prometheus Bound.* Harmondsworth: Penguin.

—— 1973. (trans.) *Euripides The Bacchae.* Harmondsworth: Penguin.

Vencl, S. 1994. The archaeology of thirst, *Journal of European Archaeology* 2 (2), 299-326.

Verpoorte, A. 2001. *Places of Art, Traces of Fire: a Contextual Approach to Anthropomorphic Figurines in the Pavlovian (Central Europe, 29-24 kyr BP).* Leiden: Faculty of Archaeology – Archaeological Studies, Leiden University, no 8, Dolní Věstonice Studies no 6.

Vilà, C. *et al.* 1997. Multiple and ancient origins of the domestic dog. *Science* 276, 1687-87.

* Vitebsky, P. 1995. *The Shaman. Voyages of the Soul: Trance, Healing and Ecstasy from Siberia to the Amazon.* Macmillan: London.

Vries, J. de 1963. *La Religion des Celtes.* Paris: Payot.

Walter, D. 2001. The medium of the message: shamanism as localized practice in the Nepal Himalayas, in Price (ed.), 105-119.

Ward, R. and Stringer, C. 1997. A molecular handle on the Neanderthals, *Nature* 388, 225-26.

Webster, J. 1999. At the end of the World: druidic and other revitalization movements in post-conquest Gaul and Britain, *Britannia* 30, 1-20.

Wellesley, K. 1964 (trans.) *Tacitus. The Histories.* Harmondsworth: Penguin.

Wender, D. 1973. *Hesiod and Theognis.* Harmondsworth: Penguin.

Wheeler, R.E.M. & T.V. 1932. *Excavations at the Prehistoric, Roman and Post-Roman site at Lydney Park, Gloucestershire.* Oxford: Oxford University Press/Society of Antiquaries of London.

* White, R. 2003. *Prehistoric Art: the symbolic journey of humankind.* New York: Harry N. Abrams.

White, R. and Bisson, M. 1998. Imagerie feminine du paléolithique: l'apport des nouvelles statuettes de Grimaldi. *Gallia Préhistoire* 40, 95-132.

Whitehouse, R. 1992. *Underground Religion: Cult and Culture in Prehistoric Italy.* London: Accordia Research Centre, University of London.

Whitley, D.S., Dorn, R.I., Simon, J.M., Rechtman, R., & Whitley, T.K. 1999. Sally's rockshelter and the archaeology of the vision quest. *Cambridge Archaeological Journal* 9:2: 221-47.

Wilbert, J. 1997. Illuminative serpents: tobacco hallucinations of the Warao. *Journal of Latin American Lore* 20(2): 317-32.

Wildfang, R.L. & Isager, J. (eds), 2000. *Divination and Portents in the Roman World.* Odense: Odense University Press.

Williams, H. 2001. An ideology of transformation: cremation rites and animal sacrifice in early Anglo-Saxon England, in Price (ed.), 193-212.

Williams, R.J., Hart, P.J. & Williams, A.T.L. 1996. *Wavendon Gate. A Late Iron Age and Roman Settlement in Milton Keynes.* Aylesbury: Buckinghamshire Archaeological Society Monograph Series 10.

Wood, J. 1989. Prophecy in Middle Welsh Tradition, in H.E. Davidson (ed.), 52-65.

—— 1997. The Horse in Welsh Folklore: A Boundary Image in Custom and Narrative, in S. Davies & N.A. Jones (eds) *The Horse in Celtic Culture.* Cardiff: University of Wales Press, 162-182.

Wooding, J. *et al.* 2000. *The Otherworld Voyage in Early Irish Literature.* Dublin: Four Courts Press.

Yellen, J. E. 1988. Barbed bone points: tradition and continuity in Saharan and sub-Saharan Africa. *African Archaeological Review* 15, 173-98.

Zachar, L. 1987. *Keltische Kunst in der Slowakei.* Bratislava: Tatran.

Zachrisson, I. and Iregren, E. 1974. *Early Norrland 5. Lappish Bear Graves in Northern Sweden: an Archaeological and Osteological Study.* Stockholm: Kungl. Vitterhets.

Zilhão, J. 2000. The Ebro frontier: a model for the late extinction of Iberian Neanderthals. In Stringer, Barton and Finlayson (eds) 2000, 111-21.

—— 2001. *Anatomically Archaic, Behaviorally Modern: the Last Neanderthals and their Destiny.* 23rd Kroon lecture.

Amsterdam: Amsterdams Archeologisch Centrum van de Universiteit van Amsterdam.

Zilhão, J. and Trinkaus, E. 2001. Troubling the Neanderthals: a reply to Langbroek's 'Trouble with Neanderthals'. *Archaeological Dialogues* 8(2), 135-42.

Zilhão, J. and Trinkaus, E. (eds) 2002. *Portrait of the Artist as a Child. The Gravettian Human Skeleton from the Abrigo do Lagar Velho and its Archaeological Context.* Lisbon: Trabalhos de Arqueologia 22.

Zvelebil, M. 1992. Hunting in farming societies: the prehistoric perspective. *Anthropozoologica* 16: 7-17.

—— 2003. People behind the lithics. Social life and social conditions of Mesolithic communities in temperate Europe. In Bevan, L. and Moore, J. (eds) *Peopling the Mesolithic in a Northern Environment*, pp. 1-26. Oxford: British Archaeological Reports International Series 1157.

Zvelebil, M. and Jordan, P. 1997. Hunter-fisher-gatherer ritual landscapes. *Analecta Praehistorica Leidensia* 29: 101-27.

Acknowledgments

The authors would like to express their gratitude to the following individuals for their help in the production of this volume, whether in the form of information or the provision of illustrative material: Jean Bagnall-Smith, Tara Bowen, Gilly Carr, Andy Chapman, Philip Crummy, Nick Griffiths, Vincent Guichard, Paul Jenkins, Anne Leaver, Keith Parfitt, Catherine Price and Robert Wilkins,. We would also like to thank all others mentioned as copyright holders in the Sources of Illustrations. We are indebted to Ivor Karavanić and Ivor Janković for their help in understanding the Krapina stratigraphy; also to Jean Clottes for his advice on the dating of Chauvet Cave. Finally, we are deeply grateful to Paul Pettitt, of the University of Sheffield, for reading through our draft text; his perceptive and helpful comments are of immense value.

SOURCES OF ILLUSTRATIONS

Abbreviations: MAG – Miranda Aldhouse-Green;
PJ – Paul Jenkins; AL – Anne Leaver

Text Figures
FRONTISPIECE: Danish National Museum, Copenhagen;
1 National Museum of Wales, drawing Tony Daly; 2 After
Cunliffe, B. (ed.) 1994, The Oxford Illustrated Prehistory of
Europe; 3 Map AL (after Mussi et al. 2000); 4 After Klein, R.
1999, The Human Career, 2nd ed., p. 476; 5 Drawing R. McLean
(after Clottes, J. & Lewis-Williams, D. 1996, The Shamans of
Prehistory, p. 14); 6 Map AL (after Mussi et al. 2000); 7
Morasvke Zemske Museum, Brno; 8 Photo SAG; 9 Reprinted
by permission of Marcel Otte and ERAUL volume 73; 10 After
Klein, R. 1999, The Human Career, 2nd ed., p. 499; 11 © Guida
Casella 1999; 12 Drawing AL (after Mussi et al. 2000); 13 Map
AL (after Mussi et al. 2000); 14 Institut für Ur-und
Frühgeschichte und Archäologie des Mittelalters, Abteilung
ältere Urgeschichte und Quartaeroekologie der Eberhard-
Karls-Universität Tübingen; 15 National Gallery, London;
16 After Ruth D. Whitehouse; 17 Photo Ruth D. Whitehouse;
18 Map AL (after Mithen 1994); 19 Oleneostrovski Mogilnik;
20 The Vedback Finds, Sollerod Museum; 21 Drawing AL
(after Coles 2000, pl. 63); 22 Drawing AL (after Coles 1999, p. 180,
fig. 13); 23 Drawing AL (after Coles 1990, fig. 62); 24 Drawing PJ;
25 Drawing AL (after Coles 1990, fig. 61); 26 Drawing AL (after
Coles 2000, pl. 69); 27 Drawing AL (after Coles 2000, pl. 70);
28 Drawing AL (after Coles 2000, pl. 57); 29 Drawing AL (after
Coles 2000, pl. 55); 30 Drawing PJ; 31 Drawing AL (after Anati
1965, pp. 192–93); 32 After D. Planck, Der Keltenfürst von
Hochdorf, Stuttgart: Landesdenkmalamt Baden-Württemburg;
33 Drawing PJ; 34 Drawing PJ; 35 Drawing PJ; 36 Drawing AL
(after Prinli 1996, p. 127); 37 Drawing AL (after Prinli 1996, p. 121);
38 Drawing PJ; 39 Drawing AL (after Anati 1965, p. 74);
40 Drawing PJ; 41 Drawing AL; 42 Drawing PJ; 43 Drawing PJ;
44 Danish National Museum, Copenhagen; 45 Photo Schloss
Gottorf Museum, Schleswig-Holstein; 46 Drawing AL;
47 Drawing Séan Goddard, with permission of Professor
Bryony Coles; 48 Drawing AL; 49 Drawing AL; 50 Drawing
PJ; 51 Drawing PJ; 52 Drawing AL; 53 Drawing PJ; 54 British
Museum, London; 55 Drawing AL (after Creighton 2000); 56
Drawing AL (after Prinli 1996); 57 Drawing PJ; 58 Drawing PJ;
59 Drawing PJ; 60 Drawing Nick Griffiths; 61 Drawing Chris
Rudd; 62 Musée des Antiquités Nationales, Saint-Germain-
en-Laye; 63 Peterborough City Museum & Art Gallery;
64 Drawing PJ; 65 National Museums & Galleries of Wales,
Cardiff; 66 Photo MAG; 67 Photo Simon James; 68 National
Museums & Galleries of Wales, Cardiff; 69 Kingston-upon-
Hull District Council Museums & Art Gallery; 70 British
Museum, London; 71 Drawing PJ; 72 Milton Keynes
Development Corporatio, with permission of Robert Williams;
73 Drawing AL; 74 Sheffield Museum; 75 Photo MAG;
76 Drawing PJ; 77 Drawing AL; 78 Kingston-upon-Hull
District Council Museums & Art Gallery; 79 Keith Parfitt,
Dover Archaeological Group; 80 Drawing AL; 81 Drawing PJ;
82 Drawing PJ; 83 British Museum, London; 84 Drawing PJ;
85 Corinium Museum, Cirencester; 86 British Museum,
London; 87 National Museums & Galleries of Wales, Cardiff;
88 Drawing AL; 89 Drawing Nick Griffiths; 90 Drawing PJ;
91 Drawing PJ; 92 Photo Jean Bagnall-Smith; 93 British
Museum, London; 94 Musée Archéologique Orléans (Photo
Bulloz); 95 Photo MAG; 96 National Museums & Galleries of
Wales, Cardiff; 97 Photo Betty Naggar; 98 Danish National
Museum, Copenhagen; 99 National Museums & Galleries of
Wales, Cardiff; 100 Drawing Barbara Crow; 101 Drawing PJ; 102
National Museums & Galleries of Wales; 103 Drawing Barbara
Crow; 104 Drawing P. J. Lopeman; 105 Worthing Museum &
Art Gallery; 106 Photo MAG; 107 Peter the Great Museum of
Anthropology & Ethnography, Russian Academy of Science,
St Petersburg; 108 Michel Lorblanchet; 109 Drawing AL

Colour Plates
1 National Museums of Scotland, Edinburgh; 2 Ministero
per i Beni e le Attivita Culturali-Soprintendenza per i Beni
Archeologici della Liguria; 3 Moravian Museum-Anthropos
Institute, Brno; 4 Jean Clottes; 5 Photo Thomas Stephan, ©
Ulmer Museum; 6 Y. Le Guillou; 7 Drawing AL; 8 Harry
Bland; 9 Dúchas, Dublin; 10 Photo MAG; 11 Photo MAG;
12 Photo MAG; 13 Danish National Museum, Copenhagen;
14 Silkeborg Museum, Denmark; 15 Moesgård Museum,
Denmark; 16 British Museum, London; 17 British Museum,
London; 18 Landesmuseum Joanneum, Graz; 19 Pamela
Johnston; 20 Service Régional de l'Archéologie de Poitou-
Charentes; 21 Photo MAG; 22 Musée des Antiquités Nationales,
Saint-Germain-en-Laye; 23 Colchester Archaeological
Trust; 24 National Museum of Ireland, Dublin

INDEX

Numerals in *italic* refer to text illustration numbers; numerals in **bold** refer to colour plate numbers.